DISRUPTED LANDSCAPES

The Environment in History: International Perspectives

Series Editors: Dolly Jørgensen, *Umea University*; David Moon, *University of York*; Christof Mauch, *LMU Munich*; Helmuth Trischler, *Deutsches Museum, Munich*.

Volume 1
Civilizing Nature: National Parks in Global Historical Perspective
Edited by Bernhard Gissibl, Sabine Höhler, and Patrick Kupper

Volume 2
Powerless Science? Science and Politics in a Toxic World
Edited by Soraya Boudia and Natalie Jas

Volume 3
Managing the Unknown: Essays on Environmental Ignorance
Edited by Frank Uekötter and Uwe Lübken

Volume 4
Creating Wilderness: A Transnational History of the Swiss National Park
Patrick Kupper
Translated by Giselle Weiss

Volume 5
Rivers, Memory, and Nation-Building: A History of the Volga and Mississippi Rivers
Dorothy Zeisler-Vralsted

Volume 6
Fault Lines: Earthquakes and Urbanism in Modern Italy
Giacomo Parrinello

Volume 7
Re/Cycling Histories: Paths to Sustainability
Edited by Ruth Oldenziel and Helmuth Trischler

Volume 8
Disrupted Landscapes: State, Peasants and the Politics of Land in Postsocialist Romania
Stefan Dorondel

Disrupted Landscapes

State, Peasants and the Politics of Land in Postsocialist Romania

Stefan Dorondel

First published in 2016 by
Berghahn Books
www.berghahnbooks.com

© 2016, 2021 Stefan Dorondel
First paperback edition published in 2021

All rights reserved. Except for the quotation of short passages for the purposes of criticism and review, no part of this book may be reproduced in any form or by any means, electronic or mechanical, including photocopying, recording, or any information storage and retrieval system now known or to be invented, without written permission of the publisher.

Library of Congress Cataloging-in-Publication Data

Dorondel, Stefan, 1968-
 Disrupted landscapes : state, peasants and the politics of land in postsocialist Romania / Stefan Dorondel.
  pages cm. -- (The environment in history : international perspectives ; volume 8)
  Includes bibliographical references and index.
  ISBN 978-1-78533-120-6 (hardback : alkaline paper) -- ISBN 978-1-78533-121-3 (ebook)
 1. Environmental policy--Romania. 2. Romania--Rural conditions. 3. Landscape changes--Romania. 4. Deforestation--Romania. 5. Peasants--Romania--Social conditions. 6. Land use--Environmental aspects--Romania. 7. Land use--Political aspects--Romania. 8. Social change--Romania. 9. Post-communism--Environmental aspects--Romania. 10. Neoliberalism--Environmental aspects--Romania. I. Title.
  GE190.R6D67 2016
  333.7309498--dc23

2015034845

British Library Cataloguing in Publication Data

A catalogue record for this book is available from the British Library

Printed in the United States

ISBN 978-1-78533-120-6 hardback
ISBN 978-1-80073-011-3 paperback
ISBN 978-1-78533-121-3 ebook

To Luminița, my wife

'Landscapes are culture before they are nature …'
—Simon Schama, *Landscape and Memory*

Contents

List of Illustrations	x
List of Figures	xi
Preface	xiii
List of Abbreviations	xvii
Introduction. Privatizing the State and the Transformation of the Agrarian Landscape	1
Chapter 1. Dragomirești and Dragova: Two Centuries of Ecological and Socio-economic Transformations	25
Chapter 2. Postsocialism as Neoliberalism: Reorganizing Society and Nature	54
Chapter 3. Bureaucrats, Patronage, Illegal Logging	64
Chapter 4. Contested Forest	95
Chapter 5. Waning Pastures	121
Chapter 6. Fragmented Lands	143
Chapter 7. Wasted Rivers	171
Conclusion: A Disrupted Landscape	189
References	203
Index	223

List of Illustrations

1.1.	The Fragmented Landscape in Dragomirești	27
1.2.	Private Pastures in Dragova	38
3.1.	Deforestation in Dragomirești, 2004	71
3.2.	Deforestation in Dragomirești, 2009	71
4.1.	The Exploitation of the Communal Forest in Dragova	108
5.1.	Bushes Taking over Pasture in Dragomirești	123
5.2.	Rudari Houses Built on the Communal Pasture	126
5.3.	Rooted Pastures of Dragova	130
6.1.	Postsocialist Land Fragmentation in Dragomirești	147
7.1.	Garbage on the River's Banks	176
7.2.	Garbage on the River's Banks (2)	176
7.3.	A Vanishing River	181

List of Figures

0.1.	Map of Romania	xviii
3.1.	Participatory Map Showing Deforestation and the Control of the State Forest	72
3.2.	Forest holdings distribution in Dragomirești	81
6.1.	Participatory Map Showing Land Fragmentation in Dragomirești	148

Preface

This book is the outcome of my trespassing shamefully on several disciplines, some of them far removed from my scientific background. I had to navigate my way through territories I was barely familiar with such as political economy, geography, agronomy or water ecology. This means that to the usual anthropologist's toolkit of concepts, methods and theories, I have added several other tools such as satellite images, more commonly employed by geographers; a more general view of land reform, such as that favoured by political economists; and explanations that have their roots in animal and river ecology. I was ill-prepared for working in disciplines so far removed from anthropology and history, the two disciplines in which I was trained. I have done this in order to provide a more comprehensive understanding of the topic – landscape cannot be examined from a single angle – and to present the reader with more complex stories about the changes the socialist state and landscape underwent. I was lucky to have the assistance of people who took my hand and guided me across these unknown territories. I am sincerely grateful to them.

The title of the book merits some explanation. By using the term 'disrupted landscape' I do not mean to imply that the socialist landscape was stable prior to the 1990s. As a reviewer of this text aptly noted, environmental historians, some of them cited in this book, have shown that the landscape and implicitly the environment have been continuously shaped in many ways throughout history (e.g. Worster 1990: 9). This is perfectly correct. Nevertheless, when referring to a 'disrupted landscape' I imply that the changes I cite are of a different order of magnitude. The socialist agricultural landscape was disrupted in many ways, first of all through industrialized forms of agriculture. Changes in land ownership, use of fertilizers and pesticides, and the introduction of monocultures drastically altered the presocialist agricultural landscape. But this disruption was somehow stable, maintained with more or less the same intensity, at least for the last twenty years that preceded the end of the regime. In contrast, postsocialism produced significant changes in terms of capital investments, access to markets and industrialization of agriculture. Thus, the disruption to the landscape was more evident and more intense in those regions that experienced radical changes in agricultural practice, especially in hilly regions. Farming has shifted from intensive, industrial agriculture practised over large areas of land to family farming on small plots using traditional methods (such as intercropping or the use of non-mechanized equipment). Here, more than in other regions, disruption of the landscape was massive, visible and dramatic. Secondly, such disruption has not only had a visual, economic and a strong environmental impact on the landscape but has wrought changes in the social fabric as well. All these four elements are intertwined and have to be understood together. This is what the title suggests.

Before acknowledgements a disclaimer seems necessary. Throughout the book I use expressions such as 'illegal logging', 'illegal loggers' or 'illegal deforestation'. This might suggest that I have adopted the state or legal point of view on such matters. I want to assure the reader that I do not use these expressions in a normative way. I use them only because I was not able to find synonyms for words that are unfortunately heavily loaded with negative associations.

As author of this book I am indebted to many institutions and people. I will start with the institutions. 'Emmy Noether-Programm' of the Deutsches Forschungsgemeinschaft (The German Research Foundation) funded my stay at Humboldt University Berlin (2003–2007) and my field research. I am greatly indebted to the Agrarian Studies Program of Yale University for the six months I spent there. This program taught me that an interdisciplinary approach is not just a term, nor a social scientist's dream – always desired, never achieved – but possible in real life. I also thank the Max Planck Institute for Social Anthropology and the University of Cambridge for granting me access to great libraries. Although I was enrolled in their programs for different projects I admit, penitently, that I also used the time for working on this book. A New Europe College Bucharest fellowship allowed me to spend ten months in an interdisciplinary academic context that gave me ideas and encouraged me to engage with different disciplines. It also allowed me to spend one month at the University of California at Berkeley, which was decisive for this book. Last but not least, special thanks to the Rachel Carson Center (RCC), an institution which not only bought me time for thinking and writing but put me in contact with scholars who helped me in innumerable ways. Without this institution and the people within it, this book would not exist. Not in this form, at least.

Many people contributed to this book through their questions, comments, suggestions, criticisms and, above all, their support and encouragement. Bill Adams, Remus Anghel, Keebet von Benda-Beckmann, Lawrence Culver, Katy Fox, Alexandra Ion, Krystyna Larkham, Diana Mincyte, Christof Mauch, Jenna Ng, Mihai Popa and Stelu Șerban read several chapters and made harsh but fair criticisms. This book owes a lot to James C. Scott and his unique way of analysing and writing. He supported me in many ways, and I am grateful to him for all I have learned from him. No less have I learned from Nancy Lee Peluso and Jeff Romm. Dora Drexler, a landscape planner, made me view landscape through her eyes, an incredibly useful experience for this book. Teresa Shawcross and James Carrier put a lot of work into reading and adjusting the Introduction and the book proposal. Sally Fenn, my linguistic guardian angel, made this book readable through her thorough work. Former fellows from the Agrarian Studies Program at Yale, members of the Resilience and Transformation in Eurasia Department from the Max Planck Institute for Social Anthropology Halle and members of the Political Ecology Group from the Department of Geography at Cambridge patiently attended to various presentations of chapters and helped me to refine my argument. During a late-night conversation in Belgrade, over a glass of wine, the late Franz von Benda-Beckmann helped me to clarify the main argument of this book. I lost the path, and he helped me find it. I retain warm memories of him. David Moon read thoroughly the whole manuscript and drew my attention to small but important inconsistencies. The final text is more coherent due to his work. Residents of the two villages where I carried out fieldwork contributed to this book with their patience in answering my questions and by tolerating me when I joined in with various activities. Among them, my host in Dragomirești, Puiu Nicolescu and his wonderful family who adopted me and took good care of me while in the field, deserve particular mention.

Finally, I owe more than words can describe to two groups of people who influenced me the most. The stormy yet friendly debates with my former co-workers in the Junior Research Group on Postsocialist Land Relations at Humboldt University in Berlin, Johannes Stahl, Daniel Müller (who taught me everything I know about participatory mapping), Phuc Xuan To, Nguyen Quang Tan, Tran Ngoc Thanh and Tatjana Thelen, helped me clarify hazy theories and thoughts swirling round my mind. The autumn 2010 cohort from the RCC deserve my gratitude for receiving me, a social anthropologist, and turning me into a person who is no longer afraid of crossing disciplinary boundaries. Lawrence Culver, Stefania Gallini, Robert Gioielli, Wilko Graf von Hardenberg, Emilian Kavalski, Patrick Kupper, Cheril Lousley, Gary Martin, Shane McCorristine, Gijs Mom, Ursula Münster, Lajos Rácz, Edmund Russell, Lisa Sideris, Jacob Tropp, Alexa Weik von Mossner: thank you, guys, for everything. It would not be right to forget the directors of the RCC, Christof Mauch and Helmut Trischler, who permanently encouraged and advised me. Christof Mauch revealed to me the scholarly advantage of putting 'more nature' into the book. Frank Uekötter also urged me in this direction, considering that a more environmental approach would particularize the book. I have left until last my profound gratitude to Thomas

Sikor, former supervisor, a mentor and a dear friend. My encounter with him changed my academic life. I have probably learnt more from him than he imagines.

My family occupies a special place. I was a lousy husband and a careless son. I hope that the time I spent away from my family while abroad is, at least partially, compensated by the publication of this book. My wife, Luminița, and my mother's efforts in putting up with my long absences from home were at least as great as my effort in writing this book. Without their understanding and support this book would never have reached the hands of its readers.

List of Abbreviations

AGR – Statistical Report for Agriculture
ASD – The Agency of State Domains
ATV – All Terrain Vehicles
CLC – County Land Commission
EU – European Union
FCW – Framework Cadre for Water
GPS – Global Positioning System
IUCN – The International Union for Conservation of Nature
LIF – Local Inspectorate of Forest
LLC – Local Land Commission
NANR – National Agency for the Natural Resources
NGO – Non-Governmental Organization
NIF – National Inspectorate of Forest
NOCGC – The National Office of Cadastre, Geodesy and Cartography
PCNP – The Piatra Craiului National Park
RAEP – The Regional Agency for Environmental Protection
SDP – The Social Democrat Party

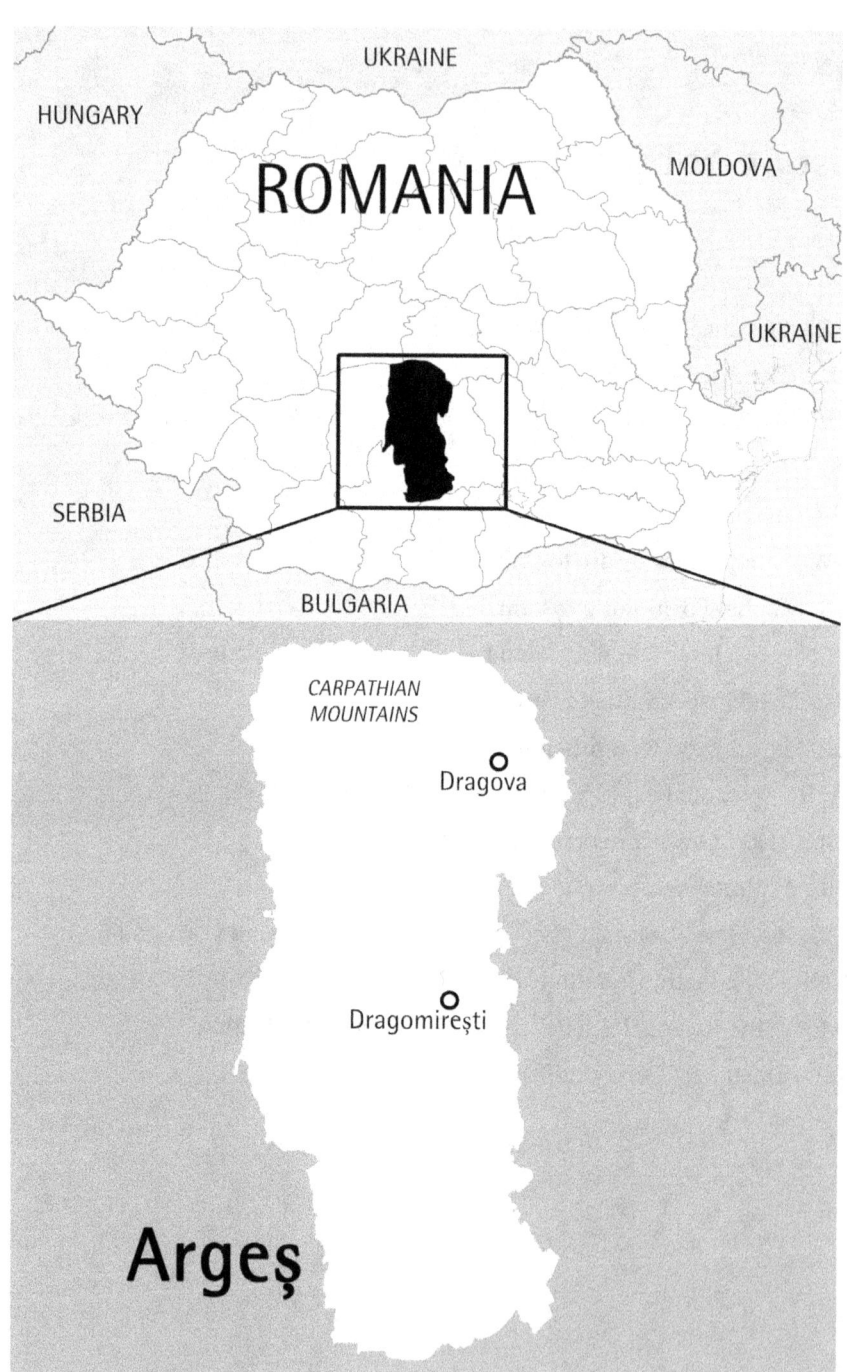

Figure 0.1. Map of Romania

Introduction
Privatizing the State and the Transformations of the Agrarian Landscape

> 'Our lives revolve around the man-made elements in the landscape.'
> —J. B. Jackson, *A Sense of Place, a Sense of Time*

December 1989. News broke of the spectacular collapse of one of the harshest dictatorial regimes in the world. Images of the crowd surrounding and then ransacking the dictatorial palace, burning books and paintings, symbolized the destruction of a highly centralized state and the people's wrath against a miscreant political regime. The helicopter carrying the dictatorial couple from the central government building roof represented, for most Romanians, the crash of a dreadful state that for years had oppressed its citizens. A few days after being chased from power, Nicolae Ceaușescu was caught, placed before an improvised jury, condemned and executed. The Romanian hyper-centralized socialist government collapsed and the public expected a democratically elected government to replace the hideous former government. The new self-appointed authorities had only a few days to take several political measures eagerly expected by the population. Land property was among the most pressing issues.[1]

While urbanites were still on the streets celebrating victory over the dictatorship, rural inhabitants were thrilled at the prospect of reclaiming the land and forests they or their parents had been forced to surrender to the state in the early 1950s. Now that the socialist state had been dismantled, the rural population became impatient to take collective farmlands back into their possession. In the months following the breakdown of the socialist regime rural inhabitants carried out spontaneous collective farm dissolution.[2] The Romanian parliament passed the first land reform law in 1991 and created local, regional and national Land Commissions, charging them with implementing land and forest restitution. The second law, passed in 2000, completed and at the same time complicated the provisions of the first law.

Land and land reform are not merely postsocialist concerns. Land has been the obsession of peasants and political reformers alike since the dawn of modern Romanian statehood. It is difficult to find a better headline to describe the societal tensions than the title of a poem published in 1894 that screams: 'We want land!'. George Coşbuc, the author of the poetry, synthesized in a poem the peasantry's primary main social and economic plea since medieval times. The number of free landholders shrank continuously during the Middle Ages whereas the number of serfs continued to grow. In 1864 serfdom was abolished, steering Romanian agriculture towards small family farms. Collectivization of agriculture, which started in 1949, brought further transformations. Private land owners were 'convinced' through violent methods to donate their land and land-related assets to collective farms.[3] Theoretically, workers on collective farms organized farm labour, sharing both the labour itself and the proceeds. In practice, the collective farms had no more autonomy than any other socialist enterprise. Besides collective farms there were state farms, which were created out of land seized from large landowners.[4] While the collective farms were not subsidized by the state, the state farms benefitted substantially from socialist state subsidies. The breakdown of the communist regime triggered a new land reform that was intended to reverse collectivization. Decollectivization, as it was termed by scholars, was the process of breaking up collective farms and restoring land and land-related assets to legitimate former owners. State farms were also dismantled and the land was privatized.[5]

Changes in landed property rights and in agrarian relations were triggered by radical political transformations experienced by the Romanian provinces in the second part of the nineteenth century and throughout the twentieth century. Until 1859, when Moldavia and Walachia were united under the name of Romanian Principalities, the provinces that constitute Romania were ruled by different powers. Despite the 1859 Union, the Romanian Principalities, as they were called, remained, at least formally, under Ottoman control until 1878. Transylvania was a relatively autonomous province under the rule of the Hungarian kingdom and between 1867 and 1918 under the Austro-Hungarian Empire. Only in 1918 was Transylvania incorporated into the Romanian state: once the Austro-Hungarian Empire had disappeared, a new nation state emerged on Europe's map. Between 1881 and 1947 Romania was an independent kingdom.[6] The installation of the communist regime in 1947 ended one political regime and installed a different one under the Soviet Union's direct supervision. This regime ended in December 1989.

Changes in political regimes and the movement of the borders throughout the twentieth century also influenced the ethnic makeup of the population of Romania. In 1919, one year after Romania incorporated Transylvania, 57.12 per cent of the Transylvania's population was ethnic Romanian, 26.46 per cent was Hungarian, almost 10 per cent was German and 3 per cent of Jewish origin. At the country level, in 1919 Romania had

28 per cent citizens belonging to different ethnic groups.[7] More than 90 years after, the 2011 census showed that out of a population exceeding 20 million almost 89 per cent is ethnic Romanian. Almost 7 per cent of the population are Hungarians, most of them located in Transylvania, and 3.3 per cent declared themselves to be Roma. The Roma population is relatively uniformly distributed across Romania. Other ethnic groups that number fewer than 20,000 are Ukrainians, Germans, Turks, Russians and Tartars.[8] In Walachia, apart from some small villages with a Bulgarian population and some Roma, most people are ethnic Romanians. Moldavia presents pretty much the same picture: a tiny Russian population, some Roma but mostly Romanian ethnics.

The nineteenth and twentieth centuries were shaken by several land reforms implemented with varying degrees of radicalism. All were declared essential in order to modernize the country's economy and society. The most radical reforms unfolded in the last sixty years: the Utopian social engineering of the last two reforms brought immense social disruption and left deep marks on the agrarian landscape. In the early 1950s the communist Utopia required the erasure of class discrimination in order to achieve a paradisiacal egalitarian social structure. Communist governments attempted to do this by nationalizing private farmland and forests and establishing collective and state farms. The quasi-elimination of property rights in agriculture during socialist times changed the agrarian landscape. Agricultural land was consolidated into large plots, and later on the means of production were mechanized in accordance with Nicolae Ceaușescu's dream of catching up with the industrialized Western countries. The postsocialist land reform yet again aimed to change agrarian relations, in order to modernize the country's economy and society. Land restitution was triggered partially by the desire to bring about historical justice and partially in order to achieve economic efficiency in the agricultural sector.[9] Postsocialist central state planners regarded land reform as a way to dismantle the collective organization of agriculture, improve the land tenure system and increase the economic efficiency of a country once dubbed the 'granary of Europe'. The centrally designed land reform had to be implemented through the lower levels of state bureaucracy: the mayor, the secretary of the mayor's office, the agricultural officer and the representative of the Local Inspectorate of Forest (LIF) were all agents of the state empowered to implement land reform provisions down to the last village. But, to paraphrase an old Romanian saying, many go out for wool and come home shorn. The local-level bureaucrats had their own economic interests, which were hardly compatible with those of central government. Central government did not foresee the local bureaucrats' opposition to land reform and the power of local social networks whose interests local bureaucrats represented and defended.[10]

By placing an emphasis on Romania as the focus of my research I am not playing a practical joke on the reader. The case of Romania, a country of a bit more than 20 million people, is not singular in the postsocialist world. The collapse of the Berlin Wall in October 1989 changed the lives of more than 100 million people in Central and Eastern Europe.[11] If we count the tremendous changes in countries in central Asia that were once part of the Soviet Union and Asian countries such as China and Vietnam, we realize that the term postsocialism can be applied to more than a quarter of the world's territory, with a population reaching around 1.5 billion.[12] The 1989 turmoil affected equally people, economy, ecology and environment. In terms of people and territories affected, the postsocialist transformation is undoubtedly the greatest transformation of modern times.

However, I do not intend to understate the complexities of so many diverse countries by employing the term 'postsocialist'. This term ought to reflect the diversity of societies and their history in the same way as socialism, which was used to designate the organization of societies and economies that differed in many ways from one country to another. For instance, Yugoslavia and Poland halted the collectivization of agriculture when socialist agricultural policies were first implemented, whereas Albania, Romania and the Soviet Union did not stop until the last piece of land was collectivized. The socialist regime in Yugoslavia was more liberal than in most of the other countries. While Yugoslavia provided thousands of *gastarbeiters* to Western Europe, Romania and Albania were virtually closed countries where even internal movement was difficult. The manner of departure from socialism was also different from country to country. When the policy of decollectivization started in the late 1980s in Vietnam – a policy known as *Đôi mói* – in Romania the centralization of land management was fiercer than ever.[13] The end of the socialist governments also came about quite differently for different countries: in Poland, Hungary and Czechoslovakia the socialist governments were peacefully removed, whereas in Romania some 1,000 people lost their lives in what was called a 'revolution'.[14] Despite following slightly different trajectories, postsocialist countries have nevertheless two general traits in common. One is the collapse of the party state and the emergence of political parties (except for Vietnam and China) which have given rise to a wider range of political ideologies, from social democrats (seen as inheritors of the communist parties) to liberals and conservatives. Second, the postsocialist governments adopted, at various stages but with few exceptions, a neoliberal philosophy concerning the market and the role of the state. Privatization of state enterprises, restoration of land and land-related assets to either former owners or to those who worked in agriculture, the privatization of forest and the opening up of the national market to global economic forces are all part of the postsocialist political picture. I present this policy more thoroughly in chapter 3. It suffices to say here that privatization of industrial enterprises and of land and forest led to a rapid evolution into a highly differentiated society.

The transformation from a state-controlled economy into a market-driven one tended to follow one of two main philosophies. One was 'shock therapy' which recommended no half measures and no gloves when privatizing state assets, imposing restrictive budgets on all economic actors and the sudden liberalization of the national market. A second philosophy, coined 'gradualism', advocated a gradual disposal of state property rights, a milder approach to privatizing state assets and restrictions in the flux of foreign capital and investments than that adopted by the 'shock therapy' philosophy.[15] Romania was among the countries that adhered to the latter philosophy, at least until 1996 when a pro-Western government came to power, limiting private investments, maintaining a strong state presence within the economy and slackening the liberalization of the market.[16]

Depending on the degree of economic and political liberalization, the actual status of postsocialist countries differs greatly. Central European countries (Poland, Hungary, Czech Republic, Slovenia and Slovakia) and the Baltic Countries were accepted into the selective club of the European Union (EU) in 2004 whereas Romania and Bulgaria were admitted only in 2007. Croatia joined as late as 2013. Serbia and Albania applied for this status in 2009 whereas the former Soviet Republics, other than the Baltic Countries, were not invited to join the EU.

The global neoliberal philosophy and governance and its political, economic, social and environmental outcomes is what binds postsocialism to postcolonialism. The term postsocialism is almost never used as an analytical term but rather designates a geographical area: Central and Eastern Europe. The term postcolonialism is used often as a theoretical paradigm but also tacitly presumes a geographical area outside Europe.[17] Both terms denote explicit or implicit opposition to the 'West' in terms of social, political and economic inequalities.[18] The two 'posts' as Verdery and Chari put it, are part of the same story in terms of epistemologies, policies, ideologies and space organization although each 'post' has its own peculiarities. Verdery and Chari plead for dropping the two 'posts' and replacing them with a unifying term: post–Cold War studies.[19] Although the aim of this book is not to compare the two 'posts', I fully acknowledge that globalization of forces producing environmental degradation affects the postsocialist countries in the same way and with the same intensity as the postcolonial ones. Thus, theories and authors which explain the causes of environmental degradation in postcolonial settings, 'married' with postsocialist studies scholarship, inform the analytical excursions of this book.

The geographic stage of the ethnographic episodes described in this book is represented by two communes, Dragomirești and Dragova, both located in Argeș County in the northern part of the province of Walachia (see Figure 0.1).[20] Both communes lie in hilly areas: Dragomirești in Sub-Carpathian hills and Dragova in the Carpathian Mountains at the border between Walachia and Transylvania. The ecology of the region largely shapes the local economy. On the surrounding hills of Dragomirești animals graze on pastures which alternate with orchards. On the top hills meadows alternate with forest whereas at the bottom of the hills a tiny strip of cropland stretches along the river. A few kilometres away can be found a huge industrial enterprise: the car factory Dacia-Renault. Thus, the local economy of Dragomirești with its three component villages is based on forest exploitation, subsistence agriculture, animal husbandry and industrial jobs. Dragova is less bewildering ecologically: located up in the mountains, the commune's three villages have large forests, meadows and pastures. The cropland is non-existent and the closest industrial factory is located some 100 kilometres away. Thus forest exploitation, animal husbandry and marketing dairy produce are the only components of the local economy. The ecological differences between the two communes are obvious. Ecology matters but so do politics, economics and social structures. I discovered the interlocks between these domains while interviewing villagers.

* * * * *

August 2004 in a household from Dragomirești village. In the shadow of the porch protecting us from the summer heat, the man before me complains about the changes his village underwent after 1989. He recounts how orchards belonging to the collective produced high-quality plums which were exported to Western European countries, the maize seeds planted were very productive and resistant to every disease and pest, and pastures belonging to the collective farms produced an impressive quality and quantity of hay. Now, he emphasizes, the new 'private' plum trees are of a different type – good enough to make *țuica* (homemade plum brandy) but not for eating: 'We also keep maize seeds from one year to another as we can't afford to buy hybrid seeds which would be more productive and more resistant to pests'. The pastures have been transformed into either land covered by bushes or built-up areas. Anyway, he assures me, there are few cows left in this village, so no need of pastures anymore. 'As for the forest, well, as we say here in the village, there are no trees left in the forest so a cuckoo would not be able to build a nest', he says, concluding with this local saying, graphically describing not only the disappearance of the forest but also the fauna which once used to populate these forests.

These stories bored me because I was concerned less about the type of plums cultivated now or the maize seeds they use than about market relations, local politics and social relationships within the village. Indeed, like other scholars of postsocialism before me, I was interested in the dismantling of the collective farm, the integration of the local economy into the wider, newly emerging capitalist economy and the new types of social relations emerging in the postsocialist period. Nevertheless, as my interlocutor pointed out, postsocialism meant reorganization not only of the society but of the natural world as well. Re-establishing private property rights over land and forest not only has economic, social and political implications; it affects local crops, trees, animals and rivers as well. As anthropologists have pointed out, decollectivization is undoubtedly a political and economic process, one that affects land tenure, the economy and local social relations.[21] However, it equally affects the type of crops cultivated, the variety of plum trees grown, and the quality of pastures and forests. More generally, land reform has changed the social, economic and political relations in the countryside but has also had environmental effects: trees, animals, plants, soils, and rivers have been put under immense pressure, subjected to dramatic changes.

This book suggests that the economic and political postsocialist transformations parallel environmental ones. By looking closer at the postsocialist changes in the natural environment I suggest, following Donald Worster, that there is a circular relationship between humans and their environment: humans influence the environment through economic and political relations and the environment influences human social relations.[22] Examining the circular relationship between humans and their environment does not suppose an equal intensity in action nor the same effect. The natural environment certainly has agency in changing the social and economic relations in rural areas. However, in this circular relationship – as I see it in this book – human action prevails and marks the landscape in a disruptive way. The effects of humans' activity on the environment have more dramatic impact and more visible consequences than the opposite. Thus, the circular relationship is not equal in both intensity and effect.[23] When I say 'environment' I mean something similar to William Cronon's understanding of 'nature': a human construction of the nonhuman world.[24] Humans shape the natural world through their social practices, and their activities make an impression on the landscape. As Denis E. Crosgrove put it, 'the ways people organize in order to produce their material lives result from and give rise to changes in relationships with their physical surroundings'.[25] Thus, by understanding changes in the agrarian landscape – that is, how the socialist landscape has been transformed into a postsocialist one – we gain a deeper understanding of the changes in local economics and politics.

In order to pinpoint how postsocialist economic and political transformations have marked the agrarian landscape and how the changed agrarian landscape has contributed to building new social relations,[26] I explore unintended outcomes of centrally designed land reform in postsocialist Romania at local level. To understand how land reform has been thwarted at the local level, I look in two directions. First, I examine villagers' local ecological responses to wider economic changes. The return to private ownership, a tenet of both neoliberal ideology and postsocialist policies, did not suddenly turn the villager into an indomitable farmer aiming to conquer the market. By trying to muddle through, the villager has brought back pre-collectivization agricultural practices such as intercropping and crop diversification. Instead of producing a boom in animal husbandry, the mountain-dwelling villager has reacted by shifting the weight of the local economy from animal husbandry to rural tourism. All these economic changes have radically reorganized the agrarian landscape. Second, this book seeks to show that local state bureaucrats have had the power to influence the outcomes of land and forest restitution in order to meet their own interests rather than those of the central government. They have thwarted the overall values and intended goals of land reform. In this way, local power relations have shaped the postsocialist agrarian landscape. Diverging from other authors working in postsocialist settings who have looked only at socio-economic relations, I include in my analysis the nonhuman world, such as land, trees, crops, waters and animals. I argue that the economy of crops and pastures is intimately linked to the economy of animals and forests; to this end, I draw links between different parts of the ecosystem and between the ecosystem and humans. I show that the decrease in the number of cattle, along with other elements of economic origin, such as the collapse of state animal complexes and the retreat of the postsocialist state from marketing processes, influence the quality of the local pastures. In fact, village pastures shrank as they became overgrown by bushes. This change is not just a biophysical one but also brings changes in the property status: the state forest inspectorate steadily marks land covered in bush as state forest. This means fewer animals to graze, less pasture needed, and so no protests among villagers as they do not need pasture anymore. Thus, although this book confers a more central role on the nonhuman agents influencing human relations in postsocialist contexts, it recognizes the importance of human action in creating new environments and landscapes.[26] By taking seriously the natural environment and the animals that populate it, as well as the outcome of human action, this book intends to add to a scarce but yet continually growing literature.[27]

The remainder of the introduction explores the book's theoretical ambit and outlines the directions the book will head in.

Land Reform and the Reorganization of the Landscape

Land reform was an attempt by postsocialist governments to impose new meanings of property on local people, attaching new values to land and utilizing a new economic language in accordance with neoliberal tenets.[28] It was part of the central state's plan to completely reorganize its socialist society, including people, economies and landscapes, and to transform it into something radically different. Postsocialist economic reforms were often neoliberal policies enacted by the national government but promoted by international financial institutions.[29] National policies regarding market relations implementation, land privatization and state withdrawal from any economic activity were thinly disguised impositions by the World Bank and International Monetary Fund missions, as I point out in chapter 3.

Postsocialist land reform led to the break-up of collective farms and land restitution to private owners in the early 1990s. As if Garrett Hardin himself had developed the land reform, governments used the 'tragedy of the commons' discourse when placing a significant emphasis on restoring private property; in this case the commons were replaced by collective and state farmland, while socialist collective farming was blamed for the failure of agriculture in Eastern Europe.[30] Private property and the market economy were expected to bring economic efficiency, responsibility for the environment and sustainable rural development. While Hungary, the Czech Republic and Poland applied 'shock therapy'- the rapid privatization of land and agricultural assets – in their attempt to transform the socialist economy into a market economy, the first Romanian postsocialist governments were rather reluctant to promote deep land reform and slow in restoring private property.[31] Nevertheless, under pressure from international organizations and the emerging civil society, Romania gradually privatized industrial and agricultural assets. Land reform was part of a more general effort of the postsocialist state to reorganize and modernize the whole society: people, economies and landscapes had to be re-arranged in order to bring the country 'into Europe'. Through re-organization of the entire economy and the landscape, the postsocialist state has proved that it shares the same DNA as any other modern state.

Modernizing economy, people and spaces means, as James C. Scott has pointed out, a simplification of the landscape – he calls it legibility – for the sake of taxation and the efficient management and control of natural resources. This high-modernist ideology, as Scott calls it, requires the state to put monetary values on natural resources and control people and spaces, all in the name of improving the human condition.[32] The process Scott has described in his seminal book only partially covers the processes of land reform and the transformation of socialist societies into new, capitalist ones.

Postsocialist land reform was meant to abolish collectivization and the nationalization of forests and to reshape rural production relations. In the process of landscape modernization described by Scott, legislators in many European countries from the nineteenth century onward were interested in removing the multitude of local tenure arrangements and agricultural practices, which were difficult to codify and thus to tax. Instead, the high modernist state imposed land property rights; each plot had a clear owner with clear boundaries to be read by the cadastral officers in their attempt to make cadastral maps, a necessary instrument in taxing the land and forest. This process is, as Scott points out, a profoundly political one. The postsocialist reformers were driven by a similar rationale: private ownership of land would turn the rural inhabitant into a capitalist farmer producing for the market. In this way, rural inhabitants' standard of life would significantly improve while their production would contribute to national economic growth and to the general welfare of the country.[33] There were political reasons as well: governmental parties were interested in enlarging their electoral base by posing as reformers and at the same time making the rural population politically dependent on the state, a.k.a., the political elite.[34]

If the rationale and ideology of the postsocialist state are to a great extent similar to that described by Scott, restoring land and forest to their previous owners has had significantly different outcomes in the field. First, the large plots of agricultural land cultivated industrially by the socialist state or the collective farms were atomized through decollectivization. Instead of large 'legible' surfaces, in Scott's terms, the state reform has created myriad parcels of land with multiple owners, as Katherine Verdery describes in the context of a village in Transylvania.[35] One of the unintended consequences of land reform was land fragmentation. Anyone travelling today in rural Romania would notice the highly fragmented landscape.[36] Although in some parts of Romania, especially in the lowland villages, people have joined new land associations in the hilly regions, landowners prefer to work their cropland, pastures and orchards individually. The stubbornness with which villagers continue to work their land is explained both by the historical evolution of the area, as they have proudly expressed their status as free landholders throughout history, and by the political economy of the postsocialist state, which emphasized private property to the detriment of collective farms. For villagers living at even higher altitudes, land fragmentation is part of their landscape history. For centuries they were small landholders, and the fences surrounding each individual plot proudly state that the land is private. Socialist collectivization did not reach them.

Such a large process as land reform, designed centrally and imposed from the top downwards, often ignores or even suppresses the practical skills and knowledge of local people acquired through long-term ecological experience, as Scott has warned us.³⁷ He calls this local knowledge and these adaptable skills *mētis*. Rural inhabitants' practical knowledge is based on an astute observation of the surrounding environment, a deep knowledge of the plants and the land they cultivate and on their immediate needs. Scientific agriculture imposed by the high-modernist state and implemented by agricultural experts not only dismisses this local knowledge and experience as unproductive but also represents, in Scott's reading, a strategy of control and appropriation.

How did postsocialist villagers, recently emerging from a differently organized society, namely a socialist one, react to these changes imposed by central governmental offices? This book argues that the reaction of villagers to these rapid changes differs from the one anticipated by central governments and their Western supervisors. Instead of being transformed into aggressive capitalist farmers, villagers rediscovered pre-collectivization agricultural practices. Once a villager reacquired his or her land, spread in several pieces throughout the commune's territory, he or she had to transform him or herself overnight from a farmer who executed the orders of the collective farm technicians into a farmer who had to make decisions concerning which crop to cultivate, when, and by what means. The collective farm aimed to cultivate a few crops intensively, following the supreme aim of the socialist government not only to achieve food sovereignty for the country but also to export agricultural products. The postsocialist landowner had a different aim and different means to achieve it. Villagers adapted fairly well to the land fragmentation by diversifying their crops, reintroducing the prewar practice of intercropping maize, beans, and pumpkin (*Curcubita pepo*) and by shifting to the type of plums more suitable for making țuica than for marketing as fresh produce. He or she had less capital, less time, and less interest in maintaining intensive cropping. In other words, farmers opted for agricultural extensification in response to the fragmentation of land.³⁸ Local agricultural practices were adapted to the new economic milieu.

Postsocialist changes were equally traumatic for those villagers who had never experienced land collectivization. Until 1989 they combined two types of economic activity: animal husbandry and its associated activities, such as the production and selling of dairy products and meat, with a still emergent rural tourism. Although these commercial activities may seem to have provided a training ground for the new capitalist society, the uncollectivized villager was also unprepared for the rapid economic changes.³⁹ Operating within the socialist market, whether legal or illegal, in a shortage economy was different from operating in a growing competitive market. While they supplied dairy products that were in short supply on the socialist state market, in the new postsocialist milieu they had to compete with cheap Western dairy products. They began to compete not only with subsidized products but with the socially valued Western agricultural products too. The opening of innumerable supermarkets, especially after 2000, led to an explosion of choice of different Western dairy brands. Thus, the once entrepreneurial peasant had to face changing consumption patterns too.[40] After 1989, the number of cattle and the labour and capital invested decreased due to all these factors.[41] Instead of intensifying animal husbandry, villagers turned to a more lucrative occupation: rural tourism. Uncollectivized villages were located at a rather high altitude in the Carpathians, and the lofty mountains, caves, cascades and 100-year-old forests surrounding those villages seemed there to be marketed to the increasing number of tourists.

The outcome of land reform was very different from that expected by the central planners. Villagers coped with the situation by resorting to local knowledge and practices, which they considered more suited to their interests. Thus I suggest that villagers resisted neoliberal governmental plans by finding their own way of dealing with them. Some rediscovered pre-war agricultural practices while others turned to new domains of activity. Thus, I suggest that improvement schemes such as land reform not only produce new forms of local knowledge and practice but also reinstate old ones that helped villagers to get by for centuries.[42]

Local State Bureaucracy and the Postsocialist Elite

So far, I have described villagers' reactions to neoliberal changes enacted by the central government. Depending on the local ecological conditions, they resisted these changes by adopting old agricultural practices or turning to new economic domains such as rural tourism. In both cases, they responded to wider economic changes in a different way to that anticipated by central planners. These local agricultural practices have environmental consequences and create a new agricultural landscape that is different from the previous socialist one.[43] However, this is not the whole story of the changing landscape. Seeing the state as a monolithic agent with a homogenous identity and practices, as Scott seems to conceive it, and as an entity represented only by prominent political figures, leaves out many intermediary levels.[44] In the case I discuss here, land reform was developed in central offices but necessarily implemented by a multitude of agencies and branches of the state at local and regional levels. It is important to identify those state actors, institutions, agencies and people, ranging from local to national level, that have contributed significantly to the reshaping of the landscape. One cannot tell the story of such radical changes in the natural landscape without a thorough description of the social activity and political practices of the parties involved.[45] I follow Joel S. Migdal who identifies four levels of state organization.⁴⁶ At the bottom of the state hierarchy are those officials who are in close contact with the population: tax collectors, police officers, teachers and all those tasked with applying state rules and regulations. These are what Michael Lipsky calls 'street level bureaucrats'; they are those who supposedly implement land reform provisions 'from the grassroots'.⁴⁷ A higher level is constituted by those bodies, local or regional, which implement policies, or those who work in local legislative offices or in courts. These officials channel resources and make decisions at local level. A third level is made up of central office staff in the capital city. These are the places where national policies are formulated and from which central resources are channelled to lower levels. Finally, the fourth level is constituted by a tiny group of top executive leaders. The four levels of state hierarchy are connected through a myriad of political and administrative threads. The relationship between higher ranked officials and lower officials is one of mutual dependence, at least in postcolonial and postsocialist countries, and it is based on an exchange: local bureaucrats provide votes for the party in power while high-ranking officials provide impunity.⁴⁸ Local state officials have at their disposal natural resources that can be easily converted into financial resources and, as I will show throughout the book, they do not feel shy about using and abusing them. As Alina Mungiu-Pippidi notes, the price of fierce competition for power in the state is the state itself and all its resources.⁴⁹ Thus, in order to understand how the state functions at a local level, one needs to document the relationship between local level officials and those higher in the hierarchy, and to show that local bureaucracy does not act autonomously but in concert with forces closer to the centre of power. Documenting this demonstrates that accountability, the mantra of every political scientist analysing the state, works vertically, from lower levels of bureaucracy towards higher levels, and not horizontally towards the citizens.

In postsocialist Romania, the local state is composed of two types of state official. Policemen, forest guards and employees in the mayor's office represent one type, which I call the local bureaucracy.⁵⁰ Higher levels of state bureaucracy appoint these officials and hold them accountable. Therefore, all these bureaucrats depend on the party in power. Thus the Romanian bureaucracy is indeed far more dependent on the higher political positions than Max Weber's Prussian bureaucrats who were in theory appointed on their own merits.⁵¹ Members of the local government and the mayor represent a second body of institutions. These individuals are elected by and should be accountable to the villagers.⁵² Although the bureaucrats I describe here share some features with the bureaucrats described by Weber, namely a special training, key knowledge and administrative skills, at the same time they differ quite substantially from the modern bureaucrats. Weber (1978: 979) presents the ethos of modern capitalist bureaucracy as free from 'arbitrary action and discretion, of *personally* (emphasized in the text) motivated favour and valuation, such we shall find to be the case among prebureaucratic forms'. The German sociologist portrays Prussian bureaucracy as 'dehumanized' in the sense that officials exclude from their administrative activity emotions or purely personal interests, acting in accordance with rules and objective considerations.[53] As I will show throughout the book, Romanian local state employees use their office positions to exploit the forest, the most valuable natural resource in rural areas, and to transform pastures into built-up spaces. Thus, local bureaucrats act in their personal advantage, avoid, if not directly break, the rules and laws of land reform and serve their superiors' political interests. In my reading, the bureaucracy I describe in this book is far from having an ethic similar to that of the Prussian bureaucracy described by Weber.

By exploring the interaction between different state officers and villagers I emphasize that there is a state presence even at local level, and that its actions directly shape the landscape. The ethnographical accounts in this book depict a state that is very much present in peoples' lives. I therefore give credit to an idea that conflicts with what some authors describe as a 'distant state' or the 'absence of the state' at local level.[54] For instance, Johannes Stahl discusses the Albanian case in which local officials extracting rent from illegal woodcutters have profoundly altered the landscape. His impressive ethnography points, however, to phenomena other than state dynamics: according to his approach, wider economic and political changes led to the retreat of the state from local life.[55] My own ethnography points in the exact opposite direction: the state, through its local level officials, is part of the daily life of the villagers and contributes significantly to forest exploitation and massive shrinkage of pasture areas. Thus, everyday political practices involving patron–client relationships and manipulation of office positions have a direct and massive impact on the local agrarian landscape.

Privatizing the State and Consequences for the Landscape

In the period following the 'revolution', the re-formation of the Romanian state at all levels, the enactment of land reform laws, and farmland and forest restitution to pre-1945 owners, took place simultaneously. The emerging postsocialist states differ in many respects from the old, settled Western states, which were, after all, the model for the postsocialist ones. The postsocialist state was built *on* the ruins of the socialist state but *with* the building materials picked up from these ruins.[56] In other words, the changes produced in the structure of the state are the outcome of a mélange of late socialist and neoliberal political institutions, ideologies and people.

In the process of decentralization, multiple centres of authority have emerged.⁵⁷ Further, privatization of socialist assets, such as land, forest or industrial factories, and market liberalization have considerably diminished the influence of the central state.⁵⁸ The creation of the Local Land Commission (LLC) aimed not only to return private property to its legitimate owners but also to make this process more accountable to local villagers. However, as many ethnographic reports show, members of the LLC were able to hijack the land reform process to serve their own interests.⁵⁹ As heads of the LLC, mayors were in a very powerful position to acquire land and agriculture-related assets such as tractors or combines from the dismantled socialist collective farms. For instance, a mayor was able to manipulate information concerning land, having access to land registers from 1945 to the present. Maps and registers simply disappeared, and the mayor usurped land that apparently had no owner. When the heir to the land showed up, the mayor was able to impede the land restitution process.⁶⁰ In many cases, the mayor's friends, who were often his political supporters, received good quality land while the legitimate owners received poor quality land.⁶¹

Most local state officials were heirs of the communist government.⁶² Although the central government was officially dismantled in December 1989, most of the local mayors and councillors remained in power. There seems to be a general agreement among anthropologists working in postsocialist countries that most of the local elite shares a socialist history. They had the advantage of having worked for the collective farms as directors and they could utilize the social networks that had been created in the postsocialist period.⁶³ Most of these former socialist elite relied on social connections that were transformed, in the postsocialist era, into market relations. The local elite now had a different connection with the central state. As Verdery pointed out, as the mayors acquired power through decentralization, the Ministry of Agriculture and Forestry had little leverage over them. This situation created immensely powerful local state officials: the mayor and the members of the local council, both elected by and therefore only accountable to the villagers, were virtually beyond the reach of the law.⁶⁴ However, the link between the centre and the local peripheries is even more complicated than this. As I have already mentioned, there is a double movement of resources and power relations from local level to the centre and vice versa: local level officials seek immunity from prosecution which is guaranteed by state officials located closer to the power centre; national politicians need votes which are usually brought in by local level bureaucrats and officials who have leverage over voters. This 'dialectical model of interaction' between the centre and the local peripheries is the perfect milieu in which to develop a patronage system at local level.⁶⁵ The existence of an extensive and politicized apparatus that once occupied pre-existing centres of power, together with those who already had access to socialist structures, represent the base for this system. In the process of new state formation, defined by Anna Grzymala-Busse and Pauline Jones Luong (2002: 536) as a 'process of elite competition over the authority to create the structured framework of policy creation and implementation', the local and central elite created institutions in which they occupied a central place to serve their personal interests.[66] As Verdery suggestively put it, the local elite represents 'their *own* state'. They simply privatized the state.[67]

These plundering officials were responsible for land reform implementation; their local interests and the political relations they have built, based on the power conferred by their offices, have contributed to physical changes in the landscape: shrinkage of pasture and deforestation are two examples of this nature transformation. Dominating people is, in this case, interconnected with the domination of the natural landscape.[68] Chapters 3 to 5 and chapter 7 ethnographically describe the local state bureaucrats' practices of outwitting the central state's plans and promoting their own interests. By bringing local state officials into the discussion I show that the state's schemes of life improvement conflict not only with local practical knowledge, Scott's *mētis*, but with the lower levels of state bureaucracy too.[69] Local state officials are those who contribute to the most significant degree to changes in the agricultural landscape.

So far, I have drawn a picture in which economic and political actions shape the natural landscape. The landscape itself also contributes to shaping human economic and political relations. Before addressing this aspect, scarcely debated so far in the literature on postsocialist transformations, let me briefly clarify how I apply the overused term 'landscape'.[70] I understand landscape as being produced through land use practices in a certain place in a certain historical moment.[71] Seeing landscape in this way suggests not only that landscape is a social product, a consequence of the human transformation of nature, but also that it involves perceptions about land, its meanings, values and struggles.[72] It encompasses the different historical meanings people attach to their land ranging from personal and social identity to social status, moral aspects and economic value.[73] In postsocialist Albania villagers cut the 'communist trees', a chestnut forest, as an expression of scorn for the collective farm and to make sure this mode of organizing the economy would never return.[74] The chestnut forest embodies equally the collective farm history, state political power and the villagers' harsh lives throughout the last half of the twentieth century.

Landscape not only bears the marks of different ideologies and of state power but also creates power and influences economies, politics and discourses. A convincing example is the establishment of national protected areas throughout the world. The constitution of national parks means, in many parts of the world, the imposition of European and North American ideas about wilderness, pristine landscape and biodiversity preservation.[75] What represents biodiversity conservation for the state or international agencies for nature protection constitutes hunting or cultivable land for villagers. As a consequence, landscape is invested with various ideologies and becomes the arena for political struggle between different groups.[76] This struggle is about imposing one's meaning on the landscape, determining what it is good for and who should define how to manage and use it. Landscape is a weapon of the powerful to be used against the weak.

Consequently, the forest becomes a contested space in which differently constructed claims over property rights have different meanings for different actors. For villagers interested in the forest as a means of livelihood and as a potential source of immediate gain, and for powerful local bureaucrats, the forest signifies wealth. The consequence is deforestation and the creation of a forestless landscape. For those interested in 'selling the scenery' the forest is an essential part of the landscape. For these actors landscape has a strong visual and aesthetic component before anything else. The forest signifies wealth for them too, but this cannot be understood outside the aesthetic element. After all, no visitor would spend money on a hike around stumps on a deforested hill. These villagers embrace the national parks' forest protection policies as supporting their own interests.

The struggle for nature becomes even more evident in the case of natural protected areas in postsocialist countries. As Wells and Williams have pointed out, in the context of a severe economic decline in postsocialist Russia, natural resources from protected areas become very attractive and represent a source of cash for a population experiencing great hardship.[77] The priorities of such a population, the meaning attached to the forest and its utility are very different to those of the state, international donors or NGOs. Consequently, two sets of practices, linked to two different ideologies, invest the landscape with different meanings and, at the same time, produce two types of landscape. In the case I will describe in chapter 4, the struggle between villagers and the national park is not only motivated by imposing ideologies; ultimately it is about granting exclusive property rights and about what Verdery calls 'effective ownership', or what villagers can or cannot do with their forests.[78]

The forest is an actor playing an essential role in determining local social dynamics. The forest has a history, interpreted differently by locals and the state, and a political life. Patronage relations have been built around the forest and local politics depends significantly on access to forest. Animals populating the forest play a central role in shaping the local economy, as I will show in chapter 5. Contributing for years to the destruction of pastures, the wild boar (*Sus scrofa*) has helped instigate the steady passage from animal husbandry to rural tourism. A pasture completely destroyed is a tragedy for a community that relies on raising animals as well as a powerful reason to look for new economic avenues. Animals such as the Carpathian brown bear (*Ursus arctos*) also embody the presence and control of the state over private forests. For many villagers from the Carpathian Mountains the presence of the state agencies monitoring private forests is not the only way the state exerts control over the forest. The brown bear, a European protected species, is for angry villagers living proof that the state still exerts property rights over private forest: the presence of the animal in *their* forest represents an attempt of the state to keep them out of the forest and an indirect claim over its usage. In this case, the agency of nonhuman actors such as animals, much discussed in the new stream of theory called multispecies ethnography (Kirksey and Helmreich 2010), has a literal meaning. This theory's intellectual genealogy lies in the work of Donna Haraway and Bruno Latour, among others, who have suggested that human relations are sometimes influenced by nonhuman actors (from inanimate things to animals). They attribute agency equally to human and nonhuman actors.[79] Kirksey and Helmreich engage with Haraway and Latour's theory but they strictly refer to biological nonhumans, that is species other than Homo sapiens. The main idea put forward by proponents of multispecies ethnography is that there is a multitude of biological organisms that shape and are shaped by political, cultural and economic forces.[80] Following this body of theory I show that nonhuman actors, such as wild animals, mediate, influence or shape local social relations and feed the political imagination and the social critique.[81] The human and the animal worlds are distinctive yet intermingling: not only do all villagers husband domestic animals as part of their livelihood but they also share with wild animals the ecology of and the property rights over a territory. It's not a peaceful cohabitation but an adversarial one. As I will show in chapter 5 the conflict with wild animals takes political, social and ethnic forms and actions as nature is always invested with cultural meanings.[82] By looking at the landscape from this perspective – following William Cronon who teaches us that animals are part of the landscape – this book suggests new ways of understanding the transformations of the natural landscape taking place in postsocialist times.[83]

Methods for Studying the State and the Agrarian Landscape

Exploring the unintended outcomes of land reform and the marks left on the postsocialist landscape requires a *bricolage* of approaches. The challenge of gaining access to intimate power relations in a small community is not easy either for ethnographer or informant. It requires the researcher to engage sometimes in unorthodox investigative techniques. Thus, I have occasionally adapted the semi-structured interview to a free conversation especially when enquiring about sensitive issues: deforestation, who gains from land and forest, or bribes for state officials. I thought of this kind of conversation as an enquiry that did not seem like an enquiry. I came to this approach when I realized that standard techniques of investigation such as the classical interview did not get me very far. People were obviously reluctant to respond to my questions even though I never asked direct questions such as, 'Have you ever bribed an official?' When it got to this point I usually closed my notebook, put my pen in the small rucksack I always carried and made it clear that the interview was over. I then continued the conversation, displaying my interest in issues such as those mentioned above *not* as a researcher but as a fellow citizen who also experiences the hardship of the transition, the abstruseness of bureaucracy and the necessity of bribing officials. At this point villagers started to complain about the way they must interact with local officials and how they manage to deal with them. Several times, I carried out interviews in unconventional places such as bars in the villages. I offered informants a beer or a bottle of wine – usually more than one, generously sponsored by Humboldt University, my employer at that time. After a first 'official' interview with innocent questions about the communist past and capitalist present of Romanian agriculture, I invited the leaders of the illegal woodcutters, the policemen, the forest guards, the mayors and the vice-mayors, one at a time, for more friendly follow-up meetings in a bar, to enjoy some drinking. In face-to-face discussions over a glass of beer, with no tape recorder or notebook on the table, people were less reluctant about giving me candid accounts of their relationships with superiors or with the political party they represented, or about how they manage to get by.

Archival documents, such as economic and social reports about the commune, should be open for public access. The law 544/2001 stipulates free access to information regarding public interests. However, in my contact with bureaucracy, at local and regional levels, it became clear that if I wanted to see any document or data at all, I needed to 'buy' the co-operation of local officials with small gifts. Some bottles of cognac for people at the County Department of Statistics, some perfume and a silk scarf for the secretary of the mayor's office, and some packages with coffee and sweets for the agricultural officer worked miracles.[84] I had good access to the information I needed.

In order to measure the changes in land use that have occurred, such as the extensification of agriculture, I have used data concerning agricultural production gathered from official documents of the mayor's office or from the regional bureau of statistics located in the county capital. Data concerning deforestation, property rights over resources and the history of land plots were obtained through participatory mapping. The objective of a participatory map is to enable villagers to carry out the interpretation of some aspects of their land resources and to point out what is important for them.[85] A map is never innocent; it stakes a claim on property rights to a territory, usually from the state's perspective ignoring at the same time local people's claims. I employed this technique, rather unusual among anthropologists, in order to allow villagers to express their points of view regarding property rights over local natural resources and the way the land is used.[86]

Local historical archives, though improperly referred to in this way, offered me some important historical documents. I was simply lucky to find in the pile of documents in a small dark room some items that I could use. More important historical information was found in unpublished manuscripts written either by those passionate about local history or by local teachers of history or geography who had to pass exams based on their research. These monographs are based on a thorough examination of local history including the environment and the economy. They are a rich source of historical and geographical information.

The following chapter will set the scene for the study by exploring the history of land use and, consequently, the economy in the two communes up to the break-up of the socialist regime.

Notes

1. Cartwright (2001).
2. Hirschhausen (1997: 120); Verdery (1995). In other postsocialist countries, Bulgaria for instance, rural inhabitants were less eager to dismantle the collective farms and claim the land back (Creed 1995). This difference, which is not the focus of this study and therefore will not be analysed here, should be ascribed to differences in agricultural politics under socialism in the two countries. As Creed (1995) points out, the illegitimacy of Nicolae Ceaușescu's political regime may have also played a certain role in the postsocialist perception of collective farms. I thank one of the anonymous peer-reviewers for drawing my attention to this issue.
3. I use 'collective farm' and 'co-operative' interchangeably throughout the book.
4. Around 95 per cent of the land was collectivized. The mountainous land, mostly pasture, remained uncollectivized. Private owners were not officially allowed to lease their land. Nevertheless, as I detail in chapter 2, those who moved into the cities used to lease their private land informally. They also had to pay high taxes to the state as well as to deliver meat, wool and living animals. See for more details Constantinescu (1972).
5. Swinnen (1997).
6. Only in 1881 did the Principle of Romania officially become a king.
7. Scurtu (1995: 8). The number of ethnic Hungarians was larger before 1918 but after the incorporation of Transylvania by Romania many Hungarians fled to Hungary. The migration continued in the 1980s during the worst years of Nicolae Ceaușescu's political regime when some 36,000 Romanian citizens, most of them Hungarians, resided in the more liberal socialist Hungary (Brubaker 1996: 158–59).

8. This data is from the National Institute of Statistics (http://www.recensamantromania.ro/wp-content/uploads/2013/07/REZULTATE-DEFINITIVE-RPL_2011.pdf), accessed 6 February 2015. There are voices, never confirmed by the official statistics, which claim that the Roma population is as large as 10 per cent of the population of Romania. What is certain is that some Roma either refuse to respond to the census question about their ethnic origin or they declare themselves Romanian ethnics.
9. Swinnen (1997).
10. Verdery (2002).
11. Bandelj (2008: xviii).
12. China and Vietnam are considered postsocialist countries in most of the academic literature. Despite the fact that the Communist Party is still the only ruling party in those countries, their economies and societies have suffered deep changes. Both countries have adopted a market economy, privatized their state enterprizes and restored land and forest to villages or private owners (Sturgeon and Sikor 2004: 16). In short, they have followed the same path as other postsocialist countries. Not all authors agree with the label 'postsocialist' for the two countries (see, for instance, Hann and Hart 2011: 137, who use the term 'reform socialism').
13. For agricultural reforms in Vietnam, see Nguyen (2005). For Albania, see Stahl (2010a).
14. This statement contains several historiographical problems, which will not be solved here. Whether it was a revolution or a coup d'état conducted by other apparatchiks is not important here. What is important though is that this moment is the beginning of a massive change in the Romanian state at all levels.
15. For more details, see Hann and Hart (2011).
16. McCollum and Schoening (2002).
17. Owczarzak (2009).
18. Owczarzak (2009: 4); cf. Todorova (2009).
19. See Chari and Verdery (2009).
20. Commune is the smallest administrative unit in Romania encompassing from one to several villages. The name of the communes, of villages and the name of all persons mentioned in this book are pseudonyms. I was specifficaly asked by some of my informants to protect their names.
21. Creed (1998); Hann (2006); Mungiu-Pippidi (2010); Verdery (2003).
22. Worster (1990).
23. I thank one of the anonymous reviewers for drawing my attention to this matter.
24. Cronon (1995).
25. Crosgrove (1998 [1984]: 5).
26. Melville (1994).
27. Gille (2009); Staddon (2009a, 2009b); Stahl (2010a).
28. Hann (2007).
29. Schwegler (2008).
30. Hardin (1968); see for instance Spoor (2009).
31. Hann and Hart (2011: 131); Mungiu-Pippidi (2010).
32. Scott (1998).
33. Sarris and Gavrilescu (1997).
34. Mungiu-Pippidi (2010).
35. Verdery (1998, 1999, 2003).
36. At national level, land restitution has fragmented the land into 14.3 million individual parcels with an average number of three parcels for each individual household

(Rusu and Pamfil 2005). Thus, the image I describe in this chapter is representative for all hilly regions in Romania.
37. Scott (1998).
38. I use the word 'extensification' as opposed to "intensification". Therefore agricultural extensification may be defined as the decrease in the amount of agricultural labour, capital investments and in the agricultural inputs per unit of worked land (Stahl 2010a).
39. For the uncollectivized farmers and their openness towards the market economy, see Stewart (1998).
40. Smith and Jehlička (2007); Mandel and Humphrey (2002).
41. I simplify a discussion that is otherwise more complicated (see Iancu and Mihăilescu 2009). Changing patterns of consumption is just one of the many causes of the decreasing number of animals in mountainous areas. The increasing cost of production and the crises the Romanian society went through in the 1990s also account for the downsizing in the number of animals. See Mincyte (2011) for a similar account in Lithuania.
42. For the production of new forms of knowledge see Li (2005).
43. Following White (1996), Schwartz (2006b) and Mincyte (2009) I consider agricultural practices an essential part of environmental activities.
44. See Herzfeld (2005: 373) for the critique of Scott (1998).
45. Weiner (2005).
46. Migdal 2001: (117–21).
47. Lipsky (1980).
48. Solnick (1998:13) suggests that high-ranking officials are 'dependent' to a certain degree on more junior officials as the latter have to implement strategies developed by the former. I suggest that this relationship is more complicated and involves movement in both directions.
49. Mungiu-Pippidi (2006).
50. Members of the local state are more numerous than I present here and include local physicians and school professors. I am interested here in naming only those bureaucrats who play a central role in changing the agrarian landscape.
51. Weber (1978: 974). I am aware that I judge the postsocialist Romanian bureaucrats against a theoretical model such as the one suggested by Weber. I am also aware of the academic literature focusing on the ethnography of bureaucracy, which shows that real bureaucracies are appointed and act very differently from Weber's ideal type of bureaucracy. As the literature has shown (see, for instance, Howe (1990)) state bureaucrats may be judgemental, interpret in a subjective manner the policy they are supposed to implement and generally act less formally than suggested by Weber's bureaucracy. However, what I try to underlie mirroring the ideal type with the 'real life' bureaucracy is the undisputed *political* power of the local state bureaucrats, which creates a highly unequal relationship between them and the villagers (see also Dorondel and Popa (2014)).
52. I have discussed elsewhere the relationship between the elected and appointed bureaucrats. For more details about this matter, see Dorondel and Popa (2014).
53. Weber (1978: 979 and 975).
54. For the 'distant state' see Bierschenk and de Olivier de Serdan (1997); for an 'absent state' see Stahl (2010a).
55. Stahl (2010a).

56. I paraphrase Stark (1996: 995) who actually pointed out that 'organizations and institutions are not rebuilding *on the ruins* but *with the ruins* of communism' (the author's emphasis).
57. Grzymala-Busse and Jones Luong (2002).
58. Kaneff (2004).
59. Mungiu-Pippidi (2010); Spoor (2009); Verdery (2002).
60. Verdery (2002).
61. Mungiu-Pippidi (2010); Verdery (1998).
62. Mungiu-Pippidi (2010).
63. Lampland (2002); Stewart (1998); Verdery (2003).
64. Verdery (2002).
65. Hann (2001: 134).
66. Grzymala-Busse and Jones Luong (2002: 536); Marcus (1983).
67. Verdery (2002: 8). I use the expression 'state privatization' differently than Hibou (2004 [1999]). While she refers to the privatization of the state as 'the spread of use of private intermediaries for an increasing number of functions formerly devolving on the state and deployment of the state' (Hibou (2004 [1999]: VIII) I use the term to designate all ways in which the state is used for certain private advantages.
68. Sachs (2003) has made a similar point for a different époque and geographical space.
69. Herzfeld (2005).
70. See Czepczynski (2008) for an attempt to consolidate some of the most important definitions of the landscape. For a historical meaning of the concept see Olwig (1996).
71. Wiersum (2004: 131).
72. Crosgrove (1998 [1984]). For an anthropological approach to the landscape seen as a cultural process that incorporates, among other meanings, a visual element, see Hirsch and O'Hanlon (1995).
73. Dorondel (2005a); Hann (1993); Verdery (2005).
74. See Stahl (2010a) for more details on this episode.
75. Neumann (1998); Gissibl et al. (2012).
76. Moore (1993); Walker and Fortmann (2003).
77. Wells and Williams (1998).
78. Verdery (2003).
79. See Haraway (1985) and Latour (1988). Some anthropologists fiercely oppose the idea of giving agency to nonhuman actors. See the short but acid critique of Tim Ingold (2008) of the idea of giving agency to inanimate things.
80. Kirksey and Helmreich (2010).
81. For a good review of human–animal relations in terms of the construction of class and race relations, see Mullin (1999). For a more recent approach on human relations with nonhuman beings, see the discussion of Kohn's 2013 book sheltered by HAU (2014). However, I am not going *stricto sensu* in the same theoretical direction.
82. Tsing (1995); Carrithers et al. (2011).
83. See Cronon (1983).
84. Students who are not familiar with field methods may find this approach to fieldwork a bit unorthodox. Accessing some of the official documents held by the mayor's office, some of them already archived, requires the assistance of the mayor's office staff. They helped me in their working time and sometimes after; I therefore considered the packets of coffee, the scarf and the perfume to be a pale attempt

to pay for their working overtime. With regard to other bureaucrats such as the policemen or the state forest guards, alcohol brought us closer and helped override the cultural differences they may have felt exist between a Ph.D. and a researcher affiliated with a German institution and themselves. Drinking with my informants meant that I performed a male local social practice (Dietler 2006). The alcohol also helped to dissolve social barriers when talking with some of the illegal forest workers. Drinking in pubs from Rudari settlement, where no Romanian villager would ever go, helped me to transgress the mistrust Rudari have in Romanians – for many good historical and political reasons. In this way, the interviews went more smoothly, and the interlocutor found himself more comfortable when recounting his illegal activity. Drinking with Rudari while they told me their stories about forest activity does not mean I deceived them in any way. At all time they were aware of my scientific interests.

85. The technical approach I took for participatory mapping is as follows: I took several GPS points at the edge of the commune following the cardinal points. A satellite image of the area based on the GPS points was ordered. Daniel Müller printed out the digitalized satellite image. On the resulting image of the village I placed a transparency. A group of five villagers was invited to take part in the discussion. In a subsequent session in the house of one villager three locals mapped their own land and forest. The agricultural officers in both communes as well as forest guards were invited to attend the discussion and to draw the state forest boundaries and the location of private land and forest. Daniel Müller then digitalized the results of the villagers' and local officials' drawings and made the maps. For more information about this technique, see Müller et al. (2003).

86. For more on the maps' political discourse, see Walker and Peters (2001). Anthropologists critique the usage of satellite images (Ingold 2000), as villagers are requested to adopt the 'bird's eye' perspective when looking at such images. However, seeing 'familiar landmarks from an unfamiliar perspective' (Jackson 1994: 3) also has advantages as it points out significant differences between different categories of villagers. For instance, there was a tremendous difference between the perceptions of illegal woodcutters and the forest owners. The former know the forest well because they have to find the best places for exploitation. The latter do not often go into the forest and thus are less able to find their way through it, but they are able to name different parts of the forest that are linked to local history. This difference points to their contrasting ways of referring to the forest: in a utilitarian way or in a more affective, though not uninterested, way.

 CHAPTER 1

Dragomirești and Dragova
Two Centuries of Ecological and Socio-economic Transformations

> 'The fight between man and nature, the desperate efforts to grab from
> the land a morsel of food, all these are of Homeric proportions.'
> —G. Bogza, *Țări de piatră, de foc și de pământ*
> *(Countries of Stone, Fire, and Earth)*

When the bus turned right off the main road that links Pitești, the Argeș county capital, to the northern part of the county, a rural landscape opened up before my eyes: a hilly village crossed by a small but still lively river, with small patches of orchards and pasture on the left side of the road and agricultural fields on the right. Patches of forest alternating with plots of deforested land still covered the peak of the hill. The bus had to make a slalom between the deep holes in the asphalt which looked 'like it had been bombed' as my host described it a few hours after my arrival in the commune. The state of the road, which links Dragomirești commune to the city capital Pitești, located 26 kilometres away, transformed travel to and from the commune into an adventure.[1] When I arrived in Dragomirești I was still able to see the signs of what used to be a region famous for its very fine orchards. The contrast between green, healthy trees and the shrivelled trees now standing in the orchards along the road was a sign that the local economy no longer puts the same value on its fruit trees.

This chapter is intended to guide the reader through the history of land use and of the local economy in Dragova and Dragomirești, the two communes from Walachia where I carried out fieldwork in 2004.[2] It sets the scene of the whole book by moving back and forth through time from the early nineteenth century to our times in order to describe the changes in the landscape. I have other reasons for conducting the reader through two centuries of local history: one is that I link changes in the agrarian landscape to the political and economic changes, showing their close interdependency. Another reason is to show that agriculture and forestry in the area were part of a national economy beginning in the nineteenth century. The rise of the socialist state, land collectivization and forest nationalization did not disrupt connections between the local economy of Dragomirești and the national and international markets. As I will show in the second part of this chapter, socialism only changed the forms and conditions of those connections to the national economy. As for Dragova, the location of the commune at the border between Walachia and Transylvania transforms it into a place of passage for people and goods. Besides, the natural scenery, spectacular forests and caves scattered throughout the area made it ideal for rural tourism, one of the pursuits that have radically transformed the local landscape.[3]

Dragomirești, a Hilly Commune

Today, Dragomirești commune comprises three villages and numbers 2,852 people. Vâlceni and Costești are located along the river Argeșelu on the surrounding terraces while Dragomirești, the administrative centre of the commune, lies along the 733 County Road. The commune comprises three ethnic groups: 933 Romanians, who represent the ethnic majority, 593 Roma people (*țigani*) and Rudari, and 99 persons belonging to other ethnic groups.[4] Out of 593 people designated as Roma, around 300 are Rudari. Roma people are designated under the generic term *țigani lăutari* (Roma fiddlers).

On ascending one of the surrounding hills one can see the landscape of the commune. The commune has 4,181 hectares. The plain along the river, 405 hectares, is the crop field. Villagers grow cereals, mostly maize and some wheat, potatoes and vegetables, all for subsistence purposes, on highly fragmented cropland. The cropland is segmented into narrow long strips of around 12 metres in width and as long as 2 kilometres. The strips cross the river and extend up the hills. This is a clear sign of the lack of any agricultural association and shows that individuals work the crop fields.

The county road that links Mioveni, a small town of slightly more than 30,000 inhabitants, to the communes along Argeșelu River divides the inhabited area into two parts. Dragomirești village developed mostly along this road. Most of the households in Dragomirești village have large backyards, some of the villagers owning up to one hectare of land of mixed cultivation. The orchards, totalling 208 hectares, grow in the middle of the pastures. Small gardens are planted next to the house. Tomatoes, onions, garlic, red and green peppers, carrots, cabbage and parsley all come from these small gardens and consumed by villagers. At the end of the pasture begins the 2,553 hectares of forest. The hill peaks, once covered by forests, look like a patchwork: the dense forest is interspersed with large deforested areas.

Most of the 698 hectares of pastures and meadows lie outside the inhabited area. Here the eye is met with the same patchwork as rather large areas

Illustration 1.1. The Fragmented Landscape in Dragomirești

of the pastures are covered with newly constructed houses. Bushes advance year by year as outposts of the forest. Cows, no more than a few dozen, graze among the bushes.

Not all households have large backyards. If the spectator turns her eyes to the southeast or northeast she will notice that most households in Costești and Vâlceni have rather small backyards packed in next to each other. Both villages lie on the hillside, on the eastern side of the river, and sometimes the small backyards are packed very close to one another on the slope of the hills. This contrast has its origin in pre-socialist times. Today, people from Dragomirești village proudly emphasize their origins as free landholders (*moșneni*) while with a slight irony sparkling in their eyes they call villagers from Vâlceni and Costești *clăcași* (serfs). Most of the former clăcași are rather poor, Dragomireștens claim, as they never had much land or forest. In retaliation, inhabitants of these two villages are ready to say to any stranger that 'people in Dragomirești are conceited and even lazy', as even though they have enough land and forest they still complain about the harshness of life.

The hilly region is suitable for the forest, natural pastures and the growing of fruit trees. Small creeks, dry for most of the year, cross the surrounding hills creating terraces suitable for fruit trees. The hills protect the village and the long strips of cropland along the river from powerful winds. The climate is temperate with no long droughts, blizzards or long wet periods. The soil constituting the flood plain was created by alluvial deposit and is well-suited to growing crops. The slopes of the surrounding hills are made of layers of clay, sand and gravel. These are not suitable for anything else but pasture. The peaks of the hills are covered with forest. The most common trees are oak (*Quercus robur*), beech (*Fagus*), hornbeam (*Carpinus betulus*), maple (*Acer platanoides*), elm (*Ulmus*), birch (*Betula*) and sycamore maple (*Acer pseudoplatanus*).

Free Small Landholders, Serfs and Land Use Practices

To some extent the area's patchy landscape and social stereotypes originate in its local history. There are few documents older than 1838 describing the village's economy and social relations in sufficient detail.[5] Until 1857, the agricultural land belonging to Dragomirești village was collectively owned by 76 of the 130 families living in the village at that time. The other 54 landless families received small plots through the agrarian reform in 1864.[6] Beginning in 1857 the collective land was shared among three ancestors (*moși*), representing the first settlers and founders of the village. All native families are descended from these three ancestors. Further, the families that had the same ancestor shared the land in long narrow strips called *chingi* (meaning 'belt' in Romanian). There was logic in having such long strips as they covered several sorts of land: cropland for cereals, hemp and flax, lower slopes for orchards and pasture and forest at the top of the hill. In this way, every family was able to obtain all types of agricultural products ranging from cereals, especially maize, to fruits, mostly plums, and hay. An area of forest as great as 574 hectares was also owned collectively until 1948, when the socialist state nationalized it.[7]

In the same period, Costești – including 86 families of serfs and 37 Roma slaves (*țigani robi*) – belonged to a nobleman.[8] The serfs were living on the nobleman's land and they had to deliver taxes both to the state (king) and to the nobleman. They also worked their master's land. The numbers illustrate the villagers' poverty: the 482 inhabitants, counting both serfs and slaves, were living in 63 huts, 23 of which were constructed underground (*bordeie*). They worked some 430 hectares of land and the orchards counted 6,110 fruit trees and 23 mulberry trees. The main crops cultivated were hemp, flax, maize, wheat and grape. These families received between 2.5 hectares and 1.5 hectares of agricultural land through the 1864 land reform.

In 1838 Vâlceni was a mixed village composed of serfs, free landholders and one nobleman. The 67 families worked 150 hectares of land, had 13 hives and, important to the local economy and that of the other two villages,

2,910 plum trees. The nobleman's land measured 1,560 hectares of cropland, pastures and orchards.

In 1864, Ioan Alexandru Cuza's land reform, the first important land reform in the Romanian history, granted land to peasants based on their agricultural inventory (the number of oxen and cows). Those who owned four oxen and a cow received five hectares in Walachia and seven hectares in Moldavia. Those with two oxen and one cow received three hectares in Walachia and five in Moldavia. Finally, villagers with no agricultural inventory received two hectares in Walachia and three in Moldavia. Peasants had to pay a certain amount of money for the land they received which was finally borrowed by the state. They had to pay back their debt in maximum 30 years. Noblemen who lost the control of up to two thirds of the arable land – although they had the right to choose the best quality land they kept – received financial compensation.[9]

Not only serfs benefitted from the 1864 land reform but the villages too. From the nobleman's land Costeşti village received 48 hectares of pasture, which had to be used communally by the inhabitants (called *islaz*). Further, the village was rewarded with another 144 hectares of pasture through the 1921 land reform, to be used communally by villagers. Dragomireşti village received 48 hectares of communal pasture in 1921 only.[10] The communal pasture was very useful as in the second part of the nineteenth century the number of animals in the three villages grew significantly. In 1838 the 320 families from the three villages owned 1,810 head of cattle (cows, oxen for work, sheep, goats and horses). By 1890 the three villages counted 2,093 head of cattle. It is true that there was also a population explosion, with 2,252 families recorded at the end of the century.[11] While the number of sheep decreased significantly from 444 to 87, the number of cows grew from 295 in 1838 to 601 heads in 1890. A possible explanation for the growing number of cattle is the land reform and the new communal pastures at the villagers' disposal. After 1864 it was easier for a family to keep a cow, having gained the right to graze their animal on the communal pasture. Besides, it was economically more viable to have cows, which give milk almost all year round, rather than sheep, which give milk for around five months in a year.

However, there were other changes in land use that were maybe more important than this one. In 1838 there were 547 draft animals (oxen and horses) while in 1890 the number increased to 730.[12] This is the sign of change in the local economy. Agriculture most probably brought some economic advantages. The local fairs, the place where people from neighbouring villages gathered to buy and sell their agricultural produce, dated from this period. Local memories of the mixture of fun – gypsy musicians playing different instruments, members of families scattered throughout the region meeting up – and commercial activities are still vivid. However, a new activity seemed to be more lucrative than agriculture and this was the exploitation of forest. This new activity required a growing number of draft animals for the wooden wagons. The timber was put into horse drawn wagons and carried either to the city located less than 30 kilometres away or to the nearest railway station, around 7 kilometres away. From here the wood was sent throughout Romania. At the end of the century the Romanian state went through an economic boom period. The creation of a national market after securing independence from the Ottoman Empire (1878), the penetration by foreign companies in the new state, was, doubtless, of much importance for the villagers as well. Forest exploitation was tempting for villagers and the landlords alike. In 1886 Perieţeanu, the landlord from Costeşti, built a railway paid from his own pocket, which connected his forest exploitation business to the railway station. The railway had to last ten years, as long as the forest was exploited. In 1889 he also built a steam chainsaw most probably to serve the locals as well. His investments show not only that the area of forest was large enough to be exploited for ten years but also that exploitation of forest was an economic activity that brought significant revenues. At the end of the century these villages became attractive to wood businessmen from Bucharest. In 1898 a businessman from Bucharest opened a frame saw in Vâlceni.[13] The documents mention other names buying and exploiting private forests in Dragomireşti.

At the dawn of the twentieth century forest exploitation was an important part of the local economy. This had multiple consequences. One was that the rush to exploit the forest contributed to massive deforestation. In 1928 the daughter of the landlord who had built the railway complained that villagers released their cows into her wood, destroying the tree saplings. This will impede the forest's growth, she added in her official complaint. In a report dated 15 October 1911 the prefect of the county describes the situation at county level: 'there are many water-powered saw mills throughout the county's territory which transform the forest into timber which is transported to southern Romania. A huge quantity of beech is transported to Bucharest'.[14] These documents prove that the once-centenarian forests were turned into a young wood in the first part of the twentieth century. Another consequence is the change in the villagers' occupational structure. In 1838, out of 281 families in the three villages, 243 families made their living exclusively from working the land. Twenty-three families made their living primarily from making wooden wheels (for horse wagons), one family from making coffins, thirteen families from working in the wood (*lemnari*) and seven from making wooden caskets. All others also had primarily non-agricultural roles such as brick maker, spinner, policeman, priest or running a small country-inn (*cârciumă*). That does not mean these families were not working the land at all, it only means that most of the household benefits came from non-agricultural activities. One hundred years later, in 1941, another statistic shows that forestry workers were almost as numerous as the agricultural workers: 104 inhabitants were forest workers while 128 were still relying on agricultural land. If we add the other occupations connected to wood work, such as horse wagon conductor (*chirigiu*), wooden wheelwright, carpenter and forest guards totalling 291 people, the total number of villagers making a living from wood products surpassed the number of those making a living exclusively from agriculture. Finally, a third consequence of the booming wood business was that for the first time the entire county, not just Dragomirești commune, experienced the importation of a foreign labour force. A document dated 1898 shows that 200 people were brought from Serbia to work in the private forest exploitations while 50 people came from Galicia for the same job.[15] The imported labour force suggests that local manpower was either scarce or more demanding than the foreign workers. In any case, villagers from Argeș County had, like their peers from Dragomirești, economic alternatives: agriculture, including the production and commercialization of *țuica* (a famous plum brandy well known throughout Romania) and the transport of wood and other goods from the villages to the nearby cities.

The most highly valued wood was beech and oak. Beech was primarily used for heating. It is a good combustible as it burns slowly, produces less smoke than any other firewood and has high heating calories. Beech started to be used in a booming furniture industry because its fibre is smooth and looks beautiful and in the construction sector because its fibre is also hard. Oak was used for the construction of railway, for buildings, and also for producing fancy, expensive furniture. The bark was used in the tanning houses as it contains a big percentage of tannin.[16] The fierce exploitation of forests must be linked to the national industry development at the beginning of the twentieth century including metallurgy, mining, railways and the communication system.[17] All these industries consumed huge quantities of different types of wood.

The cultivation of cereals was always secondary in the commune for at least two reasons: one concerns the year-round low temperature with an average of 9 degrees Celsius; second, the cropland was quite small in size, lying along the river. Until the beginning of the twentieth century, the riverbanks were irregular and the land next to the river was swampy, unfit for cultivating maize and wheat. Before collectivization, intercropping was a widespread method, maize and beans being cultivated together. The bean was planted after the maize had already started to grow so the bean plant could climb up the maize stalk. The cultivation, hoeing and harvesting was thus possible only manually, without the intervention of a machine.[18] Intercropping was a traditional response to the local ecological conditions and to the lack of availability of agricultural land. Intercropping gives a greater yield per unit of land, enhances protection against pests and diseases, and improves soil fertility.[19] It was equally dictated by the intimate knowledge of the ecology of plants and the biophysical characteristics of the land. There were unwritten rules regarding the distance between the cultivated plants, the hoeing technique, and the types of hoes peasants used in such a field.[20] Beans and maize are particularly compatible because of the root distribution between the two crops.[21] Beans contribute to fixing the nitrogen in the soil whereas maize is a great consumer of it.[22] Of course, it was not the scientific knowledge of Romanian peasants that contributed to intercropping practices but the long history of agricultural practices in this area.

Another important aspect of the local economy and land use was growing fruit trees. The climate as well as the soil made this area a paradise for fruit trees. Plums were by far the most profitable fruit for the local economy. In 1839 there were 17,483 plum trees in the three villages: that means even the poorest villagers, the Romanian serfs and the Roma slaves (*robi*), owned plum trees. Other fruit trees such as apple, pear and walnut trees (*Juglans regia*) are less significant: 693 fruit trees for the three villages.[23] The first usage of plums was plum brandy. This alcoholic beverage is of paramount cultural importance in the rural area. The cultural significance of țuica will be analysed in chapter 5. Having a special, very fruity aroma, it contains no more than 27–28 per cent alcohol.[24] It is distilled once as opposed to the famous *pălincă* (plum/apple/pear/maize brandy) in Transylvania, which is much stronger, around 50 per cent, and distilled twice. Until the end of the nineteenth century most of the plum production was used for making țuica. An 1839 document mentions that Dragomirești village had its own distillery (*povarnă*) where villagers brought the marc and firewood and made țuica.[25] This distillery must have been close to the river, probably located somewhere close to where the present-day village distillery is. This place is still called 'the Valley of Povarna'. Even earlier, in the seventeenth century, documents point to rich villagers owning their own small distilleries.[26] At the end of the nineteenth century the Dragomirești commune produced 113,600 litres of țuica. The sort of plums cultivated in the area was always rather more suitable for producing alcohol than for eating. Only towards the end of the nineteenth century were the plums dried and sold in the nearby cities. The 1911 report I cited above points out that 'only recently a professional fruit dryer was opened in Costești'. The prefect of the county suggested that the local state officials should encourage this occupation to the detriment of making țuica, thus combating alcoholism in the region.[27] The dried fruits were intended both for personal consumption and barter. Only at the beginning of the twentieth century did villagers start to cultivate different types of plums, apples and pears more suitable for sale on the market in the nearby cities.

A good part of fruit production was intended for barter: Dragomireștens offered țuica, fresh and dried fruits in exchange mainly for maize, which was always in deficit in the commune. Today, old people still remember how they used to travel with their parents or grandparents in a convoy of five or six horse carts full of fruits, țuica or firewood to the lowland villages in southern Romania.

Another occupation that brought important economic benefits for some of the villagers was raising silk worms. The nineteenth century is characterized by a significant number of mulberry trees in the commune. They constituted the food for the silk worms. In 1890 villagers from the three villages produced 270 kilograms of silk cocoons.[28] Though the socialist Romania was still one of the world's largest players in silk production in 1989, this activity disappeared in Dragomirești after the commune collectivization. This is not the only agricultural occupation that disappeared. Documents mention hemp and flax cultivation on rather a large scale. Both plants were used for making clothes locally. Villagers must have been skilled in growing this crop, as in 1885 a woman from Costești received a prize for the best quality hemp seeds. Collectivization put an end to the cultivation of these two crops.

I have emphasized so far the fact that the commune's landscape has been dramatically altered by the disappearance of certain crops. There is though a feature of the landscape that was preserved until collectivization. Land fragmentation, the long and narrow strips I described at the beginning of this chapter, is a feature of modern, early twentieth-century agriculture in the area. Land fragmentation here reflects local inheritance practices. The main heritage strategy in Walachia was for all beneficiaries to receive an equal share. In contrast with other parts of Europe, where different strategies were adopted in order to keep the family land together, in Walachia all beneficiaries, regardless of gender, inherited the same amount of land.[29] Only the girl who remained in the house or the youngest son who took care of the parents inherited the house and the garden surrounding it.[30] This system contributed massively to the fragmentation of agricultural land and originates in the division of the land in the middle of the nineteenth century. During the Medieval period the land was worked in common; at the emergence of the Romanian kingdom into modernity, land was divided up and a portion given to each family. Within a few generations, that is, in the period right before collectivization, the agricultural land became quite fragmented. Usually the boundary was marked by a plum tree or apple tree, the traditional way of separating two plots in medieval times. One document dated 12 May 1654 mentions the fringes of a plot that begins at 'Foamete [a name] apple tree' and extends 'over the Argeșelu River'. Another document dated 25 May 1709 describes the fringes of a plot 'between the marked big hazelnut tree, the mill pond, the painted oak ... and the Monastery Valley'.[31] Some of the local toponyms are still in use today and show the historical importance of trees for establishing the fringes of a land plot: Apple Tree Valley, Willow Valley, Quince Tree Valley, Nut Tree Valley, Box Thorn Valley. Another practice widely used throughout Romanian territory was that of taking the kids to land plot fringes and harshly beating them so that they would remember the land they would inherit sometime in the future.[32] With such uncertain and fluid boundary marks to deal with, the communist authorities easily produced a radical change in the landscape after collectivization.

Two features appear when analysing land use change in pre-socialist times in Dragomireşti commune. One is that forest exploitation played a major role in the local economy at the dawn of the twentieth century. Wood was easily marketable and the surrounding forest attracted a significant number of wood businessmen. It was also a major source of income not only for large forest owners but for a number of people connected with forest exploitation: forest workers, horse wagon conductors, wood wheelwrights and carpenters indirectly earned their living from forest exploitation. The most unexpected feature is that villagers had a long history of gaining an income from non-agricultural activities. A statistic from 1941 shows that out of 586 labourers only 128 were agricultural workers. Others worked as forest workers, horse wagon conductors, carpenters and for the National Railway Company. This statistic shows that villagers from Dragomireşti did not depend entirely on the land.

Forest People

At one of the edges of the commune live, mostly in poor huts, a population calling themselves Rudari. Most of the houses were built in the 1970s and 1980s, a good economic period for members of the community as some of them were hired at Dacia, a car plant. The plant opened in 1968 and absorbed many members of the Romanian rural population, including Rudari and Roma. Although Rudari were hired for unqualified jobs, such as cleaning the plant's backyard and toilets or carrying the iron chips from the production premises to a special outdoor place, the regular salary allowed them to build new houses. It was the first time in their long history that they had had a regular salary and a higher social status. There is no such thing as Rudari as far as the Romanian state is concerned but they are part of the Roma group. Their ethnic origin is much debated in the literature but most scholars consider them to be Roma, if a distinctive sub-group.[33] Roma or not, Rudari were freed in the same time as Roma people in December 1855 in Moldavia and February 1856 in Walachia.[34]

In the nineteenth century the Rudari were mentioned in the documents as river gold gatherers.[35] Their ethnonym also suggests this occupation as in Transylvania they are called *băieși* (mining workers), in Hungary and in Serbia they are called *bayasi* or *banyasi*, meaning the same thing. Sometimes in the nineteenth century, the Rudari people, for unknown reasons, changed their occupation, turning to forest exploitation. The fact that they had previously been living close to rivers must have contributed to their choosing forest as an occupation and as an ecological niche. At the end of the nineteenth century, Roma people freed few decades earlier but with no means of subsistence such as land or capital triggered what the Bulgarian scholars call 'the great Kaldarara invasion'.[36] Probably some Rudari joined the Roma, as today they are located in Bulgaria, Serbia, Hungary, Greece and the coast of Dalmatia, though under different names. The Rudari population who emigrated must have been attracted to the rich Bulgarian forest mountain areas such as Tarnovo or Varna and Burgas. Today these areas are still the most densely populated by Rudari.[37] Those who remained in the Romanian Principalities also settled in the vicinity of forests.[38] They used wood to make various types of furniture such as chairs and tables while the branches were used to weave baskets and make wooden spoons, forks, pots, spindles and brooms. Different types of wooden tools required different types of trees: from nut trees they weave baskets and wattles. For the wooden brushes they used birch branches. To carve spoons, forks and spindles Rudari needed 'soft trees' such as sycamore, maple, ash (*Fraxinus*), alder, or fruit trees which are easy to carve and pretty resistant. The oak, the beech and the poplar trees were used to make all kind of furniture. However, obtaining such wood was not a simple matter. Usually Rudari illegally cut down trees from private forests. As these trees were more expensive the probability is that forest owners reacted more promptly and aggressively to their removal. Besides, the Rudari could carry the branches on their shoulders, whereas the bigger and heavier trees they had to carry in a horse cart.[39] To the difficulties of carrying larger and heavier trunks one should add also the penalties they received. If caught with a few branches on their shoulders a Rudar might have got away without any penalty. A cart full of trunks illegally cut could have meant fines or even imprisonment.

Rudari's relationship with forest owners and the forest guards, both Romanians, has been ambiguous and tense throughout modern history. Due to their repeated forest infringements they were not particularly liked or trusted by the Romanian population. Sometimes, when they settled for a longer period of time, they built their camps on the communal pasture (islaz), impeding villagers who wished to graze their animals there; this constituted another source of tension between Rudari and the villagers. Nevertheless, almost all domestic tools used by the Romanian population in the countryside were made by Rudari. Either sold or exchanged for clothes or food, the Rudari's wooden products decorated many Romanian households. Thus, the Rudari were involved in a long-standing economic exchange with the Romanian rural population.

The relationship with the forest guards was equally ambivalent. As Rudari population lived from wood but never had property rights over forest, they had to deal with foresters. Usually, they entered the wood, wrapped up the trunk of the tree so the noise of the saw was reduced and then cut it. Sometimes when they were caught in the forest they bribed the forest guard. For half a kilo of *rachiu* (a poor quality brandy made from fruits or cereals) the forest guard turned a blind eye to Rudari illegal activities.[40] However, most of the time there were tense relations between Rudari and the forest guards. A sentence the Rudari used to describe the interwar relationship with the forest guards that I heard seventy years later almost in the same form was, 'the forest guards are as bad as dogs'. The interwar conflict with state authorities was eloquently described by one Rudar: 'You can't go into the forest because they (i.e. the forest guard) catch you; if you go to the marketplace to trade your wooden stuff they (i.e. the policemen) ask you for your permit. I don't understand these laws....'[41] The tense relations with state authorities persisted throughout the twentieth century. When they were caught by forest guards and fined, the judge invariably waived their fines, as they had no goods to be confiscated apart from their wagon-horses and their axes and saws. Moreover, they often ignored state rules that were considered exterior to their culture. On the one hand, stealing from Romanians or from other ethnic groups was considered a felony and severely punished by the elders of the community. On the other hand cutting trees illegally was not considered a felony but a legitimate way of acquiring the necessary wood for their work. It was simply considered a matter of survival and the community elders would never have punished someone for encroaching on someone else's forest.

When not settled, Rudari wander from one place to another trying to sell their products.[42] When settled, the Rudari cottages – often built below ground level and called *bordeie* – were built either deep in the forest or on the valley at the fringe of the forest. They never settled within the village but at least two or three kilometres away. Whenever they settled they chose a region with rich forest.[43] Rudari people also lived by gathering wild fruits and mushrooms, both for their personal consumption and for trading at the fairs.

The documents mention in 1838 the existence of thirty-seven families of Roma slaves (*țigani robi*) in Costești. Two of them were fiddlers; all the others were referred to as bucket makers (*căldărari*). In 1926 four families of

Rudari settled at the outskirts of Costeşti, in the valley of a dried creek. Their number increased to seventeen families by 1941 as recorded in a statistic from that year. In 1981 there were thirty-seven families, counting 169 inhabitants. When I arrived in the village, they were around three hundred persons.

Enduring Landscape of Dragova

On the road which links the two historical provinces Walachia and Transylvania a narrow path turns towards the large and mighty stone gates called the Dragova Gorges. The path follows the River Dragova, which looks as if it carved its way through the gorge. The canyon-like aspect of the gorge, with calcareous walls higher than 200 metres stretching for 8 kilometres and 50 caves spread along the Dragova River, have contributed to building the image of a savage, remote area.[44] The name of the village itself evokes large forests and the hilly aspect of the region.[45] The road winding through the gorge ends up in Dragova village. This is also the administrative centre of the commune which encompasses two other villages: Ciocănaş and Podu Dragovei. Again, the names of the two villages evoke the natural environment: Ciocănaş comes from a Slavic word meaning 'the top of a hill', 'a peak', whereas the second village translated as the 'Bridge of Dragova' depicts a nineteenth-century reality; a bridge built over a river.[46] Dragova looks like the bottom of a bucket surrounded by the Bucegi Mountain to the east, Iezer-Păpuşa and Piatra Craiului Mountain to the west. The peak of Piatra Craiului guards the surroundings with its 2,086-metre height. The 1,057 inhabitants of the commune, all Romanians, live at an altitude between 840 metres and 1,240 metres above sea level. Thus, the climate is quite cold throughout the year with an average temperature of around 8 degrees Celsius. The most northern part of Dragova has represented the border between Walachia and Transylvania since medieval times. The high altitude, the cold temperature and the location on the border also define the economic and ecological features of the commune.[47] The economy of the area since the Middle Ages has been based on animal husbandry, as the climate is too cold and the relief is too rough for cultivating cereals, on commercial activities – selling cheese, smoked meat and wood – and more recently on rural tourism. The smoked cheese, the hard cheese, the cheese kept in tree bark and the sheep pastrami were very famous products throughout the country, products that are still the pride of the village. These products were so famous that from the seventeenth century Turkish merchants came all the way from the Ottoman Empire to the area to buy them.[48]

The border location of the village enabled the inhabitants of Dragova to be involved in networks of economic exchange in the southern part of the country but also in Transylvania, which was part of the Austro-Hungarian Empire (1867–1918). Sandrea, the neighbouring village located a few kilometres north and belonging to Transylvania, was for a long time the favourite 'reservoir' for choosing a spouse. In this way, the Dragovans had a kinship network to rely on for their economic exchanges in times when relying on kin was the only option for people travelling hundreds of kilometres with their merchandise.

To a certain extent, one may say that Dragova represents a more enduring landscape than Dragomirești. A traveller through Dragova would immediately identify the source of the village's economy. On both sides of the road the green pastures, relatively well maintained, are carefully enclosed, a visible and public statement of private ownership. In fact, the enclosure of pastures not only affirms ownership but also regulates the social relations within the village. The wood enclosure protects the pasture from the neighbour's animals as well as from wild animals.

The neighbour's animals grazing on one's pasture is immediately the subject of conflict, unless the enclosure was weak and carelessly maintained by the pasture owner. The pastures are regularly fertilized with manure, the cheapest fertilizer to hand. Fertilizing the steep slopes with manure has a long history in the Carpathian Mountains, as a Romanian writer described graphically in a reportage from the interwar period: 'On a hot spring day a few people and a few oxen draining the last drop of force climb the steep slope of a hill carrying one hundred kilograms of manure.... If they didn't

Illustration 1.2. Private Pastures in Dragova

need to transport it in large quantities, hundreds, thousands of kilograms, people would carry it in their own palms, as if it was an elixir, a philosopher's stone'.[49] Taking good care of accessible pastures compensates for those that are hardly accessible and thus hard for sheep and cows to graze. The toponymy of different places such as Coasta Rea (the Bad Slope) or Coasta Dracilor (the Slope of the Devil) invokes the steepness of some slopes and the rough and hardly accessible geography of the area.

Private pastures and meadows total 1,251 hectares. To these one should add the 699 hectares of communal pasture, administered by the mayor's office and leased to those who want to graze their animals, in order to give a full picture of the extent of grazing land in the commune. The pastures are grazed by a variety of animals, including 832 bovines, 1,790 sheep and goats, 70 horses and 35 donkeys.[50] The relatively large number of horses and donkeys is explained by the necessity of hauling logs out of the forest, navigating through the deep valleys, steep slopes and the dense forests surrounding the commune. Only a traction animal would be able to negotiate its way through such thick forest.

Walking through Dragova, the eye is immediately attracted by the dense forests aligned on the top of the hills surrounding the commune, which completes the bucolic scene. The entire area has been famous since the nineteenth century for its wild centenarian forests, a mixture of coniferous and deciduous trees alternating on the alpine floor with bushes of raspberries, blackberries and cranberries and with alpine meadows. Fir trees (*Abies sp.*), spruce (*Picea sp.*) and Norway spruce (*Picea abies*) are commonly found here but beech (*Fagus*) and oak (*Quercus*) are also common, especially on the valleys. Dragova has 897 hectares of private forests, 356 hectares of collective forests and 70 hectares belonging to the commune and administered by the mayor's office. Both pastures and meadows come under two types of property rights: private and collective. Commons, *Obște* in Romanian, have a long history in this part of the country, dating back to the fifteenth century.[51] There were frictions between the kings of Walachia and noblemen on one hand and villagers from this area attempting to maintain their ancient way of economic, social and ecological organization on the other hand. At the end of the sixteenth century the villages from this area and the pastures and forests surrounding them became the property of the Walachian king. For more than two centuries villagers fought in order to buy back their lands and forests as well as their freedom from successive noblemen and Walachian kings.[52] The last important struggle was the lawsuit of 1923 when villagers' attorneys used an act dated 1797 to prove that they paid back every single penny for their collective forests.[53] Important to note is that commons were not owned by Dragovans alone but together with villagers from several neighbouring settlements, totalling 192 families owning 3,650 hectares of forest and meadows. The document proving common ownership was not only about forest but the alpine meadows in the middle of those forests as well, so important for a community of animal keepers. The long battle waged by villagers from this area is significant today because often villagers, some of them heirs of those involved in these long-standing frictions with an outside oppressor, recall these battles and their historical claims over surrounding forests, especially when struggling with the postsocialist state. Chapter 4 details villagers' claims based on historical rights when they struggle for *'their forests'* and for their right to exploit them according to their own needs with the National Park established on Dragova's territory immediately after 1990.

When I arrived in Dragova my eye was also attracted by the number of newly built houses and by those under construction. There was, obviously, a rush on building new houses or renovating the old ones, a rush which was confirmed by the statistics of the mayor's office: the number of houses had risen from 540 in 1985 to 589 in 1995 and their number rose sharply to 713 in 2005 (including houses of those who live outside the inhabited area). The simple explanation is that rural tourism has boomed since 1990. Officially, only thirteen guesthouses are registered but the small tin plates announcing availability of free rooms pinned on most gateways leave no doubts that tourism is perceived as the most important source of income in the commune.

Tourists are attracted to the local scenery, the possibility of exploring the caves around the commune, the possibility of long walks in a rough and wild area, and the excellent local food. Visitors were able to explore the area's hidden natural beauty only from the beginning of the twentieth century because until the end of the nineteenth century the trip from Podu Dragovei to Dragova was only possible on small boats up the river.[54] Thus, until the beginning of the twentieth century the three villages were hamlets whose inhabitants made their living from animal husbandry and commerce associated with dairy products and wood. Nevertheless, these villages are not new settlements on the map. Although the legend of the Dragova describes the foundation of the settlement as a grant of land and the surrounding forests from Negru Vodă (the Black King – the mythical founder of Walachia in the thirteenth century) to some outlaws, the village is first mentioned in the documents dating from 1579.[55] The Podu Dragovei village was a passage settlement since at the end of the nineteenth century some Italian constructors, famous and expensive stone workers, built a stone bridge over the river. The construction of the bridge – which does not exist any longer, having been replaced by an asphalt road – attests to the economic rise of the three villages linked to the increasing economic importance of the wood, demanded equally by the internal and external markets. Wood has been an important commodity since the late eighteenth century and it was shipped mostly to the Ottoman Empire.[56] The best houses on the shore of the Bosporus and the masts of the Ottoman ships were made with wood exploited from the Dragova area.[57] From the end of the nineteenth century and the beginning of the twentieth the documents mention the replacement of small saw mills with modern lumber enterprises. The lumber was then shipped throughout the country and abroad. There were two such enterprises in Dragova and several saw mills located along the river.[58] As in the case of Dragomirești, the industrial boom from the end of the nineteenth century and the beginning of the twentieth had given a strong impetus to wood businesses, from exploitation to processing and to sales.

Collectivization: a new agrarian landscape

The end of Second World War brought Romania under the influence of Soviet Union. Following the medieval principle *cuius regio eius religio*, meaning the winner imposes his own political and economic regime, Soviet Union imposed the socialist organization on the Romanian economy, based on state ownership. The project of collectivization, a blueprint for all countries under Soviet influence, started in Romania in 1949. It meant the imposition of state and collective forms of ownership in agriculture and a brutal collectivization and nationalization of large tracts of land and of the forest. The collectivization was a long process of thirteen years in which scholars identify three periods: a first period began in 1949 when the implementation of the collectivization strategy was carried out through violence or persuasion based on the threat of ensuing violence. A second period, between 1953 and 1956, represented a slight easing of collectivization politics. Finally, the last period ending with the declaration of the completion of collectivization in 1962 was characterized by increasing pressure and violence against peasants.[59] The politics of aggression was primarily aimed at the rich peasants (the Romanian equivalent for kulak is *chiabur*) but peasants who refused to transfer their land to the collective farms were also targeted.

Collectivization was a social engineering plan that aimed to radically change the social, economic and political features of the country. Collectivization could thus be understood from at least two perspectives. One, which I will not deal with here, is the violent aspect of imposing radical changes in agriculture.[60] The second aspect of collectivization is represented by the enforced modernization plans for Romanian agriculture. As James C. Scott has shown for the Soviet Union, collectivization had the same characteristics of high modernism throughout the world and was based on the agricultural planners' fervent belief in the benefits of huge, mechanized industrial farms.[61] Mono cropping on large tracts of land, which presupposes not only mechanized systems but also the elimination of a diversity of peasant local crops suited for subsistence farming and the introduction of cash crops, were part of the new transformation of agriculture. The 'magic of one', to use Frank Uekoetter's words, was built concomitantly with the development of science and technology which cannot be applied on fragmented agricultural plots.[62] Collectivization had a double goal: to brutally transfer land and natural resources from private hands to the state's, and to control the population economically and politically.[63] At the same time, collectivization was perceived as the socialist human being's specific adaptation to their environment and their struggle with nature in order to master it. Economically, it was a response to the globalization of the time but also an attempt to supply the entire national population with agroalimentary products and the industry with raw materials.[64]

I will shortly discuss the plan for changing pre-war Romanian agriculture, but not before adding one necessary correction. The modernization was forcefully carried out by the socialist state *against* not *for* rural inhabitants. Later in the chapter I will present several ethnographical vignettes that convey the scarcity of resources rural populations had to contend with, forced labour and the way rural inhabitants resisted state oppression. Under late socialism, though, rural inhabitants had access to both industrial wages and agricultural revenues, which made their lives slightly better.[65] These two apparently contradictory aspects of collectivization will be illuminated by ethnographic examples in the last part of the chapter.

In the dawn of collectivization Romanian agricultural land was quite fragmented: 3,142,000 family households owned less than nine million hectares of arable land, which was divided into 20,321,000 separate plots. Households had access to poor technology or no technology at all. In the early 1930s one million households had no ploughs at all whereas another 700,000 households had ploughs with wooden beams. There were an insignificant number of tractors available.[66] Nevertheless, the collectivization plans had not triggered peasants' enthusiasm: in 1949, when this process started there were only fifty-six collective farms owning 14,692 hectares. After thirteen years of violence, high taxes imposed on stubborn peasants, murders and 'dekulakization' of the rural society 10,231,000 hectares of land was collectivized.[67]

Almost 94 per cent of Romanian agricultural land was collectivized and 96 per cent of arable land was worked under collective and state ownership[68]. Approximately 95 per cent of the total number of peasant families worked for the collective or state farms.[69] The average agricultural area a collective farm disposed of was, according to Michael Cernea, 2,000 hectares which allowed the rapid mechanization and industrialization of Romanian agriculture.[70] New types of crops were added replacing the peasant ones, less suited for intensive production. For instance, in Argeș County, old peasant orchards spread over 2,500 hectares were fragmented into thousands of small plots. In the early 1960s the total area grew to 7,000 hectares grouped in several co-operatives.[71] The category of plum trees peasants used to grow allowed for production every three to four years, while the fruits were better suited for making țuica than for eating. The plum trees were replaced by new varieties and new agricultural techniques were engaged. Farms built earth terraces and left a grass band between the rows, which helped the tree to expand its roots. The hybrid maize replacing the local maize and the introduction of new agricultural techniques such as care for the density of the plants, addition of chemical fertilizers alongside the organic ones and the mechanical work contributed to a rise in productivity from 1,055 kg per hectare in 1939 to 2,740 kg per hectare in 1980. Agronomists reported higher productivity for wheat as well, from 938 kg per hectare in 1939 to 2,150 kg per hectare in 1980.[72] Again, the reader should keep in mind that usually the socialist state gained most advantage from these economic improvements, not rural inhabitants.

Rapid growth of the industry led to an increasing number of peasants involved in non-farm jobs and the emergence of a new social category: the worker-peasant. Some peasants from former collective farms, especially the young, literate and skilful were attracted by the higher social status and better salaries offered by the new industries. Whereas some of them commuted daily from their villages, and thus became fully industrial workers and part-time peasants, others preferred to leave their families for a longer period of time to work in the new industrial plants.[73] These new political economy developments affected agriculture in particular ways, as the case of Dragomirești will clearly show.

Collectivized and Uncollectivized Villages

Collectivization in Dragomirești started in 1955, later than elsewhere, mainly for two reasons. First, the small arable land plots were not suited to an economically viable co-operative. There were other attempts to abolish private property and consolidate land – a process called *întovărășiri* (associations). Dragomireștens however stayed away and this initiative died almost before starting. Only after this failed attempt did local administrators push harder in the direction of collectivization. Second, villagers of Dragomirești were free small landholders, strongly attached to their land. The economic arguments of the communist regime – that land would be consolidated and mechanized work would be possible which would improve productivity per hectares – were not strong enough to break the strong bonds between people and their lands. At the very beginning only 19 families subscribed to the collective farms totalling 46 hectares of cropland. In 1962, when collectivization was officially declared completed, the local co-operative numbered 756 families and 1,135 hectares of arable land, orchards and pastures.[74] Private forests were also nationalized in 1948, depriving peasants of an important source of their revenue. As elsewhere in Romania, Dragomireştens reacted by declaring to state officials less land and forest than they actually owned – which was possible because some of them had no papers to prove their ownership – or refusing to sign the declaration of adherence to the newly founded collective farm. Finally, almost all of them ended up as agricultural co-operative workers.

Collectivization not only changed the land use through mechanization and the use of fertilizers and pesticides but also completely changed the type of crops cultivated in the commune. Former crops such as hemp, flax or silk worms completely disappeared. Instead, the collective farm focussed on growing potatoes (on 40 hectares), cultivating maize and barley and growing fruits on 255 hectares of land. The types of plums and apples were changed to allow for better production per year and to a type of fruit more suitable for eating than for making țuica. Each year 50 to 60 tonnes of high quality fruits were exported to West Germany. Local heads of the collective farm were very careful about the quality of the fruit, as only high quality would have been acceptable to their German partners. Villagers still remember that they had to gather the fruits at dawn in order to keep the dew on them. The plums were individually packed and sent to Bucharest. The lower quality fruits were sent to the fruit canning plants in the county. The commune also became famous for the high potato productivity: in 1989 the local collective farm obtained the best potato production rate in the county, a title that villagers still proudly remember – 40 tonnes per hectare.[75] The collective farm mainly cultivated hybrid cereals which were better suited for growing earlier in the year – a good choice if one considers the altitude of the commune located around 600 metres above the sea.

An animal farm of 200 breeding bulls appeared at the beginning of the 1970s. The need for fodder meant the collective farm allocated the complex 200 hectares of intensively cultivated pasture; 2,000 sheep, sheltered in the new stables built by the collective farms, needed fodder as well, so the pastures around the commune were intensively used for this purpose.

Of course, the new developments in land use required the villagers to forgo intercropping practices. The new technological park of the collective farm encompassing nine tractors, four combines, three sowing machines and three watering machines could not be used at the same time as intercropping practices. Machinery, along with changes of crops from local to more productive hybrids, and the intensive cultivation of land and pasture was the sign of an industrialized agriculture.[76] Intercropping was possible as long as the sowing was done manually and the agriculture was mostly subsistent; when agriculture became intensive and commercial, old agricultural practices were obliterated.

Modernization and the changes in the agrarian landscape were just one side of the coin. On the other side was the harshness the collective farm workers experienced, the economic scarcity and the oppression of local authorities. Unlike the state farms, which did not have to pay back the investments from central government, the co-operatives had to return the funds invested in different facilities.[77] Moreover, the socialist state imposed low prices for the agricultural products and a cheap labour force in order to extract the surplus from rural areas. Collective farms had to cope with the continuous scarcity of labour. Young and more skilled villagers headed to new industrial factories attracted by the mirage of the city life, better salaries and higher social status. In the village there remained old people and women, which led Michael Cernea to label the process the 'feminization of agriculture'.[78] During the harvesting, the co-operatives used students, soldiers and the remaining collective farm workforce. There was no incentive for any of these categories to harvest the crops thoroughly. Whereas the first two categories were paid close to nothing, villagers also received, besides the poor cash, payment in kind. For instance, for one day of harvesting the plums a worker received two kilograms of fruits as payment. This payment was so unattractive that the collective farm leadership had difficulties in getting people into the field. The villagers reacted to the devaluation of their work by stealing agricultural products, or avoiding showing up at their workplace, finding all kind of excuses. One of the presidents of the co-operative decided to make an informal deal with the workers: if they arrived in time and harvested the plums carefully – which means not squashing the fruits – every worker would receive, at the end of the day, five kilograms of lower quality plums. These plums were at least suited for making țuica (at home, illegally, in improvised small distilleries). Colluding with the president, often workers took more than five kilograms each day. The president urged the policeman to leave the zone so that people could take the fruit home. This arrangement would have been punished with a jail sentence, if the bureaucratic hierarchy had found out. The outcome was that the following year the plum production skyrocketed: from 50 tonnes per hectares to 160.

James C. Scott classifies theft as one form of peasant resistance in relation to the authorities.[79] Instead of being involved in an open conflict, they preferred to steal or to avoid, without verbally refusing, coming to work. Stealing from the collective farm was not considered immoral nor a criminal act but a way of protesting against the oppressive state.

Less than 10 per cent of the agricultural land remained uncollectivized until the end of the socialist regime. The mountainous villages, especially, with no cropland at all or with very few, escaped the steamroller of collectivization. Dragova was such a commune. The rugged geography of the commune would not allow the cultivation of cereals or any kind of vegetables. The steep slopes are only suitable for use as pasture. In the late 1950s there was an attempt to build up a co-operative in the village but eventually the communist authorities gave up. The production was far too insignificant and the co-operative would simply not have been self-sustaining. Thus, in Dragova, villagers continued to own the land as they had done for generations.

The state was still insinuating itself into the commune: a small artificial insemination complex was build at the end of 1970s. The pastures surrounding the commune fed the animals. The bulls reared there were not of the highest quality nor did the performance of the bulls satisfy local cattle owners or other state-owned farms which sought to increase their herds.

Uncollectivized villagers had to contribute with rather high quotas for animals they bred as well as with products such as milk, cheese or sheep wool. For every cow, a villager was compelled to deliver 300 to 600 kilograms of milk per year. In exchange, the state sold them husk at a preferential price, lower than on the market. State involvement in picking up their products directly from their household, saving them time, energy and money that would have been spent going to the nearby towns' markets, was highly valued by villagers. The 1,230 cows and 2,500 sheep kept by the householders was a sign that villagers managed to make a profit from growing animals.[80] The state also ensured veterinary assistance in the commune: six people, three technicians, two inseminators and one veterinary doctor dealt with animal health in the commune. The prices villagers paid for their services were bearable. As representatives of the state, these people had, at the same time, great power in the commune and represented a strong intrusion by the state into villagers' business. The socialist state banned the slaughter of animals, being rather interested in growing their number, and those who were responsible for watching over the cattle were the veterinary and his crew. On the other side, villagers had a limited acreage of pasture allowing them to husband a limited number of animals. For instance, one informant told me that during socialism he had five hectares of grassland and a constant number of six cows. This amount of land was the perfect match for the number of animals. Any animal above this number would have created difficulties in the household, not only because of the scarcity of land but because of the lack of workforce – only the members of the family were involved in this activity – and the lack of stables. Fodder storage over winter would have required more facilities than he possessed. In order not to increase the number of animals, villagers would kill a calf overnight and report the next day to the veterinary that the calf had been sick and died. In this case they had to pay a 250 lei fine for being sloppy in their care of the animals.[81] The boldest villagers would infringe the law and slaughter the calf in order to sell it. This was an important source of cash for the households. As a highly illegal activity slaughtering took place overnight. Urbanites were usually those who bought the meat for a special occasion such a wedding party or simply for the family. Especially after the1980s, when staple foods became scarcer, selling a calf was a source of a good income, as a kilogram of veal meat was worth seventy lei. This illegal business also meant taking a high risk. If caught, a villager would have been arrested or, at best, fined with 5,000 lei, a fortune at that time.

Most of the time the cash came from selling surplus products that remained after paying their quotas to the state in local markets. Products such as cheese, milk or pastrami were very much prized by urbanites. Very often, people of Dragova established networks of urban clients through family members who had moved away from the area, through which they sold their products.[82] This commerce was off the state's radar and villagers would only report meagre gains. Dragovans felt entitled to thwart the state as a response to state policy. The socialist state established a list with prices for every product, an upper threshold price that could not be exceeded by the seller. The prices were usually low and not based on economic rationality. Uncollectivized villagers were under permanent stress, being accused of avoiding taxes, providing food staples for the black market sellers and colluding with them in enriching themselves at the expense of the 'working class'.[83]

Despite the bad press they had, Dragovans continued to rear animals. Land was still the main issue the uncollectivized villagers had to deal with. On the one hand, they could own a maximum of 10 hectares of pasture. They were not allowed to hire people outside the family, which would have turned them into a *chiabur*. On the other hand, they were pressed by the socialist state to rear more animals. Often, villagers would rent the land from those who had inherited but lived in cities and were not interested in maintaining it. The verbal agreement between the landlord and the unofficial tenant was that the tenant had to provide dairy products in exchange for the land. Sometime, the landlord simply wanted to get rid of the land and the complications attached to it and sold it to whoever was interested. There were no official papers involved, only a handwritten document and the participation of two witnesses. The official papers were only drawn up for houses, never for pastures.

Being in a remote area, few people were hired in the socialist industrial plants in the nearby cities. The closest city is 33 kilometres away, linked to the commune by a narrow, winding road. Thus, most Dragovans worked for the State Forest Company, which is not surprising since wood exploitation was one of the most important economic activities throughout modern times and it is one of the main natural resources in the county.[84] Continuing a pre-war tradition, they exploited the state forest as either wood workers or workers of the local wood processing industry. The last four private saw mills were dismantled by the socialist regime as late as the 1960s and replaced with a modern, state saw mill and three small wood exploitation enterprises.[85] The working style and the techniques of exploiting wood had suffered important changes: before 1948 workers spent up to four months in the wood living in rather insalubrious huts.[86] The forestry work became mechanized after 1950s, with workers using tractors, better chain saws and protecting equipments. New access forestry roads were constructed and connected with the county network roads. New plantations, especially of productive species such as coniferous trees, were planted at rate of 300 hectares per year. Besides, an experimental plantation was opened in a village not far away from Dragova. This experimental station was dedicated to forestry research, to observe the adaptation of new species to local conditions and to study the optimal regime of extraction and plantation.[87] This policy made it so that in 1975 the wood extraction – around 20 million cubic meters per year – was smaller than the annual volume of wood grown, which totalled some 28 million cubic meters per year.[88] The continuous state investments in the forestry industries and the construction of new wood processing factories in the cities of the county whose products were exported throughout the world had improved the working conditions of the wood workers.[89] Many villagers I talked to in 2004 were pleased with their lives under postsocialism mainly because of the consistent pensions they had after working their whole life for the State Forest Company.

Comparing Two Economic and Ecologically Different Settings

Clearly, the two communes are very different in terms of spatial organization, in natural resources, in economic coordinates and in ecological features. Dragomirești is a hilly one, giving rise to a complex use of the land, cultivating cereals, producing plum brandy from the orchards, rearing animals and managing forest. Traditionally many villagers had off-farm jobs and the communist regime transformed them into worker-peasants. The three ethnic groups co-exist in the commune but a fracture crosses the commune separating Romanian, Roma and Rudari. The other commune, a mountainous one, has a more enduring land use, the economy being based on animal husbandry and selling of dairy products. Land can only be used for pasture. They are what one may call 'entrepreneurial peasants' involved in market relations within a wider state socialist economy and maintaining a relative freedom throughout socialism. Besides, as I will show in chapter 4, the National Park founded in 1990 has completely changed the relationship of villagers with their forests. The commune is ethnically uniform, with only a

Romanian population. The very spirit of the area – a fuzzy concept, difficult to conceptualize, I am well aware – is quite different compared to the one in Dragomireşti. The personal experiences I had as an anthropologist in the two settings would help the reader understand what I seek to express here. After staying several months in my host's house in Dragomireşti I was adopted as a member of the family, participating in decisions, asked for my point of view when appropriate and, generally, fulfilling the same duties as my host's natural son. I was called by my first name and a term of endearment was used, as for the host's real son. People in the village adopted me as one of them and called me by my first name. In Dragova, in the same conditions, I was considered a client, a strange person paid by a German institution to research their lives. For every informant I talked to, I was a potential client and invited, at the end of almost all interviews, to buy smoked cheese, milk or pastrami. The mercantile spirit in the area was very different from the warm hospitality I encountered in my previous fieldwork experience.

Precisely these historical, economic and ecological differences make the comparison interesting and valuable as they show a similar outcome: deep disruptions of the agrarian landscape in postsocialist times, regardless of the contrast in local economic and ecological conditions. *Comparer ce qui est comparable* (compare what could be compared), an old French proverb says. I have dared to disobey this ancient wisdom.

Notes

1. An almost unpracticable road means that the commune was in fact poorly linked to the county capital, the largest and the most important economic city in the county, although geographically located very close.
2. I carried out eight months of fieldwork in 2004 in both communes followed by two weeks in 2006, two months in 2007 and one month in 2008. I carried out fieldwork in Dragomireşti only from August through November 2009 and from March through June 2010. Thus, my analysis refers to the period before Romania's accession to the EU in 2007.
3. This chapter draws on several unpublished local monographs. In order to avoid a fatiguing repetition of these monographs in the main text, which would make the chapter more difficult to read, I give the authors the necessary credit here. The published monographs will be cited in the main text. For Dragomireşti commune, of much help was Săvulescu (1974) and Busuiocescu (2000), while for Dragova, I have used Căciulă and Căciulă (1998). I only cite the unpublished documents from these monographs, avoiding the authors' interpretations, which are often oversimplistic and sometimes exhibit a strong nationalism.
4. County Department of Statistic Piteşti. I will detail later in the chapter the history of Rudari.
5. The village appears in sixteenth-century documents. Although several times historical documents mention quarrels over land between people from the village and outsiders, we cannot really gain a coherent account of the economy, number of

50 *Disrupted Landscapes*

people and details about land use, which is the topic of this chapter. The first statistic about these villages is dated 1838.
6. Pârnuță et al. (2003). Written documents mention an old local measurement unit called *stânjen* when giving the area of land. One stânjen means 1.96 metres.
7. The documents mention 1148 *pogoane*, another old measurement unit. One pogon measures 5011.72 square metres (Pârnuță et al. 2003: 42).
8. Until the mid nineteenth century Roma people were slaves. They were bought and sold with the land or with the village to which they belonged. Monasteries, noblemen and the king had slaves for various kinds of work. When they were freed they were never given possession of land or forest (Achim 1998).
9. See H. H. Stahl (1998 [1958], vol. III) and Micu (2012: 32 ff) for wider political and social debates on modernization of Romanian agriculture which accompanied the 1864 land reform.
10. Romania experienced three land reforms prior to the installation of the communist regime: 1864, 1921 and 1945. The fourth one is the postsocialist land reform. I have chosen to present the land use history individually for the three villages because Dragomirești commune had a variable administrative structure throughout the pre-socialist history. The present administrative configuration of the commune is a socialist creation (1956).
11. Pârnuță et al. (2003: 151).
12. Ibid.
13. Ibid. at 157.
14. Novac (2008: 143).
15. Ibid. at 65.
16. Băcanu (1999).
17. Stahl (1998 [1958], I: 215).
18. Pamfile (1913: 182).
19. Godoy and Bennett (1991). Intercropping and its benefits were quite widely debated by economists, social scientists and biologists for non-European areas (cf. Horwith 1985; Lee et al. 2006). For Eastern Europe there is no international literature, to my knowledge. I attribute the silence of anthropologists and economists to the fact that they pay attention to social, political and economic relations rather than to types of crops and agricultural practices.
20. Pamfile (1913: 183).
21. Li et al. (2006).
22. Stern (1993).
23. Pârnuță et al. (2003: 153).
24. Though almost everywhere in Romania villagers produce various alcoholic drinks, *țuica de Argeș* (the plum brandy made in Argeș) is considered as having the highest quality and it is much appreciated by both Romanians and foreigners visiting Romania.
25. Marc is the residue of grapes or other fruits after distillation.
26. Pârnuță et al. (2003: 53).
27. Novac (2008: 144).
28. In order to understand better how much 270 kilos of silk cocoon represented in the nineteenth century it suffices to say that in 1989 Romania, the second largest European producer and the sixth world producer, reported 830 tons of silk cocoon. The privatization of state farms and break up of collective farms

had passed the mulberry trees in private ownership. The new owners had no access to the market or the knowledge to continue this activity. See for more details Baiski (2005).
29. Stahl (1998 [1958]).
30. Taking care of the parents also meant organizing the funerals and the *pomana*, the meal and drink offered for the soul of dead people. Pomana was organized twice a year until the seventh year after the burial. Social and religious requirements are that only best-quality food and drink, usually țuica, be served for this occasion.
31. Pârnuță et al. (2003: 27).
32. Urechia (1895); Verdery (2003). The practice of beating children so they remember the boundaries of their land is a medieval practice widely spread in Europe (Olwig 1996).
33. Chelcea (1944); Marushiakova and Popov (1997); Stewart (2002).
34. Achim (1998).
35. Kogalnitchan (1837: 12).
36. Marushiakova and Popov (1997: 26).
37. Dorondel (2007).
38. Stahl and Piasere (1990).
39. Chelcea (1944: 76).
40. Ibid.
41. Idem: 124.
42. For this reason, Marushiakova (1992: 9) calls Rudari 'semi-nomadic artisans'.
43. Argeș County was one of the most forested in the country. This is probably the reason that a large population of Rudari, estimated in 1944 at 100,000 people, settled in Argeș (Chelcea 1944).
44. Alexiu et al. (2011).
45. Constantinescu (2006).
46. Ibid.
47. The average snow stratum lasts between 80 and 120 days per year on the Rucăr-Bran corridor and 60 to 80 days on the top of the hills (Barco and Nedelcu 1974: 46).
48. Pârnuță (1972).
49. Bogza (2011: 70).
50. Data gathered from the mayor's office of Dragova.
51. Obște means literally community, commons, but the word was also used in medieval documents to designate a whole village. It has also the meaning of 'an entire entity', something which cannot be divided (Stahl 1998 [1958]).
52. Căciulă and Căciulă (1998).
53. See *Sentința Civilă Nr. 357 din August 1923, Dosar Nr. 763/923 a Tribunalului Muscel pentru Stabilirea Drepturilor în Obștea Moșnenilor Rucăreni* [The Civil Decision No. 357 from August 1923, File No. 763/923 of the Muscel Court for Establishing the Common Property Rights of the Smallholders of Rucăr] Câmpulung-Muscel, Tipografia, Librăria și Legătoria de Cărți Gh. N. Vlădescu, 1930. This document was so important for the members of the villages involved in the lawsuit that they printed it a few years later at a local publishing house. This was the main document villagers used when they asked for restitution of the collective forest in 2000.
54. Lahovari et al. (1898–1902). The path connecting Dragova to the National Road was modernized in 1905, as a carved stone placed at the beginning of the path reminds us. This stone still exists.

55. Căciulă and Căciulă (1998).
56. After 1829 the two Romanian kingdoms, Walachia and Moldavia, enjoyed an economic boom. At this date a peace treaty was signed between the two empires, the Russian and the Ottoman, which previewed, among other things, the abolition of the economic monopoly of the Ottoman Empire over the Romanian Kingdoms, which were from then on free to export their products to other countries. This treaty has unleashed a wave of agricultural exports headed for the industrial centres of Western Europe (Madgearu 1999 [1936]).
57. Pârnuță (1972).
58. Ibid.
59. Kligman and Verdery (2011); Cătănuș and Roske (2000, 2004).
60. For an excellent analysis see Kligman and Verdery (2011) and Iordachi and Dobrincu (2009) among others.
61. Scott (1998).
62. Uekoetter (2011).
63. Scott (1998: 203).
64. Cernea (1973).
65. Not only the Romanian population benefitted from these new economic developments but also Roma people, who were hired in the socialist enterprises. From this perspective, Roma did rather well under socialism whereas in postsocialist times they experienced economic and social hardship (see, for instance, Brearly 2001).
66. The data provided in this part of the chapter comes from Cernea (1976).
67. Mungiu-Pippidi (2010: 56).
68. Socol (1999).
69. Cernea (1976).
70. Ibid. The statistical data provided by the socialist regime should be read *cum grano salis*. A joke in circulation about fake reports during the socialist era would enlighten the reader. The joke goes as follows. The agricultural agency of a Romanian county located next to the border with Hungary reported to the local Communist Party secretary – the chief responsible for everything in the county – the number of hectares of arable land that were being ploughed within the county. The Party secretary had to transmit this number up the chain of authority to the Ministry of Agriculture and Forestry in Bucharest, but she thought the figure was not satisfactory and added a further 25 per cent. The Minister of Agriculture reported this figure to the Prime Minister, who reported to Nicolae Ceaușescu the total number of hectares ploughed in Romania. As every official in the hierarchical chain thought their superior would be dissatisfied with the figure, all had added several hundred hectares to the number they received. An urgent notice reached the local agency for agriculture a few days after the report. They were urged: 'Stop ploughing! You are ploughing Hungarian land!'
71. The following data come from the work of an agronomist. See Hartia (1963).
72. Figures are from Hartia (1983: 46).
73. Cernea (1976).
74. Pârnuță et al. (2003).
75. Information from the last collective farm president. See also Pârnuță et al. (2003).
76. Goldschmidt (1947 [1978]).
77. Verdery (2003).
78. Cernea (1978).

79. Scott (1985).
80. Regarding the number of sheep, in the County Department of Statistics in Pitești only 540 were officially registered. But from oral information that I have gathered from villagers in the whole commune I calculate that there were around 2,500 animals. The official number of cows is the same as the one I arrived at from interviewing villagers.
81. In 1989, the average salary in Romania was 2,200 lei per month. In practice though this was a rather good salary. For comparison, a Dacia car – the most common automobile in Romania – was worth 70,000 lei.
82. Selling dairy products through urban networks seemed to be a common practice throughout the country. Although I was a child, growing up in a large industrial city in the eastern part of Romania, I still remember an old man coming twice a week and selling 'countryside milk' to my parents. He had his own clients in the block of apartments with whom he discussed family problems, complaining about his widower status. This was more than a peddler–client relationship; it was a social relationship built on trust. He used to borrow money from his clients as well as provide them with dairy products on credit.
83. Constantinescu (1972).
84. In the late 1960s, 43 per cent of the county territory was still covered by forests (Barco and Nedelcu 1974).
85. Localitățile (1971: 213).
86. Pârnuță (1972: 193).
87. Barco and Nedelcu (1974: 147).
88. Mușat (1980: 89).
89. The wood factories from Argeș county produced in 1970 12 per cent of the beech lumber and 17 per cent of the plywood of the country's total production (Barco and Nedelcu 1974).

 CHAPTER 2

Postsocialism as Neoliberalism
Reorganizing Society and Nature

> 'Sometimes, a huge influx of ideas rush upon the Earth and after its passage human life finds itself reorganized around new centres and new axes.'
> —Robert Musil, *The Man Without Qualities*

'Some see countries with borders. We see markets with opportunities.' This advert for a Western international bank at Amsterdam airport could serve as a motto for neoliberal ideology. New opportunities for investment, new markets that have to be conquered, new people to be turned into consumers are certainly the dream of the neoliberal project. That must have been the image the newly postsocialist states conveyed at the end of the 1980s. Where the international media saw countries with inchoate democratic governments striving to find a way out of the socialist planned economy, the neoliberal forces saw totally de-regularized markets, hundreds of millions of new consumers and endless opportunities for investment. The breakdown of the Berlin Wall opened the gate wide to a territory that had hitherto been if not out of bounds at least difficult to penetrate by international institutions, supra-national organisms and multinational companies.[1] At the beginning of the 1990s, Romania and other postsocialist states were trapped by a planned economy, a collectivized agriculture and a state-owned industry. Former socialist countries were assisted in the process of de-collectivization of agriculture and privatization of industry and natural resources by a series of international institutions such as the World Bank, the International Monetary Fund and USAID to name just a few.[2] International donors assisted these countries in order to ease the passage from planned economy to a market economy – thus helping central political decision-makers to reorganize the whole society and the natural world. Privatization of forest and agriculture and of the connected industries and liberalization of the national market was seen as one of the avenues for restructuring the socialist economy and the path towards an efficient economy and a prosperous society.[3]

This chapter briefly explores the political economy of the land reform, showing the central state master plan of land privatization with the underlying idea that private property would be economically more functional and more efficient than state-planned agriculture. Departing from socialist society, ideology and political economy, the political transformations at national level aimed to convert the socialist agrarian landscape into a capitalist one by producing new local landscapes.

New Plans for the Romanian Agriculture

One of the first governmental acts in postsocialist countries was to dismantle socialist forms of land ownership and restore private property rights. Much of the public debate about the fate of postsocialist agriculture and the associated industries linked privatization to economic efficiency, private initiative to farmers' welfare and asserted the superiority of capitalist relations over socialist economic arrangements.[4] Economic reforms were the way countries from the former socialist bloc responded to the stagnation of their economy and the social problems and poverty many of them faced at the end of 1989. In the agricultural sector the situation was even more dramatic as in the early 1990s the rural population – former collective farm employees – was landless, and villages had poor infrastructure and lacked the facilities from which the urban population benefitted. The outcome of years of socialist intensive exploitation of the land, using large quantities of fertilizers to produce bigger and bigger crops, became obvious in the early 1990s: pollution of the underground waters and of rivers with chemicals, erosion of the land and its cortege of effects such as land sliding and salt accumulation and in a number of areas natural vegetation loss.[5]

The postsocialist central state planners saw land reform as the only way to undo the collective organization of agriculture and to change the land tenure system. Land restitution was envisioned for at least two reasons: to achieve historical justice by giving land back to its historical owners and to facilitate economic efficiency in agriculture.[6] The return to private property was supposed to bring new ways of using the land, in the hope that the new landowners would produce for the new markets while new forest owners would preserve a healthy forest and the biodiversity it shelters. A new political economy of postsocialist governments rushed the retreat of the state from agricultural production, which was seen as an obstacle to agricultural development, and liberalized the internal market. At the same time, traditional international markets such as the Arabic countries and Soviet Union, the latter perceived rather as a political enemy than as a large market, were lost as the new geopolitical orientation of Romania was unidirectional – towards the West. Despite the inevitable meanderings in conducting land reform and differences between the political actors, Westernization of Romanian society in all of its components, including the biophysical world, was seen as the only possible political program and the main 'country project'. In short, at the beginning of the 1990s, the new democratic rulers showed a benevolent 'will to improve' economy, societal relations and the way the biophysical world was organized.[7]

Once the illnesses of the new postsocialist society were diagnosed, the cures were also at hand. The new economic, political and legislative changes meant to impose order on the messy reality of rural areas were devised, designed and issued by the Romanian central governments, often assisted by Western advisors.[8] The 'econolobbyists', as Janine R. Wedel calls the economic advisors paid by Western governments and international donors to advise postsocialist central governments on market reforms, were not just technical experts; they were ideological bearers and promoters of their institutions' views on economic development.[9] In fact, this transfer of knowledge, policies and governmental practices took place in a context of intense transnational interventionism in various domains such as economic, political and biodiversity. As Chris Hann has pointed out, in the early 1990s, the prevalent image of what had to be done in the agricultural sector was the one advocated by the Western advisors, themselves holders of neoliberal ideas.[10] One of the twin suppositions inherent in this new political economy was that 'through obtaining a high degree of exclusive power over things, it is postulated that agents will exercise greater care over them, invest appropriately, and generally act such that the promotion of their selfish interests will be fully consistent with the collective welfare function of their society'.[11] The other assumption was that the new landowners would produce goods for the free market for the benefit of themselves and the rest of the population alike.

As Noel Castree has shown, neoliberalism has several characteristics: privatization of state or communal land, marketization of land, which means that land becomes subject to market calculation, and the state rolls back intervention in certain areas such agriculture, market-friendly regulation, use of market proxies in the governmental sector, the strong encouragement of civil society to replace the absence or diminution of the state and the creation of 'self-sufficient' individuals and communities.[12] It is clear that most of these characteristics are also found in the policies and the vocabulary of postsocialist central governments. Another important point is, as Castree and other analysts of neoliberalism have shown, that neoliberalism is not necessarily supposed to rule out the state – although this has happened in many parts of the world – but is supposed to change its role.[13] As in the postsocialist case, the state is the promoter of the free market, of liberalization policies and of private property. The central state, through parliament and government, is the only institution that formally issues laws and regulations regarding property rights over land and forest and the way the new owner is expected to exploit it.[14] People recognize the legitimacy and the authority of this institution as the only one issuing the laws regarding both the new property rights and the conditions of exploitation of a natural resource. Recognition of both legitimacy and authority does not mean people do not challenge the state regulations or that they blindly obey them. The fact that after the 1990s there were hundreds of thousands of lawsuits concerning land restitution demonstrates that people recognize the state as the authority empowered to resolve property issues. New owners go to court, which means they appeal to a state institution when they feel that their property rights, as they perceive them, are being violated. However, they contest state legitimacy when the state turns into a direct competitor for property rights, as in the case of the newly founded national parks competing with private owners for forest.

This last example brings us to the contradictory character of the neoliberal–postsocialist project. Neoliberalism was doubtless a national project meant to revise socialist policy in agriculture and industry. It had followed, in Romania at least, a circuitous itinerary according to the ideologies and interests of parties represented in Parliament. The contradictory character of the neoliberal project is defined by at least two facts. Firstly, not only postsocialist governments imposed neoliberal values on rural people, making them innocent victims; rural people also asked for the restitution of land and forest that once belonged to their forefathers. In Romania, for instance, villagers had not waited for Parliament to pass the first Property Law (18/1991), but, based on their parents' knowledge or on the knowledge of those old enough to remember where their land was situated, took possession of their land from the collective farm.[15] The subsequent LLC had nothing to do but acknowledge the dissolution of the local collective farm and to correct the mistakes made in the process. The same strong feelings about private property are contained in the villagers' furious cry, 'This is my forest! The state should have nothing to say about my property,' when different national parks attempted to regulate access to the protected forest. Details exposed in chapter 4 will convince the reader of the villagers' fierce struggle for their private property, for the withdrawal of the state from forest ownership, and for their right to marketize the forest.

A second fact that points up the contradictory character of the neoliberal project was the ambivalent attitude of the postsocialist state. On the one hand, the central state has legislated for land and forest privatization. On the other hand the state has founded new national parks and protected areas, which means stronger state control over forest, thus weakening the position of the new private owners.

In the light of all these issues, the postsocialist project of transforming the entire socialist society may be conceived as a version of global neoliberal ideology and practice.

Establishing New Rights and New Duties

The land laws were issued over a decade; they stipulated the land and forest owners' duties and rights and instigated the mechanisms of enforcement and the enforcement institutions.[16] Law 18/1991 established two types of property ownership: private (individual and state) and public. Article 8 of the law established two ways in which one could acquire land. One was through reconstitution of property rights for those who brought their land to the co-operative or whose land was taken over by the co-operative. They and their heirs were considered legitimate owners.

A second way to acquire land was through constitution of property rights. Through this amendment, the law was aimed at those who were not entitled to receive land, as they were never owners. Those who had reconstituted their property rights received up to 10 hectares of arable land, regardless of whether they or their family brought the land to the co-operative or their land had simply been nationalized. Whereas for the hilly regions the law stipulates restitution of the same plots as before collectivization, for the flatlands the LLC can decide to restore land in a different location. Land claimants had to present a written request and historical documents which proved their ownership within forty-five days. The claimant had to prove land ownership with any kind of documents from the collective farm archives, the Agricultural Register, the original applications for joining the collective farm or any other evidence including the testimony of two witnesses.[17] Those villagers who do not want to become part of the new private farm association – in case they received their own land – had the right to receive from the newly emerged association money or payment in kind for the animals that were appropriated. Several articles refer to the duties of those who benefitted from the constitution of property rights. Owners have to refrain from selling the land for ten years. Those who break the law lose their land. Other duties were also imposed on landowners: change of land use is possible but only with the agreement of regional or national institutions such as the Ministry of Agriculture and Forestry. Soil protection is compulsory for all holders who have an obligation to prevent soil quality deterioration and to abide by the conditions stipulated in the agreement and environmental authorization for constructions of any kind. The law clearly prohibits the movement of boundary stones or other stones which delimit two private plots or the constitution of any kind of boundary stones or enclosure without official approval.

The law also created the organizations that administer and control the way the land laws are implemented. First of all, the law created two commissions that deal with decollectivization. The Liquidation Commission had to establish the way in which the assets of the collective farm, such as animals and the orchards, would be given back to those who worked for the co-operative. The Commission had also to establish the liabilities of the former co-operative such as debts to the bank. A second commission was constituted in order to establish property rights over land and forest within the commune. Article 11 empowers the mayors by making them de jure presidents of this commission. The local commission functioned under the leadership of the County Land Commission (CLC), led by the prefect.[18] The CLC has the power to validate or invalidate the LLC's decisions and the only way a landowner can change the CLC decision is by going to court.

Through the same law the central authorities for agriculture and forestry have an obligation to draw up regulations on farming systems, crop and livestock technologies and to keep evidence of the land areas that are not suitable for farm production.

As for the forest restitution, Law 18 established that former owners would receive up to 1 hectare, regardless of the size of the forest they owned before 1948. Through this law 364,379 hectares of forest were given back to former owners.[19] The new private owner has to exploit the forest in accordance with the state-established forestry rules. The law stipulated that restitution must be made in forest tracts located at the edge of the state forest or within isolated tracts. This law was completed in 1996 by the 'Forestry Code', which has established the rules of management and exploitation of public and private forests. Protection, monitoring and the exploitation of forest, and the penalties incurred for breaking the Code, were all defined by this law. Article 2 stipulates that a land covered with forestry vegetation larger than 0.25 hectare will be considered forest. The maximum size of a forest plot to be cleared is 5 hectares (Article 23). The Forestry Code stipulated that the National Inspectorate of Forest (NIF) is entitled to monitor the regeneration, management and exploitation of the public forest. The owner is obliged to replant the forest within two years of clearing. The NIF will assist the owner in cleaning and maintaining the health of the forest at the owner's expense. A vital provision of the law is that the owners have to guard their forest themselves or they should ask the local department of the NIF to provide, on a contractual basis, foresters (*pădurari*) (Article 70). Further duties are imposed on private owners: they are obliged to cut only those trees marked by the foresters and to ask for the elaboration of a scientific study of their forest plot (see below). Timber transportation must be accompanied by documents proving the legality of exploitation or the police should retain the undocumented load. If illegal cutting takes place during the night the perpetrator gets the maximum penalty (Article 97). Illegal actions can be addressed by the forest guards, the chief of forestry inspectorate or the forester engineer; these provisions in the law give them great power – akin to the powers of the police. Besides, foresters are entitled to carry firearms, which could be used against perpetrators. Foresters' ability to carry firearms, the strict hierarchy of the institution and the special green uniforms transform them into a 'green army'. In fact, they call themselves 'the second army'.[20]

If a private owner wants to cut some trees from his or her forest, he or she has first to command a 'study' concerning the status of the forest. The first step is to lodge a written request with the mayor's office. The agricultural officer verifies the property rights of the petitioner and then sends the request to the LIF (*Ocolul Silvic*). Depending on the social, economic or political position of the owner within the village, their personal relationship with the mayor or the secretary of the mayor's office or the petitioner's ability to bribe one of these officials, the request could remain in a pile of documents for quite a long time before it is sent to the LIF. The LIF is the only institution legally entitled to carry out this study. The owner has to pay for the study. The Code allows the forest owner to cut no more than 1 cubic metre for each hectare he or she owns. The forestry commission verifies again the property rights of the petitioner and the biological characteristics of the forest: the kind and age of the trees and the average growing rate of each type of tree based on the clime and the soil characteristics. Only then will the commission establish the amount of timber the owner can extract and the precise location of the extraction. The most important thing in such a study is the establishment of the type of extraction: clear cutting (*pe ras*) or just 'thinning out a dense forest' (*răritură*). Usually, only the commercial firms get permission to clear a parcel of forestland; private owners only receive permission to extract some trees from a dense forest. The LIF sends the conclusion of the study to the owner, notifying at the same time the local forester responsible for guarding the state forest in that village.[21] Then, the owner has to wait until the forester 'has time' to come and mark those trees he considers ready to be cut: the unhealthy trees or those impeding the growth of young trees. According to the Code, the forest guard should be there when the owner cuts the trees but often, as people recounted to me or I observed myself, the forester marks the lower part of the tree and then leaves. Once the forester leaves, the owner does not restrict himself to cutting only those trees that the study allows.[22] The only danger the owner faces is meeting on his way back a police patrol which could compare the quote stipulated by the official papers he has with the actual quantity of wood he is transporting. A fine of up to 20 million lei (around €600) or even a prosecution is the punishment inscribed in forestry law for such a case.[23]

The law also specifies that the improvement works will be financially supported by the state but must be approved by the forest owner. Not least for the conservation of biodiversity the forestry authorities have to support the build-up of national parks and to ensure the sustainable management of the forest ecosystems (Article 110).

Under pressure from the World Bank and the International Monetary Fund, Romania's liberal centre-right government (1996–2000) issued Law 1/2000, which was intended to change the provisions of Law 18. This law enlarged the size of the plot one could claim from 10 hectares of arable land to 50 hectares. It also increased the number of legal entities entitled to private ownership restitution: former private owners and their heirs whose agricultural land was consolidated and seized by the co-operatives with no compensation; private persons or their heirs whose land passed to the state property through expropriation; former associations, religious or educational units whose agricultural land, meadows or pastures were confiscated by the socialist state. As for the forest, this law expanded the size of forest plot to be restored to former owners up to 10 hectares. Almost 1.2 million hectares of forest were given back through this law to private owners, associations or religious entities.[24]

Land reform laws establish the institutions that have to implement, monitor and manage the regulations concerning the land and forest. The Agency of State Domains (ASD) for instance was charged with the privatization of agricultural commercial companies and with the leasing of public and private state land. ASD is under the authority of the Ministry of Agriculture and Forestry. The duty of the ASD, as the owner of the agricultural land of private state domain (land which can be sold or leased as opposed to public domain which cannot be given away), is to administer the land and to make sure it is used through concession or leasing.[25] The National Office of Cadastre, Geodesy, and Cartography (NOCGC) was charged with the execution, completion, modernization and maintenance of the national geodetic network and licenses persons capable of carrying out technical cadastral works. The county and municipal offices of the NOCGC register the boundary litigation between neighbours, owners or possessors and establish zones within localities and soil quality classes. The land reform laws also require ministries or other central state institutions to organize the cadastre in the domain of agriculture, forestry, waters, extractive industry, real estates and urbanism, roads, tourism, build-up and natural protected areas which are subject to pollution and degradation. The mayor of the locality has a duty to provide cadastral delegates with offices and accommodation for a price, as well as support for hiring auxiliary personnel when necessary, whereas the holders have a duty to allow specialist access for the execution of cadastral works.

The Ministry of Agriculture and Forestry and the NIF are the institutions that administer all public forests in Romania. The local departments of NIF participate in forest restitution collaborating with the local land commission in order to establish which areas of forest are to be restored to former owners.

These institutions and laws were created in order to reorganize society and the natural world into a new modernity, radically different from the socialist modernity and in accordance with the new capitalist requirements. The laws created new rights for private owners using neoliberal tools such as establishing clear property rights, registration of land and forest plots and issuing property titles. The underlying assumption was that only with clear property rights and clear boundaries is property able to become a valuable object that is easily marketized and commoditized.[26] The following chapters will explore villagers' responses to such assumptions.

The whole process of changes in property rights over land and forest has put the local elite into a powerful position. The LLC members in charge of land restitution were able to manipulate the land reform laws and to allocate forest and land preferentially to their friends or family members as the following chapters will explore in depth. State foresters entered into the same game and further contributed to the environmental havoc, as the next two chapters will ethnographically demonstrate.

Notes

1. I do not refer here to different Western goods, more and more difficult to find in Romania and elsewhere in contries from the socialist camp, but to economic units of production.
2. For the myriad of international donors active in Eastern Europe, see Creed and Wedel (1997) and Wedel (1998).
3. Csaki and Lerman (1997). There is an extensive literature discussing the political economy of land reform in postsocialist countries. I am not going to review it here. For a solid perspective, see for instance Spoor (2009).
4. Dorondel and Sikor (2009).
5. Muica and Zavoianu (1996); Turnock (2002).
6. Swinnen (1997).
7. Li (2007).
8. Hann (2007); Weiner (2001).
9. Wedel (1998).
10. Hann (2007).
11. Ibid. at 296.
12. Castree (2010: 1728).
13. Castree (2011); Hibou (2004 [1999]). Neoliberalism has captured the attention of many scholars in recent years. I do not intend here to review the literature. For a detailed analysis see Harvey (2005).
14. The local state is usually denied the power of making decisions about all these issues. In many parts of the world the state is one institution among others that regulate property rights over natural resources. Customary institutions such as religious ones compete with the state in sanctioning property rights and property practices. See, for instance, F. von Benda-Beckmann and K. von Benda-Beckmann (1999) for Indonesia, or de Waal (2004) and Stahl (2010a) for Albania.
15. Dorondel and Sikor (2009); von Hirschhausen (1997: 120).

16. In this book I refer only to Law 18/1991 and Law 1/2000. Law 247/2005 on the restitution *in integrum* of land and forest, whose complicated and messy effects began after I completed my fieldwork, are therefore not considered in this analysis.
17. The Agricultural Register is a book held by the mayor's office in which all persons and goods of households are registered, including the number of animals and land and forest ownership.
18. The prefect is the representative of central government in the territory. Thus, this commission has a crucial political role. The prefect is appointed by central government and leaves when a new government comes to power.
19. Popa and Popa (2013).
20. Lawrence (2005).
21. This happens in those communes where there is no Private Forest Department (PFD) as in Dragomirești. Where there is a PFD, as in Dragova, the study is sent to the private forester.
22. Cutting trees and transporting them is a strictly male job.
23. I use throughout the book the mean of the exchange rate for the year 2004, the time I carried most of my fieldwork, which is around 35,000 lei for one euro.
24. Popa and Popa (2013).
25. Pamfil (2004).
26. Dorondel and Sikor (2009).

CHAPTER 3

Bureaucrats, Patronage, Illegal Logging

'There are so few trees left in the forest that
a bird cannot find a tree to build a nest.'
—a local Romanian saying

One early morning in August 2007, I heard loud and agitated discussions in the kitchen next to my room. I thought that something bad must have happened. I dressed immediately and went into the kitchen. *Nenea* Paul and his wife, *tanti* Ana were already dressed and ready to leave.[1] They had received a phone call from the cowherd in the village as early as five o'clock in the morning. On his way to the communal pasture, driving villagers' cows, the cowherd had noticed a group of Rudari with chainsaws and horse carts in Paul's forest. He immediately suspected that Rudari were going to cut trees and called Paul. When I arrived in the kitchen, Paul had already phoned and briefed the local chief of police about the situation. I joined Paul on his way to the police station. The three of us climbed the steep hills for about an hour on a foggy morning following a rainy night. The ground was so slippery that I expressed my doubts that anyone would be able to drive a horse cart on such steep slopes and remain alive. 'Rudari can do it,' Paul said laconically. When we reached the spot, deep in the forest, we found only a few freshly cut trees, sawdust everywhere and the wheel imprints of several horse carts. The morning air was thick with a strong fresh smell of resin. The image surrounding us was deplorable: among the few standing 1-metre-high trunks, evidence of previous woodcutting activities, seven freshly cut beech trees and one oak tree lay on the ground. Obviously, the woodcutters had left the spot in a hurry. 'They must have heard us coming and run,' said the policeman, although we did not speak too much, barely able to breathe while climbing the muddy, slippery hills. Paul retorted: 'Rudari are so lazy that they don't bend down to cut trees close to the root – they cut them while standing.'

After a while, we went back home. Paul told me after we had parted company with the policeman: 'Who could have known about us coming other than the policeman? He probably called them on a mobile phone and urged them to leave. He will probably go and get his reward [i.e. money] from them later.' There is some truth in what my host said, as it was virtually impossible that the Rudari, or whoever else was present cutting trees, had heard us coming. Paul swears that he will cut down the remaining forest himself 'to get at least something' from his ownership, daring the policeman to stop him. This episode contains all the ingredients this chapter addresses: deforestation, Rudari cutting down trees, forest owners cursing Rudari and, in response to their actions, clearing their own forest, and the local state officials according protection to Rudari for their own economic gain.

This chapter and the following one explore the essential role of forest, the most valuable natural resource in the countryside. Villagers use beech for heating their houses in the long cold period from late September to mid May. Many households use firewood for cooking because Dragomirești is not yet linked to the national gas network.[2] Usually, a forest owner uses the branches and deformed trees, both beech and oak, as firewood while the straightest trees are used for construction. The oak is the most valuable tree in the area and is mainly used for building houses and fences. Thus, both types of trees are coveted both in the commune and in the southern lowland areas of the country.

This chapter also makes three further important points. First, forest plays an active role in shaping social, economic and political relations at local level. Forest empowers villagers with access to local state offices, disempowering poor villagers. The patronage relationship is built entirely on forest exploitation, as I will describe at length. Forest also ensures the subsistence of a poor ethnic group, namely Rudari, and affects the social structure of this community. Second, the dynamics of these relations show that the locus of power is at local level, rather than national level. Furthermore, access to local state offices gives advantages to some villagers over their peers. Although local power cannot be acquired without links to regional and national state officials, it must be analysed within the local context. The consequences of the local power relations are deforestation and a dramatic change in the landscape. Dragomirești's forested hills have been transformed, in postsocialist times, into a deforested landscape. Third, this chapter explores the unintended outcomes of the state's centrally designed land reform laws. Certainly, the national planners did not envision the harsh outcome of forest restitution when they planned land reform.

Ethnicity and the Postsocialist Transformations

As I will show further in this chapter, Rudari, an ethnic group classified by the Romanian state as Roma, play a key role in illegal deforestation in Romania. Although the analysis of ethnicity itself is not the real intention of this book, a brief explanation of the part ethnicity plays in Rudari experience of postsocialist transformation is provided here in order that the reader might understand the Rudari's role in the patron–client relationship and the part they play in illegal forest exploitation.

The Romanian state policy concerning land restitution, which was extensively discussed in chapter 1, created new lines of separation between the majority of Romanians and the Roma (and Rudari) population. Since Rudari never owned land or forest, the 'historical justice' restitution policy has automatically excluded them from land and forest ownership. They were not excluded merely because they belong to a certain ethnic group but because they were not legally defined as legitimate owners. Only those owners who can prove historical ownership of land and forest were compensated by the restitution laws. A proof that belonging to a minority ethnic group did not necessarily disqualify people from obtaining land restitution is that ethnic Germans or Hungarians from Transylvania who owned land and forest before collectivization received them back after 1990.[3] In the case of Rudari, by virtue of their history as propertyless 'people of the forest' as I have detailed in chapter 1, their lack of forest ownership excluded them from the land reform. Disadvantaged by the presocialist governments Rudari were, again, overlooked by the postsocialist governments' restitution policies.

Rudari were 'semi-nomadic artisans' as Elena Marushiakova puts it, and carving wood was one of their main ethnic features.[4] Access to forest was essential for an ethnic group that had worked with wood for two centuries and thus was economically dependent on forest. Their exclusion from land and forest restitution by postsocialist reformers was the painful and decisive means of turning Rudari into perfect clients.

The privatization of the industrial factories has hit the Rudari harder than any other ethnic group in Romania. The communist regime attempted to settle them – to turn them into good, obedient socialist citizens but also to control them – and hired most of them in the industrial factories or in the collective farms.[5] Under socialism, Roma and Rudari had lowly valorized jobs such as cleaning or refuse collection or similar. Despite the low positions they usually occupied they nevertheless earned a salary and their living conditions have much improved. Taking a walk within their settlement in Costești would reveal that most of their houses were built at the end of the 1970s and early 1980s. Most of them, at least in the particular case I describe in this book, had a poor educational background so were more easily dismissed by the postsocialist investors. Roma (including Rudari) have a high rate of unemployment and experienced, after 1990, a decline in living conditions.[6] Quite a high number of Rudari and Roma live today, in Dragomirești at least, on meagre social benefits.[7]

Another important issue, which I underline throughout this book when analysing the Rudari's contribution to deforestation, is their lack of political representation. As an ethnic group they refuse to be classified together with the Roma, arguing that they do not speak the Romani language, do not wear the same clothes and have different social practices.[8] Officially, Rudari are represented by Partida Romilor (Roma Political Party), but in fact they lack any representatives at regional and national level.[9] Since Rudari do not recognize their ethnic affiliation to Roma they do not see any reason for accepting political representation through the Roma Party. Consequently, the Roma Party does not engage with Rudari's specific problems (such as the lack of access to forest).

In short, the postsocialist transformations hit the Rudari population hard and forced them to turn to the forest, their historical economic niche, bringing them once again into conflict with private forest owners – all of them ethnic Romanians – and the state officials such as policemen and foresters.

Deforestation: The Beginning

Until 1989, every household received a certain amount of firewood from the LIF according to the number of rooms in the house and the number of people living there. The winter of 1990 was no exception. However, from the winter of 1991 onwards, the belt of willow planted on the riverbank was at hand for the poorest households: the willows and alder trees growing along the river constituted a source of energy for those who could not afford to pay for firewood. Within a few years Rudari and, no doubt, some poor Romanians had clear-cut the willow belt planted in the 1970s by the collective farm to protect the agricultural fields. This was possible because ownership of those trees was unclear. Formally, the collective farm was the owner, though later the National Society 'Romanian Waters', which administrates all the lakes and rivers throughout the country, claimed administration rights over the riverbank. However, in 1991, the collective farm was officially dismantled and the belt of trees was left without an owner. Both willow and alder burn quickly and do not provide many heating calories. Thus, in only a couple of years, villagers had cut extensively all trees in the vicinity of the riverbank. When I arrived in the commune, in April 2004, a mélange of debris, Coca-Cola cans and bottles and domestic rubbish had formed a garbage mountain sitting alongside the river.[10]

In 1992–1993, the mayor's office received from the LIF the communal pastures together with a small plot of black locust (*Robinia pseudacacia*). A few weeks after this transfer, Rudari and, probably, poor Romanians started to cut the trees. As the mayor's office had not arranged to guard the recently acquired forest, the plot suffered the same fate as the willow belt and the alder. A few months was all the time it required for poor villagers to clear-cut the black locust trees. Most probably, the trees could have been sold for money in either Costești – and the reader will remember that villagers from Costești were not awarded much forestland since they did not own much before nationalization – or in the lowland communes in southern Romania.

Law 18/1991 regarding forest restitution came into effect in Dragomirești at the end of 1993. The mayor's office as receiver and the LIF as donor signed a written protocol and 172 hectares passed to the mayoralty administration. The LIF restituted the 172 hectares in one single large tract and, though every household knew how much forest they had received, there was no physical demarcation of one's own forest in the field. Until 1997, the mayor's office administered the forest. Owners had to submit a written request to the mayor's office in order to establish the right to exploit a certain quantity of wood.

Having lost the black locust forest almost overnight, and motivated by the formal requirement of Law 18 that the new owners, whether state or private, assume responsibility for watching over their own forest, the mayoralty hired a retired forest ranger to guard the forest. The mayoralty preferred to hire a pensioner rather than an active ranger because he asked for less money. Forest owners feared the retired ranger. It seems that he did a good job in guarding the forest as no illegal cutting was reported under his watch. He used to ask owners to provide official papers from the mayor's office if they wanted to enter the forest at all. One could imagine the dissatisfaction of forest owners when they were asked to fill out official papers in order to exploit what they considered to be their own forest. Some villagers were more active than others in asking that the ranger be fired. Those who owned larger tracts of forest sought to exploit them, hoping for economic gains. Owners protested that as long as they could not exploit the forest as they wished, when they liked, and in the quantities they needed, they would not feel like real owners. Finally, in 1997, under pressure from the villagers, the local council decided to discharge him. Although two laws, Law 18/1991 and the Forestry Code (art. 70) ratified in 1996, require every owner to monitor his/her own forest or to hire a professional to do so, the private forest, still under the mayor's office administration, remained unguarded. Soon after this event, the mayor's office gave the forest to those villagers declared legal owners.

I will pause here for a moment and try to explain the forest owners' behaviour, which may seem irrational to those readers unfamiliar with postsocialist societies. The local villagers, in common with those elsewhere in the postsocialist world, put rather more emphasis on their rights than on their duties with regard to property ownership.[11] After almost fifty years of state regulations intruding somewhat brutally on their lives, people in postsocialist societies tend to reject most state property regulations. Although the shift in ownership from state to private hands should not change the duties of an owner, people strongly disagree with these provisions. Very often, I heard it said in the commune: 'This is *my* forest, why does the state regulate how forest should be used when the forest belongs to *me*?' The new neoliberal language of ownership created false expectations. Private property, from the villagers' point of view, means complete independence from the state; they do not accept external regulations over the way they envision the usage of the forest. Actually, owners tend to separate the rights they have from the obligations attached to their ownership rights.[12] Although the villagers know the requirements of the law, the general opinion in the commune was that looking after the forests is in fact unnecessary. Besides, many forest owners thought they could exploit the forest at will. Forest had to be an important income source. The following events proved to the forest owners that they had got the wrong end of the stick.

In 2001, the Romanian Parliament passed a new land reform law. Villagers received another 428 hectares of forest. Every legal owner could receive up to 10 hectares. Whereas in Dragomirești village there were not many villagers who owned up to 10 hectares, in Vâlceni and Costești there were several families, especially heirs of lanlords, who had owned large tracts of forest until 1948.[13] Dragomireștens have received in total 600 hectares of mostly deciduous forest. In 2003, when the mayor's office put into practice Law 1 and villagers effectively received their forests, Dragomirești villagers could have described themselves as living in a fairly prosperous commune.

Hills Without Forests

The forest owners in Dragomirești found however that their reasoning was wrong. Most of them started to cut trees as soon as the forest was under their control. However, the tree harvest served mostly domestic purposes. Beech was used mostly for firewood or fences. The LIF officially approves the extraction of only 1 cubic metre per hectare. As the winter is long in this hilly region 1 cubic metre is by no means enough. A household composed of four persons needs at least 7 cubic metres per year, if the family also uses a gas cylinder for cooking. If the family uses wood both to cook and heat the house then they need around ten cubic metres. Oak, because it is more expensive and takes longer to grow, is usually used for household construction. Most barns and stables in the commune are built from oak. Few oak trees were cut for selling the timber. In 2003 this situation changed. When I arrived in the commune, in late April 2004, the forest exploitation frenzy had just started. My first visit to the surrounding hills, soon after my arrival, bewildered me. In order to understand the extent of the disaster one should first imagine the forest and the hills surrounding Dragomirești. The forest begins at the bottom of the eastern hill and continues onto the plateau. A winding track crossing the plateau separates the private forest from the state one. The state forest lies on the eastern part of the plateau, continuing onto the eastern slopes. The forest is interspersed by large meadows, giving the landscape a patchy aspect. The slopes on both sides of the 530-metre-high hills are quite steep and small creek beds cross them. These geographical irregularities make the slopes difficult to climb and the forest difficult to exploit. The deciduous forest covering these hills consists mainly of beech and oak, but also maple, poplar (*Populus*), elm (*Ulmus*) and birch of different ages. Ten-year-old trees grow next to thirty- or forty-year-old trees, proving that these forests were exploited in different periods. When I first visited these forests, only small patches were cut. One-metre-high stumps were scattered around and tiny, still green branches left behind were the sign of hasty activity. The woodcutters were probably aware of the illegality of their actions, since they had not cut the tree closer to the root, but cut it at around one metre above the ground. This means that they lose the thickest part of the tree and thus lose money. The woodcutters first attacked the forest on the plateau. This forest was at hand and next to the track, making it easy to transport the trees with horse carts and tractors or trucks. Within only a few months in 2003, a field of one-metre-high stumps replaced what was once the plateau forest. Month after month, the activity in the forest increased and the area of felled trees increased too. The chainsaw sounded from the forest as soon as the sun set over the commune. The most intense activity definitely took place in the evenings.

After the plateau forest was clear-cut, forest exploiters targeted the forest on the steep slopes. Because of the rough terrain, using trucks was not an option anymore. Those with horse carts – and I must add that a normal cart would not do on such slopes – were now the vehicles used to move up and downwards the slopes bisected by the creeks.

When I left the commune in September 2004, only the plateau and the forest close to the top of the hill had been transformed into bare land. When I returned in 2005 and 2007, the activity in the forest was very intense. The deforested peak of the hills next to Dragomirești village, stretching for 10 kilometres, was the physical proof of this activity. When I came back again, in September 2009, the eastern hills were completely deforested and the eye could only occasionally locate a standing tree. The few trees left were either beyond the range of forest exploiters or too young to be worth the effort.

In all this time, the state forest remained almost intact. How this was possible and which social and political mechanisms produced this deforestation are the subjects of the following section.

Illustration 3.1. Deforestation in Dragomirești, 2004

Illustration 3.2. Deforestation in Dragomirești, 2009

72   *Disrupted Landscapes*

Local State Bureaucrats, Rudari and Patronage

The 600 hectares of private forest have acted as a magnet for two very different local groups: the state officials and the Rudari. These two groups occupy different positions within the commune, have two different histories and, most important, exert a tremendously different kind of leverage over each other. In the absence of any surveillance of the forest by private owners, the local state officials have turned into patrons. Rudari, who are totally dependent on forest products, both timber and non-timber, have turned into clients. The forest owners have taken action in response to this relationship but their reaction has contributed even further to deforestation.

Figure 3.1 shows that deforestation occurred only in the private forests. The state forest, which lies next to the private one, covers 1,953 hectares. The black points mark the 620 hectares of state forest under the surveillance of one single ranger. One might imagine that felling trees on such a large area of state property without fear of being caught would be easy. The challenges of forest surveillance are exacerbated by the fact that forest guards, restricted to the use of slow-moving city cars, are often forced to operate on

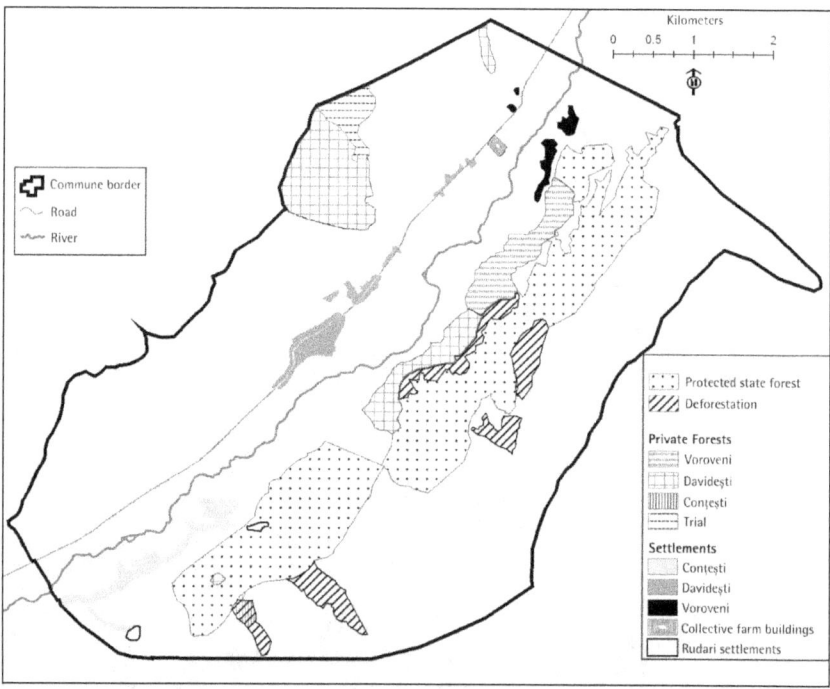

Figure 3.1. Participatory Map Showing Deforestation and the Control of the State Forest

foot.¹⁴ Even without such difficulties, the forest guard showed little interest in policing state-owned forest areas. I once joined the state forest guard on his patrol through the forest. We suddenly heard the unmistakable noise of a chainsaw. As he appeared not to be worried about the noise, I asked him if he was not afraid that the noise was coming from the state forest. 'They won't dare to cut trees in the state forest,' he told me. One must take his calm at face value: every year a national commission evaluates the status of the state forest. Every illegally cut tree has to be paid for from his own meagre salary, which does not exceed €100 per month. How was he able to retain his calm attitude in the face of these harsh sanctions? And why was it, conversely, that trees were being stolen in Dragomirești only from private forest? While villagers blame the Rudari for the theft, usually accompanied by such curses as 'They should be killed; Rudari are good for nothing but stealing wood,' the reality is more complex.

In fact, Rudari are both treated as scapegoats and used as a cheap labour force by local state officials such as policeman, forest guards and some employees of the mayor's office. It is they, via the patron–client relationship they have cultivated with these woodcutters, who are behind the theft of trees from restituted forest. There is an exchange enacted between the two groups: patrons provide protection and economic safety; clients offer a cheap labour force and various goods, such as high quality wood, and promote the patrons' political interest.

Rudari obtain information chiefly from the state forest guards as to which particular private plots may be cut in order to avoid making the 'mistake' of cutting the state forest trees for which those guards are responsible. Accurate information is vital for both woodcutters and forest guards. Imagine that in some places deep in the forest there is no line of demarcation between the private and state forest. Only a red painted sign on a tree indicates to the woodcutter that he is in a state forest. Private forest is demarcated by scratching the bark of the tree and writing the name of the owner with an indelible pencil. It is easy for an illegal woodcutter to make a mistake, especially given that most of activity takes place at night. It requires an excellent knowledge of the forest and detailed maps in order to make sure no state tree is mistakenly harvested. In exchange for information, the forest guard receives bribes and wood delivered directly to the forest guard's courtyard.

If a state ranger does catch Rudari with a cartful of wood, the Rudari cart driver bribes him – the amount of money most often mentioned was about 500,000 lei (about €15) – and provides his family with a 'gift' of high-quality wood.¹⁵ If woodcutters do not have money on them, a deferred payment is always acceptable. I was once in a car with the local chief of the forest guards. When we crossed the Rudari settlement – and there is no other way to return from the Eastern hills forest other than by crossing their settlement – the chief stopped the car next to a young Rudar. Without saying a word, as if they had a prior agreement, the young Rudar handed him 500,000 lei. 'An old debt,' the chief enlightened me. My observation is that mistrust of Romanians vis-à-vis the Rudari runs very deep. This mistrust means that no Romanian villager would ever lend money, or indeed anything else to a Rudar, much less borrow from one. Knowing the relationship between forest guards and Rudari I suspect that the money was a debt from a previous meeting in the forest.

Marian, one of the local forest guards, lives in the same courtyard as his parents. His father has erected a saw mill in their backyard. Usually, the inhabitants of all three villages use this saw mill when they need timber for houses or fences. A villager has two choices: if he has his own logs, he only pays for the mill services. If he has no forest at all, he has been unable to obtain a license to cut or his forest is too young to be harvested, then he also pays for the wood.[16] Villagers told me that most of the wood used in the saw mill comes from 'gifts' made by Rudari in exchange for different services.

George, the chief of the local police station, is another patron obtaining pocket money from illegal logging carried out by Rudari. The most important service he provides is that of offering protection against any charges villagers might bring against the Rudari. He actually fined a few Rudari when he found them with horse carts fully loaded with logs but he imposes this only on certain people and only when he knows there will be no repercussions. Most fines were imposed on poor members of the Rudari community, as the returns from their bribes are not very consistent. Paradoxically, this is another form of protection, as these poor Rudari never pay their fines. Often in court the judge does not enforce the fines, as most Rudari have no salary to pay from or properties to be foreclosed. In this way, the police officer is covering his back with the superior officers at regional level. Even if he catches them, the small quantity of wood that could be loaded in the horse wagons, around 2 cubic metres, is not enough to justify sending impoverished Rudari to court. He therefore fines them only 10 million lei.[17] Fines must be registered in a mayor's office minute. In 2006 for instance, out of 329 villagers fined only 34 persons were not Rudari. All others, 295 people, received a fine for illegal woodcutting.[18] In total 163 Rudari received fines of 10 million lei each; all the others received fines of less than 10 million lei. Several Rudari families have more than four fines, but none of them have paid yet.[19] Having their names inscribed in the register is a necessary hazard of economic survival for most of the community's members, or for the excellent economic benefits gained by those few Rudari who make a good profit from illegal logging.

The police officer mostly protects the few rich Rudari families, that is, those who own at least one truck and who provide him with larger amounts of money and timber. Whereas stealing a cartful of wood is considered a lesser crime and is punishable with a fine, a truckload of wood represents a more significant crime. A truckload could be up to 10 cubic metres or more, an offence carrying a custodial sentence. Most probably, such a criminal record would send the perpetrator to jail for several years. However, between 2003 and 2010, when I finished my field research, no such case was reported. Selective reporting allowed the local police officer to demonstrate to his superiors some success in crime prevention while enabling him to continue protecting the larger operators – the truck owners – by allowing them to circulate with unregistered trucks. Police collusion with large-scale illegal logging activity by truck-owning Rudari went still further. On several occasions, those who owned a larger area of forest complained to the County Police that theft had taken place in their forests. The Police Special Forces came in the middle of the night in order to catch the thieves but were unable to make any arrests. The forest owners complained that somebody who knew about the imminent police raid had warned the Rudari to stay home that night. They suspected that either local police officers or forest guards had given the warning.[20]

Employees of the mayor's office represent another category of patrons. They have a great deal of leverage over the Rudari. As most Rudari have neither pensions nor salaries, they receive social benefits from the state (around €20 per month). Rudari regard employees of the mayor's office as those who 'give them money'.[21] The accountant of the mayor's office, let's call him Radu, enjoys especially high status within Rudari society since he is also the cashier. Every month, a long line of Rudari forms in front of the accountant's office, expecting to receive their meagre social allowance. Most of them think that they are at the mercy of the bookkeeper and if one day he refused to give them their social allowance they would have no leverage to alter that decision. Besides, strong relationships exist between Radu and the Rudari. He lives close to the Rudari settlement (in the 'Romanian part' of Costești), knows most of them quite well, and has even offered to be godfather for some rich Rudari.[22] The bookkeeper has used this special relationship to cut 10 hectares of forest restituted to the heir of one of the landlords in Costești. This heir – let us call him Andrei – received 9 hectares of forest in 2003 in addition to the hectare received in 1991. He lives in Bucharest, the Romanian capital, and is a respected mathematician at the Institute of Mathematics of the Romanian Academy. Having a son to provide for, he thought it would be a good idea to earn some money by harvesting his forest. He sought permission to cut his forest as he heard that Rudari were illegally cutting the surrounding woods. He went to the mayor's office and asked about the legal procedure. The bookkeeper offered to help him, saying that he knew of a forest company that offered a good deal. He asked for a small amount of money in exchange for supervising the forest work and protecting the mathematician's interests. Indeed, the logging company offered Andrei a good deal, wired in advance an amount of money equal to half the final sum and started to exploit the forest. The logging company exploited less than 20 per cent of the forest when Rudari, incited by the bookkeeper, beat the forest workers and chased the company away. It took only a few weeks for the Rudari to clear-cut the forest. Meanwhile, the head of the logging company announced to Andrei that he was withdrawing his workers from the forest and himself from their business arrangement, and claimed the money back. When the distinguished professor came to the village to check on the status of his forest, he assured me in a later interview, he could not believe his eyes: the entire forest was clear-cut. A field of felled trees, some still waiting to be carried away, had replaced the old forest. He informed the local police but also complained to the General Inspectorate of Police in Bucharest. When I left the village in 2004 the investigation was nearly finished, and the bookkeeper was about to be suspended and sent to court.[23] There were rumours in the mayor's office that Radu had become too greedy and had messed with the wrong person. Another forest owner with less education and fewer connections in the country's capital would have accepted some money for the forest and dropped the complaint. This episode illustrates with more clarity than other cases, owing to the police investigation and the willingness of the victim to talk to me, how local bureaucrats abuse their position within the mayor's office to gain privileged access to the forest.

The bookkeeper is not the only mayor's office representative who delivers services to the Rudari. Iuliana, the agricultural officer, in particular provides Rudari with several other services. An essential service is to turn a blind eye when Rudari build their houses illegally on the communal pasture. As this episode will be extensively analysed in chapter 5, it suffices to mention here that this is another service the employees of the mayor's office provide to some Rudari. Moreover, most Rudari families have at least one horse. These horses graze on the communal pasture from spring to autumn. Any villager willing to use communal pasture for grazing animals has to pay a tax to the mayor's office as the legal administrator. The tax should be used to maintain the quality of the pasture. However, none of the Rudari families have ever paid for grazing rights. To this service, the mayor's office employees add another one. Any truck, tractor or car owner has to pay an annual tax to the state. Most Romanian villagers conscientiously pay this tax. There is no tractor in the Rudari settlement – they are not involved in agricultural activities – but I have seen at least eight trucks kept permanently in the settlement. In the Agricultural Register only one single truck is registered. Thus, there is one single Rudari family paying this tax. Everybody in the settlement knows, including me, that this family owns two trucks and two cars. However, they only pay tax for a single truck. The other families, who customarily own one truck, never declare them. When asked, they claim that a relative from another village owns the machine. The truck is essential for carrying the wood from Costeşti to the flatland villages in southern Romania. All people from the mayor's office know about the 'tax-free' trucks including the bookkeeper, the agricultural officer and the mayor. They do not take any action, as this is another service they provide to Rudari.[24]

The agricultural officer was in an excellent position to provide services and to demand reciprocal services. I spent the first weeks in the commune in the same office as the agricultural officer in order to gather data about the commune. I noticed that she was processing all the bureaucratic papers for Rudari. The reader should understand what this means in Romania. For any small service requested of a local state agency, a citizen has to present the request in writing (*cerere*). There is a certain structure, a certain way of using words and certain formula required, without which the cerere is not valid. As almost all Rudari are illiterate, the agricultural officer is the one who writes the cerere for them. This might seem a minor issue but it is not. Navigating through the thickets of Romanian bureaucracy, including the writing of a formal request, especially for those receiving social security, is a significant service. This bureaucratic position holds a tremendous symbolic power, the power of knowledge and writing as Michael Herzfeld put it.[25] It is not just the knowledge of writing *per se* but also the knowledge of how to address the request and the right wording to hit the claimant's target. Because they are Rudari, they are even more dependent on the agricultural officer's good will, as they have to provide documents and to make requests every six months if they want to keep receiving their social benefits. The mayor's office secretary provides this service in exchange for wood and agricultural work. For instance, she asked a few Rudari to clear her agricultural field after the harvest. They collected the maize stalks from the field, after the harvesting, transported them to the riverbanks and threw them away. This service required both human and animal labour as the Rudari transported the maize stalks with their own horse wagons.

The most important service Rudari receive from local bureaucrats is permission, for which read encouragement, to exploit the forest. Cutting and selling wood is the main activity that enables them to survive. No one from a Rudari community can imagine surviving from day to day relying only on the meagre social allowances provided by the central state.[26] Facilitating exploitation of the forest is the most important service the local state officials and bureaucrats provide to members of the Rudari community. But which exactly are the forest loss mechanisms at work in the Dragomireşti commune?

Forest Loss Mechanisms

There are two 'forest loss' mechanisms at work. The first simply involves illegal logging. Rudari with horses and carts, and their poorer companions who have nothing to offer but their labour, go into the forest and cut trees on private plots. Then, the cart's owner sells the wood either to Rudari truck owners or directly to villagers in Costeşti, including those Romanians who own no forest at all. Villagers prefer to buy firewood from Rudari, although they know very well how this wood is obtained, because it is less expensive than that sold by the NIF.[27] In several cases, Romanian villagers who keep sheep offered woodcutters lambs for Easter or cheese in exchange for the firewood. This barter is equally convenient for both sides: Rudari get food while sheep owners get firewood without lifting a finger since Rudari bring the wood into their courtyard. Sometimes they even help the shepherd to store it in the timber yard as I was able to notice myself several times.

Most often, the woodcutters sell the whole quantity of wood harvested on the day to a few rich Rudari who own trucks. Then, the truck owners transport the wood to the lowland villages in southern Romania. The truck owner needs official documents if he wants to transport such a quantity of wood. There is the danger that police could stop the truck on the highway or on the national roads to check the trucker's papers. The truck owner makes sure he is fully covered. He buys a certain amount of wood legally. He receives from the NIF a delivery order that confirms the quantity of wood he transports. Thus, the truck owner legally transports a certain amount of wood from one place to another. There is no illegality so far, one could claim. Sometimes, truck owners bribe people from the NIF to write on the delivery order a greater quantity of wood than they actually bought. In this case, the delivery order is just a fake. More often, the truck owner obtains an order for a certain quantity of wood, which is valid only for forty-eight hours. Since he already has clients and networks in southern Romania, the truck owner makes two or even three transports with the same delivery order. While the first transport is legal, the second and the third are not. That was a good way to cheat the National Roads police when they checked the trucks.[28] This mechanism was eventually uncovered by the police, who asked that the transport permit be limited to twenty-four hours. This change in the legislation made it nearly impossible to transport a second load of wood and certainly a third one with one single permit.

In these ways, Rudari transporters rapidly adapted to the new law requirements. They finally found another way of transporting wood to southern Romanian villages. The head of a private logging company issues a delivery order proving that the Rudari transporter bought 0.5 cubic metres of wood from his company. The truck owner inserts a plastic sheet between the first and the second copy of the delivery order in order to produce not two copies of the same document but two different documents. The first document remains in the custody of the logging firm, at the accounting department in case of an audit. The wood transporter takes the second document to certify the quantity and the provenance of the wood. Then, the truck owner simply adds another number in front of 0.5 cubic metres. If checked, the document will show that he is 'legally' transporting 10.5 cubic metres of wood. Both parties win from this arrangement. The logging company owner receives at least 4 million lei for each delivery order while the truck owner can transport wood he bought from poor Rudari. In this case, the penalty could be severe because the company uses falsified documents. During my stay in the commune, however, no one was arrested. One of the two young police officers from the village revealed these mechanisms to me.[29]

Sometimes, local bureaucrats proceed in a different way but still contribute to forest loss. Mayor's office employees or the forest guards 'buy the forest' very cheaply, threatening the forest owners that 'if they do not sell now for a lower amount of money they will lose their forest, because Rudari will cut it anyway.' The most advantageous business for the buyer and the most disadvantageous for the seller is the purchase of standing trees (*copaci pe picioare*); buyers negotiate additional discounts by arguing that they must pay for the cutting and transport of the trees. Owners are doubly disadvantaged in this trade since, despite their lamenting that they have 'sold the forest', they are still registered as formal owners. Since 2006, forest owners must pay a tax on deforested land that in the mayoralty official papers is registered as forest. The agricultural officer and the former vice-mayor of the commune have bought large numbers of standing trees using such threats. They paid about 10 million lei (around €300) for one hectare of forest, about 10 per cent of the market price.

Caught between the untenable alternatives of losing their forest to the 'thieving Rudari', or selling it for an intolerably low price, forest owners choose the latter, considering it the lesser of two evils. Within the patronage system the Rudari feature as a symbolic weapon in the rhetorical armoury of the wood-buyer/patrons. The traditional occupation of the Rudari becomes a threat used by local state officials in their pursuit of forest purchased through this second route mentioned above.

Some forest owners have reacted to this proposal by cutting down their own forest. Some of them admitted in interviews with me that they simply wanted 'to get something out of their own forest'. As one owner told me, he preferred to cut down his forest, bringing the timber into his own backyard and storing it there. Then he would sell it to neighbours when they needed wood rather than 'selling for nothing'. I entered several courtyards of Romanian villagers, especially in Dragomirești and Vâlceni, and noticed the large amount of wood stored in a shed behind the house.

Forest as a Local Social and Economic Player

Forest serves to promote and underpin patronage relationships. All social relations revolve around forest use in this commune. The tools that a family owns for working in the forest constitute the basis for social stratification amongst Rudari. Social stratification in this community is based on ownership of the means of production: chainsaws, horse carts and trucks for wood transportation. There are three categories of Rudari: the poorest, who have only their hands and who help to load the horse carts, those who own a chainsaw and a cart, and a few rich families who own one or more trucks. The middle group – those with a cart – is the most numerous. In the Agrarian Register, which lists all the houses, the ownership status and means of production for every household in the commune, more than half of Rudari families are listed as horse cart owners. The horse carts are important not only because their owners are less likely to be fined large amounts of money but also because they are the only means of transporting wood from steep slopes with good forest to the Rudari settlement. It is impossible for a truck, I was told, to go where a horse cart would penetrate.

The episode that opens this chapter illustrates the importance of the horse cart for Rudari. No truck would have been able to climb up that hill. The horse cart skilfully conducted by a Rudar did. All felled trees are transported from the hills to the Rudari settlement by cart. From there, those owning a truck buy the best quality wood and then transport it further to the lowland villages. Such transportation and sale is exclusively the business of a few better-off families among the Rudari. With the money gained from their wood business they have opened small shops within the Rudari settlement. Poor and middle-class Rudari buy on informal credit from these shops until they get paid for their work. The wealthy Rudari represent a kind of intermediary between local state officials and all other members of their community. Consequently, by protecting wealthy Rudari, the local state officials protect almost the entire Rudari community.

Forest is an important asset when talking about Romanian villagers' status as well. Those families owning larger forest tracts are also the most highly regarded within the community. When one asks about the most trusted families in the whole commune the names of those families who own forest come up first. Figure 3.2 shows the forest property structure of the commune. Only a few families in Dragomirești village own around 5 hectares, while in the other two commune villages a small minority owns around 1 hectare.

Forestry is the most lucrative activity in the commune. In order to describe as accurately as possible the ways in which the local elite profit from the forest I employ commodity chain analysis. This is a tool of analysis

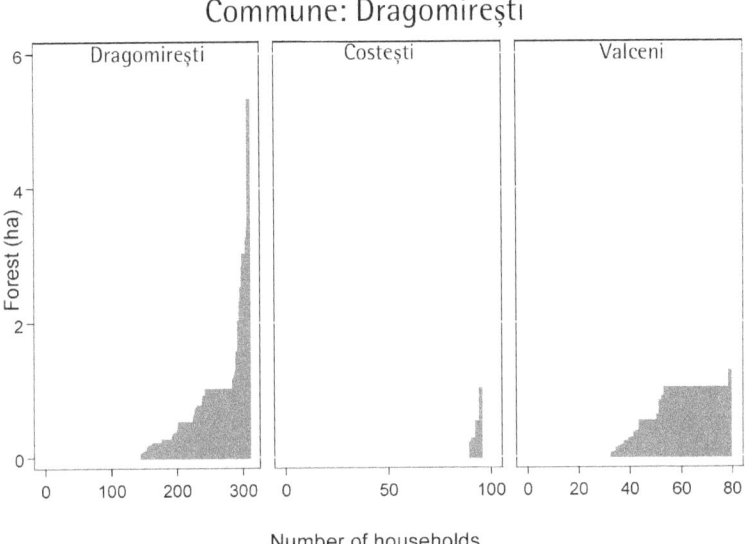

Figure 3.2. Forest holdings distribution in Dragomirești

that considers all the interlinked exchanges associated with a commodity and its constituents. Harvesting, transport, distribution, wholesale, retail, up to the final product; all these phases imply costs. By subtracting the costs for every actor involved in each of these phases one can map the final distribution of profit.[30]

A first example of the yields accrued from the wood business concerns Marian, the state forest guard. As I have described in previous pages his father has a logging company. The logging company owns a truck and a bulldozer, which are mostly used to pull felled trees out of the forest. The firm has three legal employees and five people illegally employed.[31] The monthly salary payments for all three official workers, including the truck driver, are 34 million lei (some €1,000). The five illegal workers together receive a monthly salary of 20 million lei. The firm pays a total of 54 million lei (some €1,600) in salaries each month. The income of the logging firm is earned by providing several services. First, the firm extracts wood for private forest owners. Each year the firm extracts some 2,000 cubic metres of wood, charging 800,000 lei for each cubic metre. The firm's expenses with the bulldozer amount to 300,000 lei for each cubic metre. The logging company's yield for 1 cubic metre is thus 500,000 lei. The yearly gross margin from this activity is 1 billion lei. A second service provided by the firm is plank production. Most of the fences in the commune are made of planks. Sometimes villagers come with their own logs; sometimes the logging firm provides the logs. Each year the firm gains 200 million lei, excluding the taxes they pay to the state and the 20 million they pay annually for electricity consumed by the frame saw. Usually the five illegal workers undertake this work under the supervision of Marian's father, the official owner of the company.

Another operation, which annually brings the firm a nice amount of money, is selling beech and oak logs. This operation is conducted as follows. The logging company buys 500 cubic metres of standing trees from the LIF. The company pays around 400,000 lei for 1 cubic metre of beech and 500,000 lei for 1 cubic metre of oak.[32] The main expense incurred by cutting and hauling logs from the forest to the main road is the use of a bulldozer (300,000 lei for gasoline for each cubic metre). The firm usually uses the five illegal employees to carry out this work, who receive a monthly salary from the forest guard. The Rudari usually conduct the cutting operation with their personal chainsaws and horse carts. Of course, they are rarely paid; usually the guard turning a blind eye to Rudari's cut-and-run logging is the reward for this work. The firm sells 1 cubic metre of beech for 2 million lei and 1 cubic metre of oak for 4 million lei. Oak accounts for about half of the 500 cubic metres. A simple calculation reveals that when 400,000 lei paid to the state for each cubic metre and 300,000 lei for the bulldozer's gasoline have been subtracted, the firm has gained 1.3 million lei for each cubic metre of beech. For the 250 cubic metres of beech, the firm annually earns 325 million lei. The same calculation indicates higher gains for the oak. One cubic metre of oak will fetch 4 million lei. Subtracting 500,000 lei paid to the state for each cubic metre and 300,000 for the bulldozer and assuming that the firm sells 250 cubic metres of oak per year, the annual profit made from oak is 800,000 million lei per year. The total gross margin from selling the raw logs is 1,125 billion lei.

Finally, the logging firm sells annually around twenty cubic metres of timber to an export company from outside the commune. A cubic metre of timber, after it has been processed in the frame saw, yields, according to the firm's accounts, 5 million lei. The export company picks up the timber with its own trucks. The forester's firm uses the five illegal workers to load the trucks. His expenses from this activity amount to 20 million lei for electricity to power the frame saw. The gross profit margin from this activity is 80 million lei per year. Usually, the wood for this activity comes from forest owned by the forester's father, bought over a period of years.

Counting up the sums gained from all activities, including one billion from services and inputs, plus 1,125 billion from selling trunks, plus 200 million from the plank business, plus 80 million from the timber export results in a turnover of 2,405 billion lei. Subtracting 648 million, the yearly salary of the firm's workers, gives a total of 1,757 billion lei. Subtracting again the

16 per cent for state tax, which is 280 million per year, leaves 1,479 billion lei, roughly €41,000 per year.

Here is another example of a local state bureaucrat taking economic advantage of her position over a forest owner. A young man from Bucharest inherited from his grandfather 5 hectares of forest in Dragomirești. The agricultural officer drew up all the documents concerning the forest restitution; it was her job to do that as a member of the LLC. Before doing the paper work, she suggested to the claimant that it would be nearly impossible to reclaim the forest unless she brought pressure to bear on the Land Commission. Besides, she argued, she would make sure that the forest was an old one, composed of oak, suitable for immediate exploitation. She suggested that she would take on the burden of buying the forest, though this was inappropriate under the circumstances. Probably, she argued again, Rudari would learn that this was now private forest and would cut it down 'in a second'. She offered to buy the whole forest for 20 million lei per hectare. Finally, since the young new forest owner had heard the village stories about 'Rudari cut-and-run logging' he agreed to sell it for 100 million lei (€2,750). The agricultural officer quickly drew up the paperwork and took possession of the forest. Soon after that, she sold it to an outside logging company for 1 billion lei, roughly €27,500. Subtracting the €2,750 she paid to the former owner, we see that she earned €24,750.[33] The logging company gains most from this business. According to what I have heard in the village, the logging company sold the timber on the external market, where prices are much higher than on the internal market. A hectare of forest yields 300 to 400 cubic metres of wood.[34] A cubic metre of oak lumber will fetch around €450. From 1 cubic metre of wood the logging company obtains 0.7 cubic metres of lumber. That means the company has sold 1,050 cubic metres of lumber. The other operations involved in obtaining the lumber include transport, log processing to give the lumber a certain shape, then drying it in big ovens and wrapping up the lumber in a plastic sheet. All these operations account for no more than about €100 for each cubic metre of lumber. Summing up, each cubic metre of lumber earns the logging firm an income of €350. From 5 hectares of forest the export company obtains €367,500 (€350 x 1,050 cubic metres of lumber). Subtracting €27,500, the amount paid to the agricultural officer, the company's gross profit margin is €340,000.[35]

What I have described so far represents one mechanism by which local state bureaucrats gain important advantages from exploiting local forest. These economic mechanisms reflect a legal commodity chain. Nothing described above is outlawed and therefore poses no risk for the actors involved. The gains obtained by local state bureaucrats are possible because of their position within the local state apparatus. The agricultural officer was able to manipulate the restitution papers and to obtain an immediate economic gain simply because she is the sole person from the LLC entitled to work with restitution documents, old maps and written requests. One may talk about illegitimacy or immorality, considering the position of the local state bureaucrats and their supposed duties, but no infringement of the law has taken place.

There is, however, a second, illegal commodity chain. The actors involved in this commodity chain include the forest owners, the local police officer, the forest guard and the Rudari. Due to its illegal character, and the perils involved, state bureaucrats from higher levels, from a regional and maybe national level, seem to be part of the picture. It is plausible that the chief of the county police and the chief of the LIF are involved in this network. Without them, no actions at local level would be possible. The forest owners are involved simply because they refuse to monitor the forest as Forestry Law requires. Their refusal represents an attempt to underpin their own ownership and avoid any state involvement. Private forest owners do not regard forest watch as an obligation but rather as an intrusion by the state into their private business. Villagers secretly hoped that once they got their forest back they would be able to exploit it freely without state regulations or imposed quotas. Finally, they were caught up in the vortex of logging and all they could do was 'get something out of it' by cutting down what remained after Rudari raids.

Rudari simply took advantage of unguarded forest. The poorest Rudari have teamed up with those who own a chainsaw and a horse cart in order to cut-and-run. Usually such teams are formed of two to three people, relatives or neighbours. The horse cart owner pays around 60,000 lei (less than €2) for each cartload plus food and drink. A fully loaded cart means around 2 cubic metres of wood. The team sells the wood to truck owners for 600,000 lei. Next, truck owners transport the wood, usually around eight cubic metres in each truck, to the southern villages. Here, they sell each cubic metre for around 1.5 to 1.7 million lei per cubic metre. In these lowland villages, on the Danube Valley, a cubic metre of firewood fetches around 2 million lei (€50). Villagers have not many alternatives, as willow is the most common tree in this part of the country and it is in short supply. Besides, a villager buying ten cubic metres of beech saves around 4 million lei, nearly €110, a fortune for such poor lowland villagers living from subsistence agriculture. Buying willow, a poor heat provider, for 2 million lei is not a viable business.

Now that I have explained the wood circuit, let me demonstrate the commodity chain. For an easier understanding I have calculated the distribution of profit along the wood chain for a truck. To load a truck requires four fully loaded carts, that is, 8 cubic metres. The poorest Rudari receive around €2 per cart, which is €8 for four carts. The middle-class Rudari get around 600,000 lei for 2 cubic metres of wood (a cart), which is less than €20. A cart owner receives €80 for a fully loaded truck. He pays €8 for labour and sometimes, when the local policeman catches him, he pays 500,000 lei (around €13). In this case, the team will go back for a second or even third load of wood.[36] Thus, the cart owner makes around €60 in profit on each truckload. The transporter sells a truckload for some €300. From this money, he pays €80 to cart owners and, quite often as I was told, around €40 to the National Road Police who stop every truck to extort bribes. The truck owner makes €180 profit on each load.

Commodity chain analysis highlights the risk run by each participant involved at local level. The horse wagon team usually faces high levels of risk. In 2007, the physician from Costeşti village reported fourteen Rudari with serious injuries, all caused by 'work in the woods'. The transporters also share the risk of being caught by the National Police: if prosecuted successfully, they would go to prison for several years. In order to diminish the risk, they take three or four trucks into at one time. In this way, the bribe they would have to pay if caught is more substantial and more likely therefore to tempt the road police. Several villagers told me that in some cases, the local police car accompanied the loaded trucks as far as the southern villages. If a National Police team stopped the convoy, the local police officer would use the name of the chief of the Argeş County Police, pretending that the wood was for his family. The local police officer would charge 5 million lei (€120) for such a service.[37]

George, the local head of police, earns around €13 and free quality timber for every detected cartload. The state forest guard gains money too, as he is also entitled to control the horse wagons. More important than the bribe he extracts from the horse cart owners is the protection he provides for the state forest. He is godfather to youngsters from rich Rudari families. The exchange between the forester and his godsons is that he pretends not to see the brisk evening activity in the Rudari settlement while the godsons guard the state forest against Rudari from neighbouring communes. I witnessed myself several times young Rudari heading to the state forest at sunset.

State bureaucrats at a higher level also profit indirectly from the wood business. The head of the County Police appoints the local chief of police. The rumours in the commune are that an appointment in a commune like Dragomireşti costs the appointee 200 million lei, precisely because of the wood business. The implicit assumption is that the appointee will make the money back from bribes.[38] The chief of the LIF is another actor gaining indirectly from wood business. The winning party in the national elections appoints the chief of the LIF from its own party. Consequently, he or she runs the department as long as the party remains in power. This is the main reason he or she has to make back the money he or she 'invested' in getting appointed. The LIF chief protects his local employees by not responding at all to the few villagers who complain or by organizing a formal enquiry that always concludes that no illegal action has occurred. The LIF chief does not make money from illegal logging but from legal wood extraction. A company auctions a certain tract of forest that is going to be clear-cut, let us say the equivalent of 3,000 cubic metres. The company usually exploits far more than 3,000 cubic metres.[39] The local forester and his superior will turn a blind eye in exchange for 1 billion lei, poured mostly into the chief's pockets, as one forester told me. The local forester, in turn, gains a protector for his wood business; the LIF chief protects the local forester so he can continue to conduct his wood business using Rudari labour without being questioned by his superior. Besides, the local forest guard has the unofficial duty of convincing villagers to vote for the party in power. If the party stays in power, the LIF chief remains in his post and the local forester retains his protector. This is the circle of power and money that exists around forest exploitation.

The Political Significance of the Forest

A brief glance at the figures recorded in the previous subsection is enough to understand why forest has a strong political significance. Hardly any other commodity in a rural area is of greater economic value than a forest. Thus, not surprisingly, the forest is at the very core of local politics. As an example, in the 2008 local elections the first three candidates for the mayoralty, which means those who really counted and who fought with a real chance of success, were all involved in the wood business. No local political aspiration is possible without forest control.

The local chief of forest guards, the agricultural officer and the head of the local police station all support the Social Democrat Party (SDP), which was in power at the time of my fieldwork. The forest guard can be a member of a political party and at this time was also an elected member of the local council. The agricultural officer and the police officers are public servants and cannot therefore be affiliated to a political party.[40] Formally they are not, but they visibly support the SDP by campaigning for them in elections. When the SDP mayoral candidate organized a show with folk singers in the commune, all the local state officers and bureaucrats attended it. They were not there to participate in a folk show on a sunny Sunday afternoon: they received, as did everybody else attending, buckets, pencils and caps all bearing the party logo and mingled with villagers, urging them to vote for the SDP. In a subsequent informal conversation with a Rudar he told me that the agricultural officer and other people from the mayor's office threatened that if the SDP candidate was not elected the mayoralty would cut off their social allowances. He assured me that this would cause havoc for the entire community.[41]

Their administrative powers enable local state bureaucrats to become the most efficient, albeit unofficial, political agents. They collude in this administrative territory to maintain both the political status quo and their control over forests. Access to forest is the point at which these relationships converge.

None of the postsocialist mayors attempted to prevent illegal logging. They may not have benefited materially from forest exploitation, but they benefited politically. An episode that occurred during the local electoral campaign clarifies the relationship between politics, patronage and deforestation. One of the candidates promised the Rudari elite that he would never bother them with 'forest problems' if they would not trespass on his hectare of forestland. All candidates promised that they would promote the interests of the Rudari at county level.[42] On a local television talk show, the two finalists for the office of mayor were asked what they thought about deforestation. Both of them denied that it was really occurring beyond some petty theft of branches from the forest or owners sporadically cutting down a few trees from their own forest. Next morning I met the mayoral candidates and I asked the same question. They told me that it would have been pointless trying to tackle this problem, since Rudari would in any case continue to cut the forest, as it is the only economic alternative they have. By being evasive in their answers they were keeping open the possibility of being voted in by Rudari.

Mapping Deforestation: A Postsocialist Image

The social dynamics I have described above are generally responsible for the great loss of forest and the production of a barren landscape. I do not have an official estimate of how much local forest has been lost. The unofficial estimate of ordinary villagers is that more than half of the 600 hectares of private forest has been illegally cut. The hills without forest surrounding the commune are a living proof of the villagers' estimate.

The analysis I provide in this chapter is by no means an isolated case in postsocialist Romania. Despite the local variations in ecological, economic and political conditions, the ethnographic reports highlight the same social dynamics throughout Romanian forests leading to dramatic changes in the landscape. For instance, 100 timber exploitation companies operate in one single hilly, heavily forested commune in Eastern Romania.[43] The mayor, who is the most important local wood businessperson, owns 16 saw mills. Other local state officials such as the members of the local council and the local foresters support his business. All of them own saw mills and earn good money from illegal logging. The local bureaucrats benefit from political support at higher levels, from prominent SDP members at national level or from high-ranking state officials in the NIF. At the other end of the wood business are poor people, hauling timber out of the forest for local logging companies, using their pair of oxen, or those illegally employed by the local timber exploitation companies.[44]

Private forests are not the only targets in this whirlwind of illegal exploitation. The common forest (named differently in different parts of Romania as *Obște* or *Composesorat*) has also been savagely exploited by those entrusted with its good management.[45] Several anthropologists have pointed out that throughout Romania, it is local state officers and bureaucrats who actually profit economically from the common forests while the commoners get little benefit, if any.[46] The story is the same as the one provided in this chapter: patron–client relations are key to illegal logging practices at local level; local state officials fiercely exploit the forest, whether private or common, while collusion between local state bureaucrats and central state officials is the main force behind illegal forest exploitation. Political power, ranging from local to national, is the common thread running through this story of illegal logging. The outcome is severe deforestation, ecological damage and the loss of biodiversity.

At national level, the forest's status does not look good at all. There are 6.38 million hectares of forestland in Romania – 26.7 per cent of the total national territory – of which 4.2 million hectares are public forest while the rest belongs to private owners, communities or different institutions such as the church.[47] A 2006 World Bank Report on Romanian forestry estimates that illegal logging in private forests accounts for 40 per cent of the wood harvested. In the National Plan for Fighting Against Illegal Logging the estimate of forest which has been clear-cut is raised to 32,524 hectares, while 95,077 hectares of forest have been damaged by illegal logging.[48] Despite evidence of heavy deforestation, other reports are more optimistic. David Turnock points out that in southwestern Romania the woodland is relatively stable and is regenerating naturally.[49] Seven years after the first law on forest privatization, in 1998, out of 337,000 hectares only 10,600 hectares had been cut. Despite this optimistic assessment, forests remains under pressure because of widespread poverty, while high demand for firewood is continually encouraged by a limited natural gas distribution network at national level.

The destruction of forests is not peculiar to Romania. Virtually all of the postsocialist countries have gone through the same process. In Albania, the dense forest decreased from 31 per cent of the country's total land surface in 1991 to 25 per cent in 2001. The reports show that only 30 to 40 per cent of logging actually carried out in this country is legal. The forest guards lack the capacity and the will to enforce regulations in the state forests. Rent-seeking state officials reap the economic benefits of drastic deforestation. Local residents, forest authorities, logging companies and unlicensed woodcutters were all in the rush to cut down trees.[50] In the Republic of Moldova, a former republic of the Soviet Union that gained independence in 1991, there is no private forest. In the early 1990s, Moldova had 325,000 hectares of forest. During 1991–1996, some 1.27 million cubic metres of wood was illegally extracted, totalling at least US $70 million, leaving behind a degraded state forest, eroded soils and poor pastures.[51] As in the case of Romania, the Bulgarian state has restored forest to former owners and their heirs. The land reform laws never encompassed those ethnic groups that had never enjoyed property rights over forest.[52] The *Kopanari* population – Romanian Rudari who migrated to Bulgaria in the nineteenth century – have forged patron–client relationships with rich local villagers, usually members of the local councils or foresters. The local elite use Kopanari population, as poor as their Romanian peers and equally excluded from political representation and economic opportunities, as cheap labour to carry out illegal logging in the state forest.[53] Throughout Bulgaria, rural communities heavily rely on access to natural resources, particularly forest.[54] Deciduous wood is particularly prized for burning while spruce and fir are useful for building.[55] Staddon reports that in a small region of the Razlog Basin, in Bulgaria, around one million cubic metres of wood has been illegally cut as compared to five million which were legally exploited.[56] Forest, as the most valuable natural resource accessible to rural people, suffers not only from the petty acts of wood theft, which has helped villagers to survive, but also from extended illegal logging conducted by what is usually called 'the wood mafia'.[57] The 'shadowy mafia', as Staddon and Grykień called it, reaps quick profits through the export of raw logs or by selling them to local producers.[58] Further, illegal forest exploitation is encouraged by several factors including high unemployment rates, the ease of access to relatively plentiful mature forests and the small number of foresters.[59]

In Ukraine, the 10.8 million hectares of forest are state-owned. In this country the forest dynamics are slightly different from those I have presented so far, simply because the state owns both the forest and the wood-processing companies. Studies based on satellite image analysis have pointed out that Ukrainian forests are also under siege from woodcutters, one of the main reasons being corruption among high-level state bureaucrats combined with the poverty of local people.[60] In Russia, the state owns the forest and auctions and leases it to private logging companies. The local management units were privatized in the mid 1990s. Actually, the employees were given stocks but no capital or technologies were directed to them. The result was that these units were not able to compete at the auctions and most of these companies went bankrupt, the dismissed employees contributing to the massive out-migration from rural areas.[61] The outcome was deforestation and the usual retinue accompanying this process: forest fragmentation, soil erosion and loss of biodiversity. In short, cross-national studies of the forestry sector in countries from Central and Eastern Europe point out the high rates of forest disturbance after 1990.[62] This is, most probably, the effect of the illegal exploitation of forests.[63] In turn, incompetent and inconsistent governmental policy, the political power of logging companies, lack of transparency, the poverty of rural inhabitants, the lack of economic opportunities and, last but not least, the corruption of the forest staff at different levels are the causes of illegal forest exploitation.[64]

Postsocialist Asian countries have also experienced heavy losses of forest. Vietnam, for instance, began the devolution of state forest to households in the early 1990s. However, most of the forestland was given to local level state-owned units. Further, the politically appointed leaders at local level decided which households would receive forest and which were excluded from allocation. The ethnographic reports show that only wealthier households, whose members had political connections, customary rights or labour capacity, were able to exploit the forest. Poor households, though equally entitled to forest allocation, had no capacity to reap economic benefits.[65] Illegal logging has many causes in Vietnam, which I am not going to explore in detail here. Sikor and To identify a complex of factors essential to understanding the rush on forest in Vietnam which has to do with both the struggle for forest use at local level and the national policy seeking to consolidate state authority over forests. The criminalization of commercial logging – a governmental attempt to consolidate its power over natural resources – empowered wholesalers and powerful brokers to control the timber trade.[66]

Hills left without forests seem to be a fairly representative image of most postsocialist countries. It looks like the central planners responsible for land reform laws did not foresee the outcomes of forest restitution. Privatizing forest had to be the way to more sustainable forest exploitation and economic improvements of forest owners' lives, according to the tenet of neoliberal ideology. The massive loss of forest was not the aim of forest privatization. By manipulating the law, by taking advantage of their strengthened position through decentralization, and by triggering the reaction of forest owners who contributed further to deforestation, local state bureaucrats have subverted the initial vision of central planners. Equally they have altered the postsocialist landscape.

Notes

This chapter has been partially published under the title, '"They should be killed." Forest restitution, ethnic groups and patronage in post-socialist Romania', in *The Rights and Wrongs of Land Restitution. 'Restoring What Was Ours'*, eds. D. Fay and D. James (New York: Routledge-Cavendish, 2009), 43–65.

1. *Nenea* and *tanti* have the same meaning in Romanian language as uncle and aunt. These are also appellatives for an older male or a female. In order for a young person to use these appellatives, s/he should be intimately connected to that person.
2. In the late 1990s, the mayoralty stopped the introduction of a gas pipe due to lack of funds.
3. Verdery (1998). See also Kaneff (1998) for the land reform and the reinforcement of ethnic boundaries in Bulgaria.
4. Marushiakova (1993). See also Dorondel (2007).
5. Achim (1998).
6. Zamfir and Zamfir (1993).
7. Dorondel and Popa (2014).
8. See, for instance, Sorescu-Marinković (2013) for more details about possible differences in the legal system between Rudari and Roma.
9. For more details, see McGarry (2008).
10. There is no garbage service in the commune and both villagers and the mayor's office consider the riverbank as a dumping area. See chapter 7 for more details.
11. Howarth (1998).
12. Sikor (2006).
13. A landlord from Costești had, in 1948, almost 1,000 hectares of forest. Nevertheless his heir received 9 hectares of forest, added to the 1 hectare he got back in 1993.
14. The forest guard watching the state forest owns a Dacia car dating from late 1989. Very often, the car broke down and he confessed to me that several times he had to replace the car axle and the wheel spring out of his own meagre salary. These two components suffered most from the rugged, hilly terrain.
15. There is no fixed bribe but this was the amount of money most often quoted, in whispers, by Rudari and villagers.
16. I use 'he' because this is exclusively a man's job. I never heard of a woman going to a saw mill. Even widows ask a male member of the family or a neighbour to help them in this regard.
17. This amount of money, equivalent to €300 – twice the national average salary in 2004 – is still quite significant for a rural family.
18. The data comes from the mayor's office register. I thank the mayor's office tax collector who allowed me to study his books. It was easy to differentiate between entries for Rudari and others, as I know every family name in the commune.
19. The research was carried out during the summer of 2007.
20. The Forestry Code (Art. 76) requires that any police control in forestry matters must be carried out in the presence of at least one forest guard.
21. Every family receiving social support has to be socially and economically re-evaluated every six months. This means test (*ancheta socială*) is supposed to be carried out by social workers. As there were none in the commune in 2004, the agricultural officer fulfilled this role. Two young women from the County Council in Pitești regularly visited the commune to sign and confirm the agricultural officer's means test. They

never double-checked the real situation in the field. Thus the agricultural officer and other mayor's office employees have an important leverage over Rudari. As many authors have pointed out (see, for instance, von Benda-Beckmann et al. (2000) [1994], Mungiu-Pippidi (2010) or Thelen et al. (2011)) social security has not only an economic function but also constitutes a strong political control especially in patron–client relationships where social security programs may be used as leverage to gain political or electoral support.

22. The literature on symbolic kinship is too extensive to be quoted here. This exceeds the aim of this chapter. It is important to note though that godfatherhood represents an important tie among villagers, as strong as the blood kinship. The godparenthood is 'a social relationship between two groups of people or between two persons with a different status which requires a donor and a recipient' (Hammel (1980: 2); for the Romanian case, see Vasile (2012)). Godparenthood also denotes a complex system of services.
23. The prosecutor was not able or did not want to prove the link between Rudari and the bookkeeper. The bookkeeper was discharged, resumed his post within the mayor's office and was elected mayor of the commune in 2008.
24. The relationship between the Rudari population and the employees of the mayor's office is more complicated than indicated here. For a more general picture of these relations, see Dorondel and Popa (2014).
25. Herzfeld (1992).
26. The ethnic discrimination against Roma and Rudari within the labour market makes it impossible for these ethnic groups to find a job outside the commune (ANES (2007)). This renders Rudari totally dependent on social allowances.
27. NIF provides a service of forest exploitation. An auction takes place and a private firm gains the right to cut a certain quantity of wood. The poorer quality wood is then sold to whoever needs firewood, usually local people. It is understandable that these production costs, which must cover trees, state expenses and the private firm's expenses, are far higher than those incurred by Rudari.
28. Usually such transports took place during the night. A visitor would certainly be surprised by the dynamics of working practice within a Rudari settlement: all day long the settlement looks deserted, apart from kids playing on the dusty road, but at sunset the settlement becomes very lively. After 20:00 the whole settlement becomes very animated, as it is time to load the trucks.
29. There are three police officers in Dragomirești commune. The policeman accused of corruption I refer to is the head of the local station. The other two are young people, respected by the villagers as I was told with several occasions. Both of them are also students at the college and they see themselves as representatives of a new generation of police officers, doing their jobs in the peoples' service, immune to corruption and obeying only the law. Their boss is much feared and disrespected in the commune. Villagers consider him 'shady'. Sometimes, the relationship between the head of the local police and the two subordinates is tense, as I noticed on several occasions. For instance, I witnessed an incident where one young officer had stopped a truck driven by a Rudar who had no documents at all. Just as the young officer was preparing to confiscate the wood the senior officer came and said: 'Leave him alone, I know this man; he has papers but left them at home.' The young policeman had to obey the order although his face registered high dissatisfaction. In 2006, the head of the local police station was caught in the act of taking money from a Rudar. He was dismissed

but never prosecuted, though he was forced to retire (see the newspaper *Cotidianul*, 11 October 2006). The rumours, supported by the newspaper article, were that had his case come to court it would have become known that he had given information about the bribe to his superiors, at regional and maybe national level. In 2007, when I came back in the commune, he had already moved away.
30. Ribot (1998).
31. All the data and prices were provided by Marian in one of the interviews.
32. I compared the amount of money the company paid with the official data from a study on timber auctions in Romania (Saphores et al. (2006: 45)). According to this study, 1 cubic metre of beech was auctioned in Argeș County for 800,000 lei and 1 cubic metre of oak for 1,491,153 lei. The forest guard's explanation for such a price difference was that he usually bids for areas that are difficult to exploit, such as steep slopes and deep valleys, which reduces the price of the wood. Officially, he uses a bulldozer to extract the logs. Unofficially, he sometimes employs Rudari with their carts and strong horses in exchange for allowing them to practise cut-and-run logging.
33. In order to avoid high taxes imposed by the Romanian state the following practice has become widely established in Romania. A notary draws up the sell/buy contract. Both parties agree in advance to quote a very low price in the official contract. Thus, both parties avoid paying higher taxes, to the notary as well as to the state.
34. Grodzińskca et al. (2004).
35. I did not add taxes to this sum of money because the Romanian state gives a tax refund to Romanian export firms as an encouragement to export goods. This is the general rule. I have no information regarding whether or not this particular firm received the tax back.
36. This happens no more often than once a week.
37. While staying amongst Rudari I never personally saw a police car escorting their trucks. Even if it is just a fabricated story it nevertheless demonstrates the strong links between rich Rudari families and the local police officer. Nevertheless, the newspapers recently reported that police cars with lights on had escorted trucks loaded with smuggled cigarettes (*România Liberă*, Friday, 18 February 2011).
38. I have this information from one of the young police officers of the commune. He was strongly against this practice as he made it clear to me.
39. Saphores et al. (2006).
40. Other categories of citizens who cannot affiliate to a party are professional soldiers, members of the Intelligence Services and public functionaries.
41. Local state officials cannot simply refuse to pay social allowances to those eligible to receive them. But my informant seemed convinced by the power of mayor's office employees to withhold such payments.
42. Rudari generally have two requirements. One is 0.4 hectare of land to be allocated to each family for housing. This requirement reflects their unease about building their new houses on the communal pasture. The second is access to running water. In 2008, the Rudari still drew water from an incredibly insanitary spring that looked rather like a hole in the ground containing dirty water.
43. I draw on Vasile (2009).
44. Vasile (2009).
45. I cannot discuss in detail here the avatars of the common forest. This would take me too far away from the main discussion. For more details, see Vasile (2009); Vasile and Mǎntescu (2009).

46. Vasile (2009); Vasile and Măntescu (2009); Chiburte (2008).
47. Romsilva (2011).
48. Plan Național (2010). At a workshop organized by Oxford University and the Institute of Geography, Bucharest at Comana, 19–20 September 2006, a high-ranking official from the NIF who attended the workshop declared that until 1999, before Law 1/2000 was passed, 30,000 hectares of private forest had been clear-cut. The official estimated the monetary value of this deforestation at US$1.5 billion. Regardless of the real figures, which are hard to estimate, the disastrous outcome for Romanian forest remains a fact.
49. Turnock (2002).
50. Stahl (2010b).
51. Gulca (2008).
52. Stoyanov (1999).
53. Dorondel (2007).
54. Cellarius (2004).
55. Staddon and Grykień (2009).
56. Staddon (2009).
57. Interestingly enough, the Romanian media also talk about a 'wood mafia' when describing the chain of local, regional and national politicians involved in illegal wood business.
58. Staddon and Grykień (2009: 110).
59. Staddon (2001).
60. Kuemmerle et al. (2009); Nijnik and Kooten (2000).
61. Eikeland and Riabova (2002).
62. Kuemmerle et al. (2007).
63. These studies are based on the analysis of remote sensing data, a methodology that does not allow for descriptions of the economic and political mechanisms behind forest loss but only the forest loss itself.
64. Bouriaud (2005).
65. Sikor and Nguyen (2007).
66. Sikor and To (2011).

 CHAPTER 4

Contested Forest

> 'Broadly speaking, their idea was to tear down the forests and replace them with cars. It wasn't a conscious, considered plan; it was worse than that. They had no idea where they were heading, but they went there all the same, whistling on their way and after them came the flood, the downpour (or, rather, the acid rain).'
> —Fr. Beigbeder, *Was £9.99 now £6.99*

On a cold morning in mid September 2004 I was waiting in front of the Dragova mayor's office for the usual lorry that, at this time of the day, was supposed to pass hourly. Since I had arrived in the commune, every morning, except Sundays, several lorries had driven up to the northern part of the commune to load logs. The lorries passed by again in the afternoon, loaded with heavy wood, heading south. After more than an hour of waiting, desperate to reach the northern part of the commune in order to take GPS points, I entered the mayor's office. One of the functionaries enlightened me: 'There are no trucks going up today because the control team is coming from the Ministry of Agriculture and Forestry.' The mayor, whose wife owns the log firm, had temporarily halted any forest activity. Forest exploitation would resume next morning, after the senior officials had left. Indeed, the next day, it took me less than half an hour of waiting until a lorry had arrived. One hour later I reached the northern point of the commune. A desolate landscape had opened up in front of my eyes: as far as one could see, a large field of felled trees lay at my feet. Hundreds of trunks of varying length and thickness waited in rows to be loaded in the lorries. 'Is it possible to cut trees on the National Park's territory? Isn't this forest under protection?' I naively asked the lorry driver. 'Well, this is the communal forest and, with the approval of the park, it is possible to cut it. The mayor's firm got the approval,' the driver assured me. My companion, a villager with good knowledge of the commune's territory,[1] commented bitterly after we moved some distance away and the driver could not hear him: 'When I wanted to cut a tree from my own forest the park would not allow me. Nevertheless, the mayor has obtained the park's approval to clear-cut the whole communal forest.'

This story prefigures and illustrates the content of this chapter. The National Park administration operates a double standard when it comes to forest protection. While forest owners have difficulties in exploiting their own forest, due to the park's opposition, plundering local officials exploit the forest on an industrial scale. National Park administration, local state officials and forest owners find themselves locked in a struggle for rights to the surrounding forest. Each party has different methods, tools and ideas about how to access forest. The outcome of this struggle is the spoliation of the forest and the creation of a forestless landscape.

Disputing Forest: Villagers Against the Park

In 1990, villagers were thrilled at the prospect of getting back their forests. For centuries, wood and other forest products have constituted an important part of their livelihood. Forest privatization was an economic shock for the entire community, as I have described in a previous chapter. Law 18/1991 stipulated that private forest must be returned to former owners, up to 1 hectare per owner. Law 1/2000 referred to the restitution of private forest, up to 10 hectares this time, and also of collective and communal forest. A total of 879 hectares of forest passed to private hands and 70 hectares of forest passed to the commune. Both tracts of forest were situated in the protection zone within the territory of the Piatra Craiului National Park (PCNP).

The steady development of the park has coincided with the forest restitution carried out during ten years of land reform. In 1990, a first law established 8,100 hectares of forestland as a National Park. The park was not founded from scratch; its kernel represented 440 hectares of forestland declared a nature reserve in 1938. Between 1990 and 2004 the park was extended to 14,773 hectares. According to the Plan of Management, the main act stipulating which activities are permitted in the park, the aim of the park is to protect the forest's biodiversity and to maintain 'traditional land use' in the area.[2] Land reform laws that attempt to restore historical justice make no specific mention of preventing the restitution of protected forest. Thus, there is a mixture of property rights to the park's territory. Thirteen per cent of the forest and 20 per cent of the meadows belong to individuals. The state owns 40 per cent of the forest and no meadows at all. The rest of the park is owned by a number of local authorities with jurisdiction over land bordering the park and by *Obști* (the administrative body of the collective forest). Nevertheless, ROMSILVA administers 58 per cent of the total territory of the park, which includes forest, meadows and rock formations, while the other owners, including private individuals, the *Obștea* and the local councils, administer the remaining 42 per cent.[3]

Following IUCN guidelines the park's forest is zoned into different categories. The core zone of the park representing 683 hectares is the scientific reserve. Any other activity in this forest, besides scientific endeavour, is forbidden. Following IUCN Category II, a second zone was designated 'the central area of the park' where only traditional activities such as grazing are allowed. Finally, there is a third zone of protected land where certain economic activities such as rural tourism and forest use are allowed, according to IUCN Category V.[4] Regardless of the property rights, the park administration has the ultimate decision regarding any activity on the park's territory. That means a forest owner, be it an individual or a community, cannot decide freely on the management of his or her own forest and meadows but has to obey the park's rules. This decision was even more difficult for the other forest owners to accept as until 2003 there were no physical borders to mark the park's boundaries. Forest owners accuse the park's manager of regarding the forest as a kind of ownerless space, to be claimed by the state – despite the fact that other state agencies implement land reform and conduct the forest restitution. A common utterance I often heard in the commune was: 'Am I the owner of this forest or does the park own it? If I am the owner, I don't see any reason to obey the park's rules. If I'm not the owner, then the park's administrators (or other state agency involved in forest restitution) should take back this plot and give me another one somewhere else.'[5]

These two intertwined actions – forest restitution to former owners and the constitution of the park – have triggered a clash between two competing ways of understanding the history of the surrounding nature, including biodiversity, forests and meadows, and different ways of building and legitimizing claims over the environment.[6] Ultimately, the clash is between two competing ways of perceiving the use of natural resources and more broadly, of the natural environment. The park promotes an 'environmentalist' approach as stated in the management plan: 'The PCNP's main aim is the protection and the conservation of some representative samples of the biogeographic national space containing some special valuable natural elements of physical-geographic, flora, fauna, hydrology, geology, palaeontology, soil, or of any other part of nature. The park offers the possibility for scientific research and educational, touristic and recreational visits.'[7] According to this statement and to the general manager of the park, the PCNP aims to serve the wider public interest.[8] The values promoted by the park are 'non-utilitarian' and intentionally are national, even international, values. Forest within the park is conceived as a crucial element in carbon sequestration, the production of ozone and in watershed and soil protection. No less important is the landscape and the shelter of protected species: over 300 fungi species, lichens (such as *Bucegia romanica*), flora including Great Yellow Gentian (*Gentiana lutea*), Fragrant Orchid (*Gymnadenia conopsea*) and Military

Orchid (*Orchis militaris*), to name only a few, and valuable fauna such as bear, lynx, wild boar and martens, among others.⁹ The general manager of the park complained to me that deforestation will result in damage even for the locals as in rainy springs, water torrents run onto the hill slopes, damaging vegetation and eroding the soil. 'It will not be long before landslides sweep away the village's houses,' he declared apocalyptically, picturing the outcomes of deforestation. 'Forest restitution means stabbing to death the green lung of Romania' was his final emotive plea against forest restitution. The park's mission as stated by the general manager and the management plan is congruent with the wider *raison d'être* of the state that, theoretically, serves the public good. From this perspective, retaining decision-making power over the park forestland¹⁰ management is necessary not only to control a valuable natural resource but also as part of a complicated process of establishing state authority.¹¹

Villagers base their claim on rather more 'utilitarian' values. Their arguments are historical: the forestland belonged to their forefathers and it was always used for local livelihood. Villagers questioned me almost aggressively on several occasions when I kept asking about the role of the park in maintaining biodiversity: 'Where was the park when my grandfather owned forest there?' they asked, waving their hands in the direction of the park. Their claim to the forest is based on local history and on the livelihood argument. Forest is first and foremost a source of heat and a building material. Since the commune lies at an altitude of between 854 and 1264 metres, spring comes very late, in May, and the weather turns quite cold in September.¹² A large quantity of wood is necessary to heat the houses and to cook. Even though most of the houses today are built with bricks or concrete, villagers still build their barns and stables as well as their fences from beech or fir. Restricting wood extraction makes life difficult in this region. Thus, the park's establishment was perceived as an attempt by the state to limit land reform and maintain control over natural resources, people and the local economy. Villagers are harshly critical of the state's interference in their property rights.¹³

The villagers' grudge against various state agencies was exacerbated by the NIF's decision to give back forest in a tract that had already been exploited in the last years of the communist regime. Although in the official papers this tract was described as 'forest', in fact, only young trees and bushes grew there. Villagers considered this affront as an attempt by the state to trick them once again.

The two 'ideologies of landscape', to use Walker and Fortmann's words, conflict: one seeks to delegitimize the state, which regards the forest as a public good and biodiversity as a value.¹⁴ This discourse is a vehicle for broader actions against the state and its policy of forest regulation. Delegitimizing the state reinforces self-legitimization, which is based on a history of forest ownership and the argument of a long period of habitation in the area: villagers were there long before the park. The park manager's discourse dismisses this view and engages the language of science and both national and international interests: biodiversity and nature preservation as well as land degradation represent an interpretative framework which leaves people out of the picture, emphasizing first and foremost the fate of the natural world.

The park and the villagers employ different tools to appropriate their claims. Villagers have at their disposal what James C. Scott calls the 'weapons of the weak': whenever they can they overgraze their own meadows by bringing more sheep than agreed with the park officials.[15] For instance, they bring not only their own sheep to graze but also sheep belonging to their relatives from villages around. Park rangers calculate the number of sheep each meadow is able to support, basing their estimate on the types of soil, plants and location of the meadow within the park. Above this number, grazing is not sustainable but damages the meadow, argues the park's general director. Shepherds contest the scientific evaluation based on their forefathers' and their own experience, considering it just an attempt by the park to restrict their access. Villagers distrust the park's assessment of local nature and contest the value of the local flora by describing the protected flora as being nothing more than 'just a bloody weed'.[16] Cutting trees without asking the ranger's permission and without the technical study that is supposed to accompany the logging is another weapon in the villagers' arsenal. Usually villagers log for domestic purposes, so they do not clear-cut. As I have shown in a previous chapter, scientific forestry requires an impact study (*studiu de amenajare*) before any wood extraction. The quantity of wood to be extracted depends on many variables but very important are the growing rate of the forest, the type of tree and the type of soil. The study also takes into account the wood extraction quota established at county level. Villagers often ignore the necessity of the impact study and go straight into the wood to cut the tree they find fit for their purposes. In an impact study the trees to be marked for cutting would be the trees with less monetary value, that is, trees with twisted trunks, or infested by fir bark bugs (*Ips typographus*). A twisted tree would not be useful for house construction or for making board fences but for firewood only.

Villagers not only log without permission but also haul the logs through the wood and, against the scientific forestry norms, push them across the steep slopes to reach the main road. This way they avoid the forestry roads and unexpected and undesired contacts with a park ranger. This practice not only affects the seedling and vegetation slopes but the ragged branches end up in the river running parallel with the road, changing its course and contributing to floods.

When the park finally started to mark its field boundaries, in the summer of 2003, villagers reacted by destroying the landmarks. Every few days the park employees discovered that the landmarks were missing or were simply destroyed. It took some time, the park's director assured me, before villagers gave up such acts.

The park managers have incomparably more sophisticated tools for forest appropriation. In 2005, a large satellite image was displayed in the main hall of the mayor's office. The image represents the park's entire territory with the borders marked in bold. The image also shows the zones, including the protected zone and private forests. Officially, the satellite image was displayed there for villagers' information. Nevertheless, such an image is never innocent but a warning to trespassers and a metaphor for property claims.[17] There is no better place to make a statement than the hall of the mayor's office. Located in the centre of the commune, the mayor's office is the main administrative body and embodies the power of the state. People come here regularly to pick up various documents or to make different official requests. Even though only few villagers can read the satellite image properly, most of them understand the meaning of the park's borders, which are emphasized with yellow on a dark grey background. I was there several times while villagers remained for quite a long time in front of the image, trying to locate their own forestland. The fact that few villagers are able to read this map is frustrating and gives them a feeling of uncertainty. This image gives the park the same power and privilege as writing gives to the state bureaucracy.[18] The park makes property claims and dominates through knowledge and high technology.

Another tool is provided by the international discourse on climate change and on the urgency of nature preservation, and by the international programmes that implement measures of biodiversity preservation. Natura 2000, a European network of conservation areas destined for EU country members as well as the candidate countries, is such a programme. The PCNP is one of the five Romanian areas included in this network beginning with June 2003. Through this program, the director succeeded in securing several projects worth €500,000 which are aimed at those people who have forest on the park's territory. The director seeks to change the local economy of villages located on the borders of the park: he hopes that people will make a steady passage from forest exploitation and animal husbandry to rural tourism. The motto of the park's director is probably the motto of any director of protected areas in this world and he sums it up in these words: 'I want people (i.e. forest owners) out of the park!' The myth of pristine forest, untouched by humans, still haunts the imagination of most parks' managers across the globe, hence their attempt to deny locals any right to the forest.

The Romanian national government's negotiations with EU institutions during the period before accession,[19] together with the international programs of biodiversity preservation, provide the park with ammunition in its struggle with local villagers. The park's manager openly recognized that 'the attitudes of local and regional offices and bureaucrats have radically changed since the negotiations started. We now have much stronger support from them than before negotiations'. The manager's words are not just a trope but the acknowledgement of an enforcement tool of forestland appropriation, as the following episode shows.

In September 2004, the park general manager asked the mayor to convene a local council meeting in order to approve the nationalization of a small area of forestland of only 1,500 square metres, though conveniently located close to the main road.[20] The park biologists had discovered that an endangered plant on the EU red list, a marigold (*Ligularia sibirica*), grew in this small area. The manager not only wanted to protect the plant but also intended to fence the area and to capture a water source, located on the same spot, in order to rebalance the water regime of the soil. This small area of forestland was also going to benefit from several posters announcing to visitors the importance of the plant. The only obstacle to the implementation of these measures was Mihai Gorovei, a villager who owned the plot and who stubbornly refused to give up the land. Moreover, the villager had plans to sell that plot to whoever would pay him a good price; since the plot is located on the riverbank and close to the main road it is perfectly suited to build a tourist centre. In the conference room of the mayor's office several state officials from the County Council, Prefecture and the Regional Agency for Environmental Protection (RAEP) eloquently championed the park's request to local councillors. State bureaucrats underlined that this was not a good time to waive biodiversity protection while the national government was holding ongoing negotiations with the EU. 'All the European countries are watching us,' said the RAEP representative. The representative of the Prefecture raised the stakes by suggesting that denying the park's request would cast the central government in a bad light in the eyes of their European partners, which might have a negative impact on the following year's communal budget.[21] They also invoked current international concerns over environmental protection and suggested that protecting this particular plant would attract national and international visitors, to the benefit of villagers and the local budget.

Eventually, the councillors decided to approve the park's request. The following day, with a suspect and unprecedented efficiency on the part of the state bureaucrats the decision was written, sent to the Prefecture, approved by the prefect in his capacity as central government representative in the territory and a topographer was sent to Dragova to re-measure Gorovei's plot. Within less than a week, a new ownership title was issued and the park received the coveted plot. The cantankerous owner was not even asked to present his point of view during the state officials meeting; he was only notified of the need to attend the re-measurements of his plot.

This episode says much about the way international ideologies are implemented down to village level and the way local politicians and bureaucrats take up global ideas such as biodiversity and forest conservation in order to use them for claiming property rights over forest. Local politics is more than anything else about access to natural resources and any weapon to acquire more will do. The global discourse on nature conservation is a powerful weapon wielded by local officials against forest owners. As formal referees between the park and the villagers local officials should help both sites to negotiate a better agreement. Instead, they use their position to weaken the forest owners' position when this serves their own interests. Their political connections with high-level state authorities, as the visit of the President of the Senate described in chapter 5 will clearly show, offer them impunity. When I asked Gorovei why he did not protest against the mayor's decision to nationalize his plot he replied bitterly, 'The mayor has connections at high level. If you fight against him, you fight against the state. You can't win when you fight against the state.' In fact, Gorovei's struggle for his own land ended before it began. Besides complaining to his neighbours about the injustice he suffered he did not take any concrete action to recover the plot.

Another informant complaining about the mayor's decisions in favour of the park administration pointed to political connections with high-ranking state officials: 'I was there when the mayor was called by the prefect. They seemed to be on very friendly terms. All people from this village know that he has excellent connections with people from central government. We know his power.' Forest owners not only acknowledge the power of the mayor but confirm Michael Herzfeld's interpretation of passive attitudes observed among villagers from Greece: fighting against state bureaucracy is like fighting against fate.[22] This attitude illustrates both how citizens perceive the state and how they interpret their failure to obtain something from the bureaucrats, considers Herzfeld. The mayor exploits his political connections with senior officials as well as the villagers' passivity in the face of his actions and offers support to the park administration against villagers. His support for the park's actions is not for free, as in return he expects the park administration to keep a close eye regarding his wood business.

Imagining State Control over Forest: The Carpathian Bear

The bear (*Ursus arctos*) is symbolic of a particular episode in the struggle between the park administration and villagers. During my stay in Dragova I heard villagers complaining many times that the park administration has brought bears into the area. Several people swore that they had seen with their own eyes helicopters bringing large cages in which only bears would fit. When I asked the park's director he enlightened me, laughing: 'Those were not bear cages; they were wooden shelters for visitors being installed in the park'. But he proudly acknowledged the existence of bears within the park. It is worth noting that Romania has the largest brown bear population in Europe (excepting Russia), more than 6,500 bears, and the highest densities of 90 to 220 bears per 1,000 square kilometres (Knapp 2006). It is a strictly protected species but can be also hunted when the population exceeds a certain number.

Whether the park administration flew in bears or not is not important here. More important is the role of the bear within the local public discourse. Forest owners perceive the bear as a state instrument of forest control. Some of them interpreted this action as another mechanism used by the state to impede their access to the forest. They know from media reports that Romania has the highest rate of human injuries in Europe – 18 people killed and 101 severely injured between 1990 and 1999.[23] They also fear for their livestock as throughout Romania over 4,500 livestock killings were reported during this period.[24] More importantly, villagers fear that if the bear is sighted in *their* forest, the park will simply nationalize it. Thus, as in the case of the wild boar described in chapter 5, the Carpathian bear became a public enemy in Dragova, an undesirable beast haunting the surrounding forests, an incarnation of the state restrictions imposed to forest owners. For villagers the Carpathian bear is an alien trespassing on their territory – since it was flown in from somewhere else – and a challenger of their ancient property rights over the surrounding forest. In the local imagination, the bear has ceased to be a wild animal; it is a political tool of forest appropriation.

Nevertheless, not all inhabitants of Dragova are unhappy with the existence of the bear and with the park's restrictions. Those inhabitants who own guesthouses and do not depend on forest livelihoods are interested in supporting the park's actions. For them, the forest is part of the landscape. For these actors, landscape has a strong visual and aesthetic component, before anything else. As one informant, the owner of a large guesthouse in the commune, told me, 'We sell nature and landscape.' Guesthouse owners also associate the forest with revenue, but this cannot be understood outside the aesthetic element. Cutting down the forest strikes directly at the heart of their business. After all, nobody spends money on a hike among stumps of a recently felled forest.

Preserving forest and biodiversity attracts visitors. Media images with 'scavenger bears' coming down from the mountains to find food in the garbage bins in the outskirts of the city of Brasov, located just 60 kilometres away, attracted hundreds of visitors worldwide. Those involved in rural tourism hoped that bears 'visiting' Dragova would constitute a magnet for photo-trophy hunters. The existence of the park, a preserved forest and a rich biodiversity, including bears, serves their economic interests. Without knowing it, they resonate with the wildlife experts who studied other geographical areas, and whose studies showed the financial benefits of conserving biodiversity for local communities: tourists are attracted by the large animals and are willing to pay substantial amounts of money to see different species in their own environment.[25]

The few villagers who do not own forest within the park are rather indifferent on this issue. Nevertheless, the two categories of villagers who do not speak out against the park are not advocates for the trees or the bears. The former group does not actually defend the environment, only their right to use it. They think of the environment in terms of distribution of costs and benefits, as Daniel Klooster pointed out in the case of Mexico.[26] As for the latter group, they simply avoid a confrontation with the mighty state.

Villagers' practices as described so far doubtlessly affect the environment but, as the park manager agrees, they are responsible for only 10 per cent of deforestation. 'Weapons of the weak', as presented earlier in this chapter, produce minimal deforestation. The most significant damage is inflicted by the logging firms and by the industrial exploitation of the forest. This type of forest exploitation is intrinsically linked to political positions and to the local state office holders.

Refereeing Disputes

Defusing friction between villagers and the park's administration is the role of the local bureaucrats: the mayor, the vice-mayor and the local council members. These officials supposedly mediate between various state agencies, institutions and levels of state. They constitute the main channels of communication between regional and national government and local people. All villagers' complaints against the state go through the mayor's office. Most laws issued by the central state are in practice implemented by the mayor's office employees. Thus, the mayor's office is the pivotal administrative and political centre in the commune.

Instead of refereeing the dispute between the park and forest owners, local officials follow their own private interest. The mayor of the commune stands quite clearly with other officials when negotiating between the park administration and forest owners. Not only is he the head of the local land restitution commission, thus having the power to manipulate documents and to make choices about forest allocation, but also the administrative laws empower him to approve, deny or at least delay wood exploitation licences for small forest owners. A good example was the re-nationalization of Gorovei's small forestland. The mayor was very active in convincing Gorovei to give up his land. He promised not to ask to see Gorovei's logging licence when he next saw him emerging from the forest with wood. It must be said that, because there is a single road running from north to south of the commune, through the village and passing in front of the mayor's office, it is virtually impossible for employees to fail to see wood being transported. The mayor sided with the park simply because it serves his own economic interests. Often, his wife's logging firm interferes with the park's interests. In order to please the park administration he manipulated the forest restitution process in an attempt to allocate private forest outside the park.

A short forest history is necessary here in order that the reader may understand the whole story. Villagers owned two types of collective forest before nationalization: one was *Obștea Mare* (the large collective forest), a forest owned collectively by several surrounding villages; there was also an *Obștea Mică* (the small collective forest), the forest covering a small mountain on the territory of the commune belonging to several richer families.[27] The difference between the two was not only that the latter was much smaller than the former but also that only a few families owned it in common. Ownership documents regarding *Obștea Mică* dating back to the 1930s mention the size of the forest as 52 *fârtare*. The document, hidden during the socialist era for forty years by one of the inheritors of the forest, identifies the families who collectively own the forest but does not mention the area's boundaries. Being a medieval local unit of measurement, fârtare disappeared after World War II in the process of land and forest nationalization. It was an attempt by the socialist state to unify all measurement units in order to have a clear picture of the natural resources at its disposal and to display the authority of the new state. The restitution laws use the hectare and its subdivisions as the only official measurement unit recognized by the state when handing back land and forest. The right to establish the unit of measurement at both the national and local level not only points to the sovereignty and the authority of the state, once again demonstrated openly, but also makes the state a major player in land reform.[28] The decision to transform fârtare into hectares belonged to the local land commission. The mayor who runs the commission decided that 1 fârtar equalled 3 hectares instead of 6, as village elders remembered. Instead of 312 hectares of forest those families ought to have received, they got back half. On the other half of the mountain, which luckily is located outside the park, the mayor gave land to several families who had owned forestland before nationalization but who categorically refused to accept land within the park as restitution. This way the mayor had satisfied through this move both the forest owners who refused to accept forestland within the park and the park administration consequently experienced less trouble from forest owners. The mayor expects in turn to mollify the park administration and enable his wife's logging firm to exploit forest within the park. Yet, this was not the only reason for halving the *Obştea Mică*. Since it is a forest outside the park, the mayor considered it to be easier for his wife's logging firm to exploit, provided the forest owners agreed to his terms and price. Coincidentally or not, forest owners agreed.

Forest Access and Political Positions

Several villagers told me during the local electoral campaign in 2004 that the main stake for any elected mayor is control over the forest. Indeed, in Romania, mayors have important powers, including the power of twisting the meaning of land reform by making decisions at the local level about land to be restored.[29] As the head of the local land commission the mayor had allocated private forest plots preferentially. Several families received 'good' tracts of forest while others received 'bad' ones. Local taxonomy of the forest considers good forest to be areas with trees old enough to be exploited for construction needs and located in an accessible area. A forest unexploited for the last 70 to 80 years is more economically valuable than a forest exploited 10 to 20 years ago. The trees composing the forest also make a huge difference: beech and spruce are better suited to construction needs than other tree species but beech has more caloric value as firewood than the spruce. Thus, a good forest implies the existence of both species. The rugged geography of the commune makes forest location a vital element of forest exploitation. An old forest yet located in the middle of the park, on the steep slopes or in the deep valleys away from any forestry road, is worthless. Thus, families who received good forest, mostly villagers from Podu, the largest of the villages in the commune and therefore the one with the largest constituency, have voted consistently for the current mayor. As he was born in Podu, he knows the village well and villagers perceive him as one of them. Some of them were not entitled to receive forest as they or their families had no forest ownership before nationalization yet they received forestland. It seems that the mayor made his allocation of good forest tracts conditional on their agreement that his wife's logging firm would be granted permission to exploit parts of the forest.

Several people from the commune received unexpectedly good forest; this was unexpected as they were too old to remain all day in the mayor's office lobbying the mayor for good forest, as some younger families did. Nevertheless Angela, a 65-year-old widow, received 4 hectares of an excellent mix of deciduous and spruce forest located close to the main road. This was an ideal location for exploitation of the forest. Angela was thrilled when the mayor's wife offered her €4,000 for the 4 hectares of forest and she sold it on the spot. Living off a meagre monthly pension of €100, Angela thought she was making a great deal when she heard the mayor's proposition. She actually felt that she had earned some money from this forest, which had belonged to her family for some generations. A few weeks after the deal was cut, the logging firm started to exploit the forest.

Another example of manipulating forest history during land reform is that of Vasile Nicolescu, who owned a few hectares of forest very close to his father's household. When his father died he moved into his house, which is located at the edge of the commune. It was a good place for him, close to their family meadow, vital for their sheep, and close to the family's forest. The 4 hectares of wood 'fall on their house' (*pădurea cade pe casă*) as he usually says, meaning that the forest starts from the edge of his household. Not only is this forest old enough to be exploited for wood construction but it also belonged to Nicolescu's grandfather. Being so close to his household, the forest is relatively safe, as potential wood thefts would stop short of illegal logging. Besides, transportation of wood is easy and does not necessitate trespassing onto other properties. Many villagers came to blows with each other in such cases, because hauling trunks over somebody else's pasture makes it useless for the following year. Obtaining agreement to haul trunks across a private pasture requires a lot of persuasion and a certain amount of money to pay the pasture owner. Thus, a forest close to the household is the dream of any forest holder from Dragova. When the snow comes, he cuts several trees and transports them by sled to the house. Since the distance from the forest to his house is quite short he does not need to engage people other than his own two sons to transport the wood. In 1991 he claimed 1 hectare from this forest and received it. In 2000, he requested the other 3 hectares, hoping to have his 4 hectares of forest in the same spot. However, this forest was too good to escape the mayor's interest. Because Vasile's daughter Maria works at the mayor's office, the mayor hampered the restitution for as long as he could. When Maria took her two weeks of summer vacation and left the village, the mayor rushed through the restitution of Vasile's 3 hectares. A good friend and supporter of the mayor during the electoral campaign received it, despite the fact that the new owner was not entitled to forest at all.

The exploitation of these small forest plots brought a fortune to the mayor's family. Nevertheless, the story does not end here. New opportunities opened up for the mayor's family when the state decided to restitute 70 hectares of communal forest.

Communal forest is the outcome of a tacit understanding among World War II veterans. Those who fought in the war received in 1945 from the state, as a sign of royal gratitude for their courage, small forest plots. In 1948 when the communist state decided to nationalize all forests, the veterans decided to offer their forest to the village.[30] Nevertheless, shortly after this event the forest was nationalized anyway. Law 1 repaired this injustice in 2000 by granting restitution to the community. This forest is intended for communal purposes only: it should provide wood for heating communal buildings such as the dispensary, schools and the church. This forest also provides wood at lower prices for those persons from the commune who have no forest at all and are too poor to buy it or too old to be able to work it. In short, according to the 1948 donors' will the communal forest should serve communal public interests and ensure social security services for the needy.

In the spring of 2004, the local council members decided, in response to a request from the mayor, to allow the exploitation of the 70 hectares to repair the public roads. There are two main public roads: one that runs up to Ciocănaș, the third village in the commune, and the main road, which crosses the commune from north to south. While the former is almost impracticable from October to March due to the heavy snow and serves only a couple of hundreds of inhabitants, the latter is essential for the commune's connection with the outside world. Both the main road and a few of the small bridges that cross the Dragova River have suffered damage caused by lorries belonging to the logging companies. The mayor's wife's logging

Illustration 4.1. The Exploitation of the Communal Forest in Dragova

company is not the only one operating in the region but it is definitely the most active. The lorries are particularly destructive in autumn, when heavy rains make the road almost impassable. Then, fully loaded lorries leave deep wheel tracks in the road that fill with rainwater. When the water is gone the mud mixed with gravel becomes as tough as concrete. After a few years of forest exploitation the road has been transformed into a nightmare for private car drivers, for both visitors and locals. Although some of the mayor's political opponents suggested that logging firms should also pay a communal road tax, since the visitors pay for their cars, in the end, with the support of friends from the council, the tax for the logging firms' lorries was vetoed. Clear-cutting the communal forest remained the only financial source for repairing the road. The next step was the organization of a public auction.[31] Predictably, the logging firm owned by the mayor's wife won.

Before considering further the exploitation of communal forest, let us take a step back to see the whole picture. Central governments have devised auctions as the main mechanism for eradicating corruption and putting the private and state logging companies on an equal footing. The auction should be advertised publicly thirty days in advance. In this way, all potential participants are able to prepare the necessary documents for attending the auction (Saphores et al. 2006). In the particular case I describe here, the mayor, taking advantage of his political position, succeeded in delaying the auction announcement until a few days before it started. The announcement was advertised in a small local newspaper. Only his wife's firm and a friend's logging firm were able to hand in the application while other potential participants had no time to prepare the documents. For an auction to be valid, it is compulsory for at least two bidders to compete. The friend's firm was not seriously committed to winning so they bid in such a way as to ensure the other firm won. Allegedly, the mayor's wife's firm won several auctions.[32] Not only did the mayor's wife apparently win the auction, thanks to her husband's support; she also continued to benefit from it. The episode which opens this chapter should be regarded as an example of political support: while other logging companies are spot-checked regularly 'on blind' without prior warning by the representatives of the Ministry of Agriculture and Forestry, the logging firm belonging to the mayor's wife knew about the control check the day before. The mission of such controls is to check if the auctioned forest plot is exploited according to forestry rules. Often, as logging workers have confirmed to me, firms would cut more than they declared at auction. They would neither clear the land after the exploitation to facilitate the reforestation process nor did they replant it after the exploitation was completed, as the forestry rules stipulate. Besides, the caterpillars of machines specialized for wood exploitation cause serious damage to the steep slopes, hindering the natural re-growth of the forest.

The case of communal forest illustrates the political mechanisms of forest exploitation. Private and public interests are intertwined in this case and the border between the two becomes blurred. The situation could be summarized as follows: public money goes to private pockets to repair public roads destroyed by private interests. While one private firm reaps the economic benefits of exploiting the communal forest, the whole community pays for the externalities. Putting asphalt on the main road, at least along the inhabited area, benefitted the entire community. Yet, the asphalt laid previously was destroyed by the logging firm's heavy lorries, which are exempted from taxation. The owner of the lorries gets public money to repair what he actually destroyed in his own interest. Although I agree with the authors who suggest that everywhere in the world some public services are co-produced by public and private actors I still need to emphasize the uniqueness of the situation I describe here: one actor who contributes massively to the destruction of the road in his private interests requests public money to fix it and gains, for the second time, in the process.[33]

The mayor is the most important local factor in deforestation in Dragova but not the only one. The vice-mayor – a member of the National Liberal Party, a flourishing local businessman and the owner of three guesthouses in the village – started his business with the money earned from clear-cutting of 3 hectares of forest. His grandfather owned the 3 hectares before nationalization. Each of his three offspring claimed 1 hectare of forest in 1991. The vice-mayor's mother was one of them. Before receiving the ownership title but knowing exactly which parcel of land was going to be restituted to the family, the vice-mayor clear-cut the forest on all 3 hectares. As a member of the local land commission he knew for certain that there is no legal penalty for exploiting the forest in such a case. When the 3 hectares were given back, all inheritors had undifferentiated rights until each individual's rights were decided in court. The law simply does not specify what should happen if one individual or family of the three cuts down the entire forest before succession is completed. The single legal barrier against forest exploitation in this particular case was the forestry code. Nevertheless, the forestry code stipulates technical issues, such as the necessity of a technical study, the approval of the mayor and the marking of the trees by the forest guard. The property rights aspect had to be technically established by the mayor as the head of the land commission. Although the two are political enemies they collude over access to natural resources. This mutual support was evident on several occasions, including the vice-mayor's opposition to the introduction of a tax for logging firm's lorries or the coalition between the two against a guesthouse owner in competition with the vice-mayor.[34]

All these episodes clearly point to the pressures on surrounding forests. The demand for forest is motivated by short-term economic benefits. Economic interests prevail over any environmental argument.

The Economy and the Politics of the Forest

As was apparent in the case of Dragomirești forest, commodity chain analysis can provide an approximate but nevertheless clear picture of the benefits derived from forest. I provide the case of Angela, who sold her forest to the mayor's. I do not have irrefutable proof of how much money the logging firm made from the 5 hectares but I estimate a profit of at least €200,000. Angela received €4,000 for 5 hectares of forest. When she closed the deal with the logging firm she declared a smaller sum than the amount she actually received, in order to avoid paying high taxes to the notary. Angela paid around €200 in taxes. Thus, her profit was roughly €3,800. The logging firm works with a team of five people. The whole team earns 90,000 lei for each cubic metre (approximately €2.5). Every week the forest workers cut about 100 cubic metres. Thus, the whole team earns 9 million lei per week (€250). That is some €50 for each worker per week. A forest worker has around €200 per month if the weather is fine and does not rain. On rainy days they cannot work so they are not paid. Forest workers live in poor conditions in huts made of iron plate and often suffer accidents. The firm also has three lorry drivers whose salary is around 4 million lei per month (a bit over €100). From four hectares of forest the firm obtains 1,200 to 1,600 cubic metres. My estimate is based on Grodzińskca et al. (2004) which points out that 1 hectare of Carpathian forest comprises between 300 to 400 cubic metres.[35] The price of the timber at the time of this research was €200 to €380 for 1 cubic metre of beech and €95 to €140 for 1 cubic metre of spruce if the wood is exported. The potential revenue is between €142,500 and €760,000. Now, subtracting the costs of the firm, which includes €1,000 per month for forest workers, €300 for the drivers and the gasoline costs which amounts to roughly €400 per month, we see that the firm spends €1,700 per month. The forest was clear-cut in roughly three to four months, considering that forest workers cut weekly 100 cubic metres. Subtracting all costs, the logging firm pays the workers and drivers €5,100 to €6,800 over the three months. To this amount we add the €4,000 paid to Angela and the taxes to the Romanian state. Even if we count the total costs of the firm as €20,000, including the taxes the firm has to pay to the Romanian state, it is still apparent that this was great business for the logging firm.

The above calculation explains why forest is so enticing to the local elite and became the main political stake. During the electoral campaign forest was central to local political debates as it was obvious that controlling politics at local level means controlling forest access. Forest is the gateway to wealth in rural Romania.

New Practices, New Landscapes

A comparison between Dragova and Dragomireşti points to different local dynamics concerning the issue of deforestation but which result in the same outcome in terms of landscape. In Dragomireşti forest cutting was mostly illegal. Rudari and Romanian villagers have cut down private forests with regrettable consequences for the landscape. Within only a few years, the hills surrounding the commune have been transformed into a deserted landscape: the Rudari loggers left behind hundreds of hectares of 1-metre-high trunks surrounded by a mess of branches. Romanian villagers have cut the trees more thoroughly to a few centimetres above the ground. While the Romanian villagers explain that the way Rudari have cut the forest reflects Rudari's moral deficiency – suggesting they are too lazy to bend down to reach the tree roots – the real explanation has to do with the general conditions under which the Rudari exploit the forest. Rudari work mostly during the night and know their actions are illegal. Thus, they try to finish their work as quickly as possible. Bending right down to the ground would take more time to cut a tree because of the inconvenient body position when cutting; also because the tree trunk is thicker close to the ground. As most of the wood will be sold as firewood, there is not much demand for the thick part of the trunk.

In Dragova, logging companies carry out most of the logging. The mayor's political manoeuvres may sometimes be illegal or at least immoral according to the community's standards and the auctions are rigged, but the forest exploitation itself is carried out to professional standards. Nevertheless, once the exploitation is over the logging firm 'forgets' to clear the ground in order to help the natural reforestation or to replant the exploited plot. Thus, regeneration of the forest is impeded or at least it is made more difficult.

Although there are two different local social dynamics regarding forest exploitation the fate of the forestland is similar. In the case of Dragomireşti, forest has a double status and a double meaning: in the official documents of the mayor's office the forest is still there on the hills as long as no bureaucrat officially communicates to higher offices that the forest has vanished. According to the Forestry Code (Art. 37), the local authorities can grant animal owners the right to graze their animals in the forest under certain conditions and for a limited number of animals. Certain herdsmen received the right to graze their animals in the forest. Other animal owners ignore the local officials and simply graze their animals in the forest. The Forestry Code forbids in Article 71 'grazing in the forestland where forest is recovering ... and on plantations that are younger than ten years and with vegetation lower than three metres is strictly forbidden'. Thus, legally, if the status of the forest is 'recovering forest' then villagers should not be granted the right to graze on the hills. Nevertheless, the Mayor's Office employees are operating within the law as long as the forest officially still exists.

More critical damage is inflicted on deforested areas by the villagers' goats, as one pensioned local forest engineer assured me. A goat is not just an economically efficient animal that is easy to keep. As compared to a cow, a goat is not an animal demanding special grass, grazing all types of plants and weeds. Nevertheless, when grazing in a deforested area, goats do more damage than sheep and cows. As one famous interwar Romanian forester once said, 'When a goat eyes a certain tract of forest, there is immediately a drought.'[36] This saying reflects the strong feelings of foresters against goat owners and against the destructive potential of this animal.

For villagers, forest has a different meaning: they call forest that land which is covered by trees; once the trees have been extracted, whether legally or illegally, a forestland ceases to be considered forest and the owner's property rights are suspended. This land becomes nobody's property or everyone's property. Thus sheep owners usually graze their animals in these places, as nobody claims ownership of this forestland any longer.

In Dragova, the fact that the logging firms' owners are strongly connected with people who hold high state office enables them to ignore the forestry norm, which clearly stipulates that logging firms have an obligation to clear the land after exploitation for the young vegetation to grow. Moreover, the owners of the exploited forest have a duty to replant the exploited plot within two years. Villagers like Angela who sold their forest to logging firms to exploit it are to be held responsible for replanting the plot. According to the Forestry Code in Article 67, if the owner does not comply with these regulations the LIF must replant the plot and then claim the funds from the forest owner. I returned in the village almost every year until 2010 and I have never heard of a single plot being reforested either by the owner or by the LIF. Besides, when villagers claim that 'they sold the forest', they actually mean that they sold the standing trees and the right to exploit them. However the remaining forestland, even if treeless, is still legally owned by the owner. Logging firms have no incentive to buy the whole forest – trees and the ground underneath – as they would be held responsible for the reforestation process. All forest owners I interviewed strongly claimed that 'they sold the forest' not the trees; thus they are not interested anymore in the fate of the forestland. The forest owners' misconception of what forest actually is – by separating the trees from the land on which they stand – has as a consequence, as in the case of Dragomirești: the creation of a forestless landscape. The different meanings that villagers, local bureaucrats and forest loggers attach to forestland lead to the creation of deforested zones where no vegetation grows. This makes natural reforestation difficult, if not impossible.

National Parks and the Struggle for Forest in the Postsocialist World

The tense relations between the PCNP and local villagers, is not coincidental in postsocialist Romania. The example of the Buila-Vânturarița Park in the southern part of the country shows a pattern of reactions similar to the one described above. The park was founded in 2004 by an NGO.[37] The Obștea (association of collective forest owners) owns most of the forest in the core-protected area. Local forest owners simply refused to recognize the existence of the park and, therefore, interference by the state in their wood business. The conflict between the two parties has mostly the same coordinates as the conflict between villagers from Dragova and the PCNP. Local residents accused the state of creating a core zone that is far larger than it should be and alleged that the park's regulations imposed on them represents a *de facto* expropriation. Villagers accused the park of imperialism and considered it as embodying the mighty state's power with its appetite for acquiring natural resources. Conversely, the park managers accused the members of the Obștea of placing their economic interests above environmental ones. The two parties were once more in dispute over forestry and grazing practices: the park insists that villagers should extract only fallen trees (a practice which would sanitize the forest and help it to grow healthier) and not clear-cut the forest. Villagers should also graze the alpine pastures with sheep, not with goats as they currently do. The vision of the young park experts, based on science, environmental laws and global importance of the protected areas, stands in opposition to the villagers' arguments, which are concerned with economic, historical and property rights issues. Obștea members uphold the importance of forest for supporting the livelihood of local people and the fact that the park was just recently created; they also emphasize their rights that have been acquired through land reform laws.

Similar conflicts are to be found throughout the postsocialist world. Białowieża National Park, a large temperate mixed forest lying at the border between Poland and Belarus, was the subject of a heated dispute between experts, scientists and ecologists representing the state and villagers in postsocialist Poland.³⁸ The Polish scientists plead for extending the borders of the national park and for restrictions in forest exploitation and grazing practices. The biological scientists consider that such restrictions in agricultural and forest activities of inhabitants from surrounding villages, most of them of Belarus ethnic origin, would bring back to life a primaeval forest, a forest untouched by man. George Peterken, an ecologist who studied forests from the northern temperate regions, points out that far from being untouched by human activities the Białowieża forest in its current shape is the result of intense economic and ecological activities such as grazing cattle, bee keeping, the collection of litter for fertilizer, the manufacture of charcoal and potash and hunting.³⁹ Using patriotic arguments, attaching a powerful national symbolism to Białowieża forest and to some of its wild animal inhabitants, such as the bison and the white-tailed eagle, the scientists and environmental NGOs seek to return the land 'to a closed, primaeval forest, largely emptied of people'.⁴⁰ The environmental NGOs and scientists appealed to powerful international organizations such as the World Wide Fund for Nature or Birdlife International for support and organized campaigns and street marches in the city capital to support the enlargement of the park. Ignoring villagers' concerns that they will lose their access to berries, mushrooms, herbs and firewood, the park's experts orchestrated an international Internet campaign in support of the park. The whole story developed within the context of Poland's negotiations with the EU for accession and the Białowieża forest represented, as Stuart Franklin suggests, a 'green visiting card' for Polish authorities.⁴¹

When officials wanted to transform the Slitere Reserve, on the Baltic Sea coast in Latvia, into a national park, villagers next to the reserve feared that the park would impose restrictions on traditional land use.⁴² Local residents making their living from gathering firewood, grazing their animals and picking mushrooms and berries sold in the nearby markets were concerned that these activities were going to be banned within the park. Residents defined their relation with nature in strictly economic terms. Despite the assurance of the director that these activities would be encouraged and despite the idyllic picture he portrayed of future tourism development bringing good money to the area, villagers remained reluctant to accept the transformation of the surrounding forestland into a park.⁴³

The struggle between the parks and local people is also well illustrated by the Albanian Prespa National Park.⁴⁴ This park was founded with both conservation and development as goals. Thus, more than 85 per cent of the park's territory was designated a development zone and only a small part was declared strictly a conservation zone. Villagers from around the park have faced land use restrictions and prohibitions such as the utilization of pesticides and fertilizers and the extraction of wood and non-timber forest products without permission from the administration. For local people who depend largely on agriculture and animal husbandry, the park administration had to reduce the impact of these prohibitions for locals by issuing a list of 'temporary exceptions'. The 'long-standing traditional agricultural activities', as it stands in the Management Plan, are permitted if they do not harm the environment.[45] Cutting wood is also possible if the activity allows the forest to regenerate. Local people contest the park's regulations and continue to use high quantities of pesticides and fertilizers while herdsmen simply ignore the regulations. Goat herders continue to bring their animals to the forest and feed them with leaves and young branches of deciduous trees. Other shepherds ignore the park's calendar for grazing and bring their animals to the pasture as they see fit. Imposing top-down restrictions and ignoring local people when the management plan was drawn up were among the state's tools in building Prespa National Park. The German Agency for Cooperation also supported the park by selectively funding several households in order to change the weight of the local economy from agriculture and animal husbandry to rural tourism.

Further east, Russia faces the same problems.[46] National parks there have a fairly recent history as the first one was founded in 1983. Nevertheless, control over the land was not transferred to the parks or to other governmental agencies and local people continue to use the land without restrictions. Since the decentralization process started in early 1990 and the central government shifted control over natural resources to regional governments a dramatic increase in illegal activities has been observed. The prolonged postsocialist economic crisis, the high rates of inflation and the lack of employment opportunities turned the villagers' attention to natural resources. Poaching endangered species with great market value such as the Siberian tiger, grazing cattle or clear-cut logging in buffer zones, and the construction of roads through the protected areas are just a few of the violations noted by Wells and Williams.[47] The newly established large private farms use pesticide and intensive tilling which have destroyed the soil microfauna in protected areas while small landowning farmers and herdsmen have encroached on protected areas in south-central Siberia. All these have a strong negative impact on biodiversity conservation but constitute a safety valve in terms of local people's livelihood.

Even when establishing a new park contributes to the revitalization of local cultures, as in the case of the Tunda Park among Buriats in south-central Siberia, and the residents strongly support the principles on which the park has been created, it is very uncertain whether the goal of conservation has been met or not.[48] Despite the fact that the park has been founded on the principle of protecting nature and, at the same time, conserving the cultural heritage and people's livelihood, an undesired outcome has been an intensification of the timber harvesting in order to meet the local contribution to the park's budget. As part of a cultural revitalization movement, the foundation of the park sought to bring more autonomy to local people at the end of the socialist period and after the collapse of the Berlin Wall, and to restore their natural resources. This case appears to offer a counterargument to the idea that relations between people and park officials are adversarial in postsocialist countries. Nevertheless, as Katherine Metzo mentions, conservation activity was merely an appropriation of state tools by a local intelligentsia in order to transform not only the environment but local power relations as well.[49]

Several examples could be added but they would point to similar dynamics. These short accounts highlight several general postsocialist characteristics. One is that there is a sharp clash of interests between local people and different state agencies managing the national parks. The priorities of such populations, the meanings they attach to the forest and its utility are very different from those of the state, of the international institutions that protect nature, and of the NGOs. While for most local people, from Central Europe to Russia, forest is the main source of livelihood and a matter of historical rights, for the central state and international institutions forest is a matter of biodiversity conservation and environmental protection. Consequently, the land use practices seen from these two perspectives seem pretty much opposed. This struggle is ultimately about imposing one's meaning over what the landscape is, what it is good for and who should define the ways it is managed and used.

The two parties give different weight to rights and obligations attached to property: local people emphasize their rights, whereas state environmental agencies and the international donors underline the duties of forest owners as Thomas Sikor has clearly pointed out regarding the Protected Landscape Area Bílé Karpati in the Czech Republic.[50] Further, international institutions put intense pressure on central governments to issue restrictive environmental policies and to overrule local governments and local people. Conversely, the local political elite uses the global environmental discourse and EU countries' negotiation for accession, as in the case of Romania and Poland, as a weapon against villagers' agricultural and forestry practices. Often, these pressures serve local private interests.

The park, that is the state, frequently imposes its vision and ideas about forest landscape. It has superior means to engage in this struggle: new technologies, such as satellite images, a staff of army-like rangers and, not least, local level bureaucrats and officers who have a personal economic interest in supporting the park administration. On the other side, villagers employ the 'weapons of the weak' by ignoring the park's restrictions or encroaching on the park's territory.

The establishment of national parks has meant, in many parts of the world, the imposition of European ideas about wilderness, pristine landscape and biodiversity preservation.[51] Consequently, it has meant a clash between local people whose hunting or cultivation land has changed into a place of biodiversity conservation, and the state or international environmental institutions. The imposition of protected areas throughout the world comes up against local agricultural and forestry practices and begets protests, trespassing, intensive grazing, illegal hunting and illegal logging. Often, international conservationist institutions impose new policies, or at least support the national policies that restrict local people's access to natural resources.[52] Bram Büscher has coined the term 'inverted commons' to describe the phenomenon of creating a sort of global ecological commons in postcolonial countries that supposedly exceed the rights of local people to their own environment: nevertheless it is local people who pay the price for preserving these inverted commons.[53] It is always the local elite, be they conservationists, rangers, professional foresters or members of the local governments, who win out in this clash.[54]

A question springs to mind regarding these developments: is there anything specific to postsocialist countries as compared to postcolonial ones about the struggle between local people and the national parks? After all, the accounts provided so far could be found in most of the ethnographies on parks in postcolonial countries. The postsocialist specificity relates, I would argue, to the incoherent position of the state: while one state institution decides to restitute the land and forest, another one decides to establish a new park or a new protected area. While one state institution gives rights to the new forest owners, the other suspends them. The two actions unfold almost simultaneously. Even more, in most accounts from postcolonial countries local people claim a customary right to the forest while the postcolonial state tries hard to deny it.[55] In the postsocialist case the state first recognizes the legal historical rights of inhabitants over the forest but then chooses to minimize them. In the process, local bureaucrats and politicians win while the forest owners bear most of the negative consequences of this legal morass. These scorched earth actions leave deep scars in the landscape: large deforested surfaces with little chance of regenerating in the coming years. A new landscape is emerging before our eyes.

Notes

1. I paid a local to show me the most northern point of the commune, which is not marked in the field.
2. Plan (2004: 2).
3. Ibid.; Verghelet et al. (2003).

4. Plan (2004: 2); Verghelet et al. (2003: 15).
5. Dorondel (2011a).
6. The further description is based on Dorondel (2011a).
7. Plan (2004: 1).
8. I interviewed the park's manager in September 2004.
9. Ioras et al. (2001).
10. I include in this category forest and meadows.
11. Sikor et al. (2009).
12. The average temperature in this region is 7 degrees Celsius. In the summer the temperature rarely rises above 20 degrees.
13. Dorondel (2011a).
14. See Walker and Fortmann (2003).
15. Scott (1985).
16. Dorondel (2011a).
17. Walker and Peters (2001).
18. Regarding the power of administrative knowledge and writing see Weber (1978) and more recently Herzfeld (2005) and Hull (2008).
19. Romania joined the EU in 2007. Before the act was signed, there was a thorough negotiation between ministers or their deputies and the European Council concerning the legislative changes which had to be operational before the actual accession started in 1999. Negotiations on Environment, one of thirty-one chapters to negotiate, were among the most difficult as Romania had a long way go to catch up with the other EU countries (for details, see Infoeuropa (2007)).
20. The written request to the Prefecture of the Argeş county, dated 17.09.2004, found in the mayoralty's archive and my own observations during the Local Council meeting.
21. Most of the communal budget comes from the national government which allocates money based on requests from the local mayor's office. Usually, communes receive less than they ask for.
22. Herzfeld (1992).
23. This figure is obsolete since in the last two years alone around ten people were either severely injured or killed by the Carpathian bear as reported by the Romanian newspapers.
24. Knapp (2006).
25. Naidoo et al. (2011).
26. Klooster (2006).
27. For more details about collective forest in Romania and its management before 1948, see Stahl (1998 [1955]). For postsocialist restitution of collective forest, see Vasile (2008a) and Vasile and Măntescu (2009).
28. For more about the units of measurements and the state, see Kula (1984) and Scott (1998).
29. Verdery (2002).
30. On 30 December 1947 King Mihai I was compelled to resign. At that moment Romania was transformed from a kingdom into a 'popular republic'.
31. Several Ministerial Orders issued from 1991 to 1998 force the public administration to organize auctions for the exploitation of public forests.
32. See Saphores et al. (2006) and Bouriaud and Marzano (2013) for similar cases in other parts of Romania.

33. See, for instance, Bierschenk (2014). This feature is not specific to postsocialist societies. As Peluso (2007) shows, in many parts of the world privatization or the new enclosures of natural resources involve an alliance of state and private capital. Thus, the distinction between private and public becomes more and more blurred.
34. More about the colluding agreements and support between the mayor and the vice-mayor in Dorondel (2011b).
35. Grodzińskca et al. (2004).
36. Marian Drăgoi, professor at the Faculty of Forestry, University of Suceava, personal communication.
37. The example is based on Vasile (2008b).
38. I draw on Franklin (2002).
39. Peterken (1996: 73). See also Franklin (2002).
40. Franklin (2002: 1474).
41. Ibid.
42. The case is presented in detail in Schwartz (2006a).
43. Ibid.
44. This account is based on Stahl et al. (2009).
45. Stahl et al. (2009).
46. I draw on Wells and Williams (1998) when presenting the Russian case.
47. Wells and Williams (2002).
48. The example draws on Metzo (2009).
49. Metzo (2009).
50. Sikor (2006).
51. Neumann (1998).
52. There is a huge literature on 'parks against people' in postcolonial countries. It is beyond the scope of this chapter to review it. West et al. (2006) provides a useful insight into this topic.
53. Büscher (2012).
54. Sodikoff (2007); Vandergeest and Peluso (2006); Zingerli (2005).
55. Moore (1993); Neumann (1998); Tsing (2001).

 CHAPTER 5

Waning Pastures

> 'The cattle are then transformed from a practical object,
> so to speak, into a moral one.'
> —Robert Musil, *The Man Without Qualities*

Imagine a time traveller visiting Dragomirești and Dragova in the late 1980s. She would have seen the built-up area of the two communes, strictly regulated by construction laws and codes of practice, and surrounded by large tracts of forest and pasture. The traveller would have immediately understood that in both communes animal husbandry was an important component of the local economy. The eastern part of Dragomirești was covered by pasture that was used for trialling different types of fodder (*pajiștea model*). The surrounding hills were covered partially with forest and partially with meadows. The built-up area of Dragova had developed in socialist times along the main road but it was quite concentrated around the village administrative centre.[1] The inhabited area was also surrounded by carefully maintained pastures.

Twenty years on, the traveller sees a different landscape. In Dragomirești, the pastures have been considerably reduced. Hectares of what was formerly the pasture on the east hill are now covered with bushes and tall weeds. The pasture on the southern hill, close to the Rudari settlement, is now partially covered by bushes, up to the peak, and partially with new, although visibly poor, houses scattered at the bottom of the hill. In Dragova, our traveller sees the new guesthouses, some still under construction, others just finished, going up on the pastures close to the main road. The time traveller could see that the inhabited area has expanded since the socialist period whereas the pastures along the roadside have virtually disappeared. This chapter tells the story of these waning pastures and explains how a 'forest of houses' has sprung up in postsocialist times in both communes. It also analyses the role played by particular wild animals whose ecology intersects with that of humans in the area.

Vanishing Pastures, Building New Huts

Flipping through the official papers of the Mayor's office in Dragomirești one could count 698 hectares of land listed under the heading 'pastures and meadows'.[2] In 1989 there were 526 hectares of pastures and 110 hectares of meadows, most of them belonging either to the state or the collective farm. Looking at these figures it is obvious that the pastures grew from 636 hectares in 1989 to 698 hectares in 2003. The increase in pasture can be explained in terms of a decrease in arable land and orchards, as I will explain in the following chapter. In the first years after decollectivization pastures seem to have grown in importance in the local economy. Besides, it was easy to transform an orchard or cropland into pasture; one had only to refrain from ploughing the land or from investing in maintaining the fruit trees for several years.

After 1990, the experimental pasture, which belonged to the state, was given back to the community whereas after dismantling the collective farm its pastures and meadows were given back to former owners. Today, pasture can be either privately or publicly owned. Public pasture (*islaz*) is managed by the mayor's office and is used by villagers to graze their animals. Villagers who keep animals have also their private pastures, some in their garden – a term usually used to distinguish between the pasture and the villagers' backyards. For some villagers, garden is the appropriate term since there is a mixture of land use on these plots: pasture is mixed with orchard and, if situated close to the houses, with small vegetable gardens. The plots that serve solely as pastures are those that lie far from the houses on the surrounding hills. Only the land located close to the village is enriched with manure whereas the meadows, located at quite a distance from the village, are left to regenerate naturally. Their owners mow them every year but do not use natural or chemical fertilizers to improve the quality and the production of hay.[3]

Private pastures and meadows are rarely grazed in the summer. The hay is cut twice or even three times per season, left on the ground to dry and then gathered into large haystacks. This hay serves as winter fodder. Economically, the fact that pastures close to the house are not grazed demonstrates prudent planning: it is convenient for villagers to build up haystacks behind their stables since the workforce usually consists of family members only. Grazing meadows located quite far from the house do not make sense either for at least two reasons. First, the annual tax to the mayor's office, which permits one to graze one's animals on the communal pasture, is fairly modest. Second, there is a cowman, a local pensioner wishing to supplement his income, who takes the cows to the communal pasture every morning, watches over them during the day and brings them back in the evening. He receives payment from those villagers who entrust their cows to him.

The public pastures are theoretically maintained and fertilized by their administrator, which is the mayoralty. When pastures were under the management of the co-operative they were carefully maintained. Pastures were separated into parcels of land by fences; after three weeks of grazing animals, that area was left to regenerate. The co-operative also used natural and chemical fertilizers to spread on pastures. Every four to five years the pasture was re-sown. After 1990, the only funds the mayoralty had for investing in the communal pastures was the tax levied from cattle owners. All successive mayors have refused to raise this tax, mainly for electoral reasons. Usually unemployed villagers on social benefits carry out work on the communal pasture. The vast majority of them are Rudari.[4] As they do not have animals to graze, except for the horses they graze illegally on the communal pasture next to their settlement, they have no incentive at all to do a thorough job.

In 2004, when I started my fieldwork, one of the first observations I made was that the pastures were in a poor condition and steadily shrinking. A pasture in poor condition means that the grass has been replaced by tall weeds as a consequence of a lack of investment in cutting the weed or in resowing the grass together with disorganized grazing. Bushes, an outpost of the forest, have taken over the pastures

Not only is the lack of thorough maintenance to be blamed for the weeds and the encroachment of the forest but the constant decrease in grazing too. Whereas in 1989 there were 1,411 cows and 1,923 sheep in the whole commune, in 1996 only 547 cows and 432 sheep remained. In 2004 the

Illustration 5.1. Bushes Taking over Pasture in Dragomireşti

number of cows slightly increased to 599 whereas the number of sheep slightly decreased to 421. These figures reflect a national reality; they are congruent with the decrease in cattle in Romania after 1989, from a little over 7 million head of cattle to around 2.8 million. From some 16 million in 1989 sheep decreased to around 9 million head in 2004.[5] As for the village horses, their number increased significantly from 131 in 1989 to 183 in 2004.[6] The increasing number of horses after 1990 does not reflect the Romanian villagers' agricultural needs but rather to those of the Rudari. As I have explained in chapter 3, they are the deforestation squad. They need horses for transporting wood from the forest to their households before selling it to richer Rudari. Forest restitution to private owners unfolded at the same pace as the increase in the number of horses owned by Rudari.

Thus, the statistics show us that year after year there were fewer and fewer animals to graze the islaz. Again, this phenomenon can be explained in terms of the prevailing political economy. As I will explain in more detail in the following chapter, Romanian agriculture suffered from the lack of state subsidies, from the withdrawal of the state from the economy generally and from agriculture in particular, leaving producers to manage themselves. Thus, the vast majority of Dragomireștens keep one cow to supplement food for household consumption and not for selling dairy products. The liberalization of the market allowed, at least after 2000, large Western supermarkets to open stores everywhere in Romania. Several such supermarkets have opened in Mioveni, the small town close to Dragomirești. Keeping a cow, thus ensuring a supply of milk and cheese for the household, made economic sense in the early years of political change when galloping inflation changed the price of food every other hour.[7] After 2000, when the Romanian economy began to stabilize and food prices became more stable, keeping a cow ceased to be economically viable. It no longer paid to invest money and work in obtaining fodder when it was cheaper to buy dairy products from the supermarket than to keep a cow. This was the reasoning expressed by every villager I talked to. The only argument for keeping a cow was the uncontested higher quality of local dairy products as compared to the supermarket ones.[8] The situation I describe here is not unique or specific to Romania but is familiar in other postsocialist countries as well. In post-Soviet Estonia, for instance, the consumption of Western goods is not a matter of displaying personal wealth or social status but rather proof of the re-Westernization of the country.[9] The 'mirage of hypermarket' goods has appeared also in the Czech Republic and Poland, competing with food produced locally – although there is not an outright rejection of traditional food in these countries.[10]

The lack of funds for maintaining the pastures, the apathy demonstrated by social benefits workers whose job it is to clear the communal pastures and the lack of interest shown both by the mayor's office and the villagers have all contributed to the annual encroachment of bushes on communal pasture. Villagers complain not so much about the quality of the pasture but about the lack of any protest on the part of mayoralty employees at state foresters annually marking the most advanced young trees with the stamp that claims the trees as state property. Forest restitution was severely condemned by state foresters and one of the reasons was that they were afraid of being fired – less forest to watch over means less need for forest guards. Marking the young trees with the state's stamp allows them to report larger forested areas as still belonging to the state. Although one can barely call bushes a young forest and villagers loudly contest the state definition of forest, state foresters continue to mark the most advanced trees. The advancement of the bushes has brought about a slow change in at least two directions: changes in property rights since once marked, the new young trees pass into state ownership, together with the land underneath. The trees in this case become the outpost soldiers of the state, conquering new lands, while forest (even in its bushy phase) becomes the instrument of the state regaining control over land. When this happens on private pasture – and several villagers complained about such abusive behaviour on the part of state foresters – forest becomes the enemy that swallows private pasture and spits back state forestland. The second change is in land use. Pastures are steadily transformed into forest, which means the laws under which this land is managed are changing as well. Once designated as forest, the land comes under Forestry Code rules and can only be managed accordingly.

Yet, the most severe transformation of all imposed on the pastures has to be the illegal building of new houses on communal pasture. Looking through the mayor's official papers I observed that out of eighty-six households built in the Rudari settlement thirty-five have been illegally constructed. When I use the term 'illegal' I mean by this that no authorization was issued by the mayor's office for the construction of these houses and the house 'owners' have no legal rights over the land on which they are built. The mayor's office has the power to authorize any construction on the commune's territory but only within the established residential area. Even if local authorities had wanted to release such an authorization, it would have been illegal since the new Rudari houses were erected on land designated as pasture in the official papers. No change in land use is allowed at local level; such change requires authorization from the Ministry of Agriculture and Forestry. Thus, in the official papers, the land that now serves as a residential area is defined as islaz and the owner and manager of the land is still the mayor's office.

From the moment Rudari first settled in the commune they have occupied a narrow valley on the edge of the village, next to the communal pasture. For almost a century, they did not expand their settlement. After the 1990s, as a result of greater access to the forest, the inhabitants of the settlement grew from 169 people to more than 300. This expansion of the population has required more houses. The only land at their disposal was the communal pasture. One by one, houses were erected on the surrounding hills. None of them had documents of ownership for the land. They simply built houses when the family outgrew their traditional one- or two-room dwellings. As most of the courtyards are too small to accommodate a new construction, building on the pastures next to their valley was their only option.

Most of these houses are poor, with no electricity, no running water or any other facility. Built from a mixture of clay and wood the new houses are insalubrious while the electric cables come from nearby houses belonging to another family member. Long cables of more than 100 metres hanging in the air, supported by wooden poles and linking two houses, is not an unusual sight in this community. Since the new owners have no documents to prove their land ownership or legal authorization to build, the electricity company cannot hook them up to the national grid. The toilet is outside, behind the house – when there is a toilet at all. Usually, Rudari cook outside, in their backyard, as the kitchens are small and poorly equipped.

The mayor's office employees, especially the agricultural officer, the vice-mayor and the mayor are the bureaucrats responsible for enforcing the law concerning land use. They have not taken any direct action against Rudari yet all know about the illegal expansion. Although the Romanian population

Illustration 5.2. Rudari Houses Built on the Communal Pasture

shuns the Rudari settlement, the new houses are clearly visible from a distance. The local authorities turn a blind eye because of the patron–client relationship between Rudari and local state bureaucrats. Local state officers use Rudari as a cheap labour force for forest exploitation and as scapegoats for deforestation. In return, they have looked the other way when Rudari have illegally erected their houses on communal pasture. The usual defence offered by the state employees when reproached for their passive attitude toward this illegal land use is: 'Rudari are poor; they cannot afford to buy land anywhere else. We can't simply demolish their houses as they have nowhere else to go.' During every electoral campaign all Romanian candidates have promised Rudari that they will bring a representative of the County Cadastral Office, at the mayor's expense, to draw up the cadastral map of the area. This would be the first step towards granting the Rudari property rights and, in the process, changing the land use from pasture to residential. Needless to say, in 2010 when I left the field, the status of those houses was still illegal and their inhabitants were still outlawed.

I have described the patron–client relationships, the economic gains made by state officers from private forest exploitation and the environmental havoc produced by these relationships in chapter 3. What I emphasize here are the effective changes in land use not recorded in the local state official papers. In fact, there is a huge discrepancy between the statistics – hectares officially described as 'pasture' – and the land actually used as pasture. Though officially today the pasture is larger than it was in the socialist period, in practice the pasture has shrunk and its quality is worse than it was twenty-four years ago.

Further, I examine the way in which Rudari have reacted against their exploiters and patrons.

Snakes as Avatars of an Uncivilized Settlement

Those Rudari who live in illegal huts constantly complain about the snakes that have invaded their settlement. Inhabitants of those houses built most recently and who therefore live closest to the bushes encroaching on the pasture are the most vocal.[11] One day, Tinu, father of two small children living in a hut neighbouring the thick bushes showed me a hole of a few centimetres in diameter made at the foundation of his one-room clay built house. He complained that he had plugged up the hole several times but the snakes continued to appear. That morning he had even found a snake under his bed and he feared for his children.

Several times I myself witnessed dead, non-poisonous snakes no longer than 50 centimetres lying in the middle of the road that crosses the Rudari's settlement. All members of the community also complain that the small and insalubrious pond that has formed in their valley shelters a 'big snake'. They fear for the safety of their children but also for their few domestic animals. They blame the snake for the disappearance of small animals such as cats, small dogs or chickens from the backyards situated next to the pond. Some members of the community swore that they saw in the bushes surrounding the pond a large snake 'as thick as a solid man's arm'. The man who recounted this brandished his right arm to demonstrate to me how big the snake was. The solid and muscled arm of a daily forest worker used to physical work, cutting thick trees and carrying heavy trunks, being used as a measurement unit for the reptile expressed how terrified they are.

Whether such a big snake exists or not is not the issue here. The biologists would certainly argue that Romania does not shelter large snakes such as the one villagers described as terrorizing their community. For sure, the grass snake (*Natrix natrix*), a water lover, the water snake (*Natrix tesselata*) and the smooth snake (*Coronella austriaca*), which live in bushes or at edge of the forests, are part of the local fauna.[12] The local environment is perfectly suitable for such reptiles: they eat frogs, tadpoles, small lizards and small fish – all to be found in the insalubrious pond lying in the middle of Rudari settlement. These snakes also need bushes, leaves and hay to build a nest for hatching their eggs.[13] The ecology of humans and of wild animals overlaps in this case. In the last years of socialism, due to the high quantity of pesticides used and intensive agriculture the snakes became more rare as they retreated to the forest. Once the bushes started to take over the pastures after the breakup of the collective farm the snakes became more numerous and started to come closer to human settlements.

The snake is used here as an avatar for poverty and exclusion. Not only is the Rudari settlement built at the edge of the commune, but the illegal houses are also built outside the inhabited area, closer to the bushes. The snake is the metaphor for their social and political marginality and a non-political and indirect way of criticizing the state and local bureaucrats who constantly refuse to offer Rudari decent places to build their houses. The snake attack stories speak about the precarious housing situation, the poor living conditions and about social and economic marginality. It is difficult to find a more suitable symbol of nature as opposed to civilization, of un-habitable condition as opposed to inhabited area than the snake. Besides, several Rudari use the snake example to point up that they live outside the inhabited area, with no minimum standard of living conditions such as electricity, running water and safety from predators.

Rudari are aware of their economic dependency on powerful local bureaucrats who could evict them within days; this is the main reason, in my opinion, why they do not engage in an open confrontation. The return of nature as represented by bushes and snakes give them a perfect opportunity to engage in a social and political critique without openly attacking their protectors-cum-exploiters: a usage of the 'weapons of the weak' at its best.

Wild Boar as Public Enemy

On a late October morning in 2004 I noticed a disturbance in front of the mayor's office in Dragova. The cleaning lady brushed the latest leaves that had fallen from the trees in the mayor's office's backyard while other employees made the final preparations for an important visit. The president of the Romanian Senate, who is the second most powerful man in the Romanian state, after the president, was going to visit the village and mingle with the locals. He was invited by the mayor in an attempt to show he had political connections at the highest level and display his unchallenged authority in the area. Even though there was an electoral campaign running, the fact that such a powerful and influential politician made a detour and stopped in a small remote village of 500 inhabitants was impressive equally for local constituents and for the mayor's political competitors. Several villagers were present as they had important grievances to transmit to those who run the country. Nicolae Văcăroiu, former prime minister of Romania, arrived at around noon, greeted the crowd which had grown significantly to around sixty people, and then spent twenty minutes in a private discussion with the mayor and several other local SDP politicians. Then Mr. Văcăroiu stood on the mayor's office stairs and, after praising the mayor's management qualities which were visible throughout the village, asked which were the most pressing issues confronting the villagers. He offered to be their voice in central government. I expected the first issue people raised would be linked to forest restitution. Although this was indeed the second most pressing issue, the most urgent was the problem of the wild boars.

These animals annually root up the pastures, especially those lying up on the mountain, at a distance from the inhabited area. Villagers complained that every year the number of boars grew and so did the damage they caused. For people who rely on animal husbandry, rooted up pastures lies at the heart of their business. As in the case of Dragomirești, private pastures located close to the inhabited area of Dragova or in the villagers' backyards are rarely grazed. Villagers prefer to graze their animals on the communal land and pay an annual tax. Meadows and pastures located far from the village are only mowed and the hay stacked in villagers' backyards. Year after year the wild boars break down the wooden fences that enclose these pastures and destroy them. The mountainous meadows and pastures are surrounded by state and private forests, which provide a perfect habitat for the wild boar. In its quest

Illustration 5.3. Rooted Pastures of Dragova

for bulbs and field rats' nests the boar roots up the pastures located at the edge of the forests.[14] A rooted up pasture means that the grass and other plant roots are pulled up from the soil and quickly dry out as illustration 5.3 shows.

Such a pasture cannot be mowed or grazed until the following year. The loss is total. The boar is shy and mostly nocturnal so villagers cannot protect their fields effectively. The ecology of this wild animal conflicts and competes with the ecology of humans, to the detriment of the latter. Hunting the boar is not a solution either, as only those who are authorized hunters can hold a firearm, and they are allowed to shoot the boar only if they pay a certain amount of money. Thus, pasture owners are powerless to prevent the annual destruction of their land.

The damage inflicted by wild boar has contributed to a certain extent to the shift in the local economy from animal husbandry to rural tourism. Pastures located at a distance from the village, regularly destroyed by the wild boar, became useless to their owners who consequently had trouble providing sufficient winter hay for their animals. The pastures have changed from being an asset to a liability. The problems caused by wild boars have triggered the decision, for some of them, to switch their household's economic strategy from animal husbandry to rural tourism. In this way, several villagers assured me, the family would not depend anymore on the caprice of nature. In addition to the damage inflicted by wild boar a villager strictly specializing in animal husbandry is also at the mercy of the weather. Since pastures and meadows are not irrigated, a dry year could mean less fodder and thus a drastic reduction in the number of cattle. By switching to rural tourism villagers have attempted to ensure that wild boars and the weather lottery play a less significant role in their household income.

Land, Tourism and Politics

It is not as if one day the villagers decided to stop keeping animals and selling dairy produce and the next day opened a guesthouse. Changes in the economic strategies of Dragova householders unfolded over time, after 1990, and this shift should be understood as the emphasis shifting from one activity to the other. The number of cows constantly decreased to 832 in 2004 from 1,230 in 1989.[15] This is perhaps surprising in the context of the restitution of meadows and pastures to former owners and of the restitution of 699 hectares of communal pasture to the mayor's office. This pasture is in addition to 289 hectares of pastures and meadows also given back through restitution laws. Thus, if in 1989 villagers of Dragova had at their disposal 1,017 hectares of pastures and meadows, this had grown to 2,011 hectares (including the communal pasture) by 2004. Despite the larger area of grassland at their disposal in postsocialist times there are fewer cows in the commune than during socialism. The explanations I gave in the first part of the chapter fit this case too: the withdrawal of the state from involvement in agriculture, cutting state subsidies, the privatization of connected industries and liberalization of the market all contributed to changes in the local economy of Dragova.

The fact that some villagers turned to rural tourism should not come as a surprise. The two economic sectors are closely connected. Visitors are attracted to Dragova not only by the beautiful scenery and by the possibility of hiking in the National Park but also by the possibility of consuming fresh local products such as milk, smoked cheese, cheese kept in oak bark and pastrami.

After the 1990s, villagers recognized an opportunity to exploit the local landscape through developing rural tourism. The cave had attracted visitors since the interwar period and the number of visitors had grown steadily since the early 1950s. Villagers began to supplement their income by making a few of the nicer rooms in their house available to visitors, while members of the family squeezed into one or two rooms. Even today many houses have tin plaques announcing to the potential visitor that they have free rooms. Since this activity was, and still is, an unofficial business, villagers do not pay any tax to the mayor's office or anywhere else. Nor would they declare this business on a census. From my interviews and my own observations though, there are few houses in the village that would not open their doors to visitors.

Some villagers had money to invest in building a guesthouse equipped with all necessary facilities. The growing number of houses, from 540 in 1985 to 585 in 1995, can only be explained by the fact that new guesthouses were built.[16] Dragova is not an exception in Romania. Between 2000 and 2005 for instance, the accommodation capacity at national level in houses used for rural tourism grew from 100 per cent to 314.64 per cent.[17] This trend should also be put in the context of steady growth of the national economy after 2000 and of urbanites able to afford to spend their vacation in places such as Dragova. In the peak seasons, in winter and in summer, it is quite difficult to find a room to rent. Most customers book rooms well in advance. For instance, in 2007 customers booked their rooms in September for the winter feasts (23 December to 3 January).

Opening a guesthouse is not cheap, though, and presupposes that large profits can be made. In Dragova, several rich people including members of the local council, the mayor and the vice-mayor have erected new guesthouses. Most of the local political elite has first made money from forest exploitation, as I have shown in chapter 4. With few exceptions, those able to build a guesthouse are those connected to a local state office and who were involved in forest exploitation as well. It is important for anyone who decides to build a guesthouse to be somehow connected to the mayor's office, as one needs the mayor's office authorization of construction and the cooperation of the mayor's office with changes in the zone planning. If the pasture to be converted into a residential area is not already within the inhabited zone then the mayor's office has to seek approval from the Ministries in Bucharest to change the category of land use. This means more paperwork for the mayor's office employees hence the link between guesthouse ownership and state office holders.

The next example of a local council member who owns a restaurant, conveniently located in the centre of Dragova village, just one kilometre away from the much-visited cave, proves the importance of local political position for doing rural tourism. The bus station is located close to his restaurant. When his business started to boom he extended the beer garden and also the car park, which had become too small for the volume of external visitors. The beer garden is particularly attractive as it has a 20-metre-high mountain wall behind, and nice views of the forest and the purling spring. Being disturbed by villagers waiting for the bus in front of his beer garden he convinced the other members of the local council to move the bus station to some 60 metres away. Then he extended the private parking area for his restaurant visitors. The allegations were that he even extended the beer garden a few metres onto public land. The restaurant owner received support in his crusade against the bus travellers from the mayor himself who, in exchange, benefitted from our councillor's support in the wood business. In a similar case, Petronela, a young lady who offered accommodation in her newly built guesthouse and also had a small shop where she sold local traditional food items was refused authorization from the mayor's office to build a small car park. She needed the parking for the shop clients and also for her guesthouse visitors. Not only did she not receive the parking authorization but the mayor threatened her with a fine on the pretext that she lacked some other authorization. She finally had to dismantle her food shop.

The only difference between the two cases is that one concerns a member of the local council who belongs to the same political party as the mayor and is a supporter of the mayor's wood business. If Petronela had been a member of the local political elite or at least on good terms with the mayor she would probably have obtained her authorization. The importance of political contacts for developing rural tourism was made even clearer when the PCNP organized a competition for EU funds intended for those who owned forest or land within the park's territory. The funds came from the EU with a clear intention to support and encourage villagers in re-orientating their business from forest exploitation to more sustainable activities such as rural tourism. The amount of money an applicant could receive was between €1,500 and €10,000. The only possible applicants were guesthouse owners who wanted to upgrade their guesthouses. From Dragova the only person to receive funds was the wife of the councillor who owns the beer garden. She was in the best position to access the EU funds: she knew from her husband about the application well before anyone else in the commune and their guesthouse is located right in the centre of Dragova, quite close to the cave.

As with any commercial activity, rural tourism can involve fierce competition among guesthouse owners, and the struggle is not always played straight. The land next to the cave and the restaurant built there represented a postsocialist Eldorado for any potential investor in tourism. Thus the heirs of the historical owner representing one party and the vice-mayor and the mayor representing another party have carried on a long guerrilla war to acquire the restaurant and the small adjacent plot. Rada, the present owner, is the daughter of the man who built the restaurant in 1939. Having the mountain walls behind the restaurant, the spring and the forest in front and to the right the entrance of the cave, the restaurant was in an excellent location for visitors to relax and constituted a lucrative business for the owner. In 1950 the communist regime nationalized the restaurant but the owner was kept on as a waiter. For almost fifty years the restaurant belonged to the local co-operative.[18] In 1996, when the neoliberal government came to power, Rada sued the co-operative and, supported by two members of her family, as well as members of the local council, she succeeded in getting the restaurant back. From this moment the mayor and the vice-mayor mounted a guerrilla war. The restaurant represents a powerful competitor for the vice-mayor's restaurant, which is located further away from the cave. The mayor's office repeatedly asked the Environmental Guard (*Garda de Mediu*)[19] to verify whether the restaurant owner was violating any environmental laws. Thus, Rada is constantly under pressure from the state offices obeying the mayor's orders. This was just one episode in the merciless political struggle for land in Dragova.

Rugged Geography, Property, Conflicts

The tourism business in Dragova became so financially attractive that several people from Bucharest opened guesthouses there after buying small pasture plots located in or close to the inhabited area. As a consequence, the price of land in Dragova skyrocketed and the land market became far more buoyant than the one in Dragomirești. From 1997 to 2004, 185 transactions were registered at the mayor's office. However, the location of the land traded is not insignificant. Because of the rugged geography of the region – and remember that until the end of the nineteenth century Dragova could be visited only by boat along the river – the location of the land, which is usually grassland, is crucial. Thus, the value of the land varies substantially depending on its location. The land located close to the main road becomes very attractive because of the opportunity of erecting a guesthouse whereas the land located up in the mountain becomes less and less attractive. Since only the principal road which links Dragova to the exterior world is covered with asphalt, the other roads, especially those which go up to Ciocănaș village are almost impracticable with a city car. During the rainy seasons (spring and autumn) only a strong off-road car is able to climb these roads. Consequently, building a guesthouse on these plots is unfeasible simply because there are not many visitors who would wish to stay in such a remote place. The location of the guesthouse was one of the main considerations for park officials when evaluating applications for the EU funds. Petronela, the local guesthouse owner mentioned earlier, applied for EU funding. One of the main objections raised by the evaluators was that her guesthouse is not located on the main road. They asked her: 'Who do you think would bring his/her Mercedes up these steep slopes?' She was turned down mainly on the basis of the location of her guesthouse.

The wild boar and its feeding habits play a central role in devaluing the pastures located outside the village but this is not the only factor. Even if this pasture has not been trashed by wild boar, the simple fact that the owner has to walk at least half an hour until he or she reaches it is already a problem. More than in Dragomirești, the geography of the area makes the difference between a valuable site and a useless one. Whereas in Dragomirești most villagers have rather large backyards that ascend the gentle slopes where they shelter their animals, Dragovans have small backyards. This means that villagers keep their animals in barns located on the pastures beyond their gardens. If this plot is located conveniently close to the household, this is an advantage to the animal owner. If the plot is at the edge of the commune it becomes a burden in terms of keeping animals or the land's market value. These are the twin reasons why pastures located within the inhabited area or found close to the main road became valuable assets for their owners whereas those located further away became a liability.

If a plot is not located on the road and lacks an access road then that land can be totally useless. In one case, a landowner who had recently inherited a pasture refused access to Radu, his neighbour, who owned a pasture next to his. At the same time, the new neighbour suggested that he would be interested in buying Radu's land, which he said was worthless without an access road. Radu complained to the mayor's office but the new owner produced a cadastral map of the area showing that no access road is mentioned. The parents of the two owners had had a verbal agreement about the passageway, an argument presented by Radu who also mentioned that the two neighbouring families had previously lived side by side without conflict. The new owner remained inflexible, emphasizing the rigours of the law against trespassing. Finally, Radu decided to accept the disadvantageous deal but, he told me, he just 'wants to get on his neighbour's nerves a bit more' before selling him the land.

This short story is by no means unique. Changes in the economy of the village from animal husbandry to rural tourism have triggered several harsh conflicts between neighbours concerning access roads. One young lady, let us call her Tina, decided to open a guesthouse in her large backyard.[20] She inherited this plot from her grandmother and she wanted to take advantage of her inheritance. After building a small new guesthouse she invested around €1,200 more to chamfer the 15-metre road which serves two households. The two households, Tina's and her neighbour's, are located on the peak of a small but steep hill and the road links the two households to the main road, which runs around 6 metres below. One day, Tina simply blocked her neighbours' access to the newly chamfered road, urging her neighbour to build her own access road. Her reason was strictly economic; she applied to PHARE funds to expand her guesthouse but the evaluator who came to inspect the project asked her, laughing: 'Who would you expect to venture up here on such a bad road? You need to repair the road and to add some stones in order to make it look like a real road.' This was the reason she chamfered the road and refused her neighbours access – her neighbours' cows would simply destroy the road and 'the dung on the road is just disgusting and offends visitors'. Besides, she wanted her investments to have clear property rights and to be able to control her property. The history of this road is as old as 1903 and reveals generational changes in the relationship between villagers but also between villagers and their natural environment. Two brothers constructed the road in 1903; they had erected houses next to each other on the peak of the hill. In daily use as both households drove their cows to and from pasture, the road suffered further erosion by the heavy rains of 1966. The grandsons of those men who built the road signed an agreement that allowed one of them – Tina's grandfather – to buy the small strip of land that constituted the road, but gave both families the right to use it. The handwritten agreement was signed and dated October 1973. At the bottom of the paper the two brothers forbade future generations to change this agreement. Since then, both families had used the road until Tina's decision to block it.

The two neighbours posed different arguments based on two generational views on social relations and on the link with the nonhuman world. Tina, a young investor in local tourism, based her claims on economic and judicial arguments, and on the necessity for clear, individual property rights for her investment. Her opponent, a lady of around sixty years old, based her claims on historical arguments, and on the fact that the old road (*drum bătrânesc*) was supposed to be used by the members of both families. She also based her arguments on ethical grounds: if her family built another road, as Tina suggested, it would have to be on a slope which is so steep that the cows could not climb it. Her final argument was that it would not be possible to carry her mother's coffin down the hill on such a road (her mother was ninety years old). Whereas Tina sees this road in strictly economic terms her neighbour points to the history of the road and to the social relations. Land is a commodity in Tina's view, while her neighbour regards it as a way to foster social relations.

This conflict not only is about different generational attitudes to the land but also illustrates the conflict between two types of economic activity in the commune. The interests of rural tourism may conflict with the interests of animal husbandry. Tourism as an economic activity is spatially selective – one cannot build a guesthouse just anywhere – and generates competition for the space.[21] The conflict between guesthouse owners and those keen to exploit the forest, described largely in chapter 4, illustrates the same competition for land. Guesthouse owners are interested in preserving nature; this is the reason that some of them periodically clear plastic bags and other detritus from the river and why they are critical of the wood business of the mayor, whose trucks destroy the roads and disturb the silence of nature. They also want to 'sell nature' but in a non-destructive way. The struggle for the environment is in fact the struggle over defining nature: what nature is, how it should be used and who has the right to appropriate it is a matter of harsh debate, struggles and negotiations.

Pasture and Politics

In both field sites, pastures have suffered tremendous changes in the post-socialist era. Although there are different local social and economic mechanisms at play there are two common features that explain the shrinkage of the pasture. First, the political economy of the country led, in both cases, to a decreasing interest in animal husbandry. This has in turn led to less maintenance of the pasture, both in terms of its quality and size, and more room for manoeuvre for local state bureaucrats. Second, those villagers involved in expanding the built-up area are those who had a vested political and economic interest in so doing; they all hold local state office.

There is nevertheless a major difference between the two cases. The mechanisms by which the pastures are transformed into built-up areas are significantly different in the two communes as are the economic consequences for the entire community. In Dragomirești, local state bureaucrats paid their debts to Rudari, their clients, by not taking administrative action when land use was drastically changed. This was an illegal action from the central state perspective, a brutal interference with its functions and commandments, though in part well intentioned: the poor Rudari need a shelter over their heads. In Dragova, the process through which land use was changed was legal – mostly because it involved a change in land use within areas that are already inhabited. The local state offices were involved in authorizing the construction plans since the pastures were privately owned and located within an area that had already been developed. From this point of view the central state was neither involved nor vexed. Building guesthouses on land previously used as pastures was economically beneficial for most villagers, including those who remained in the animal husbandry business, as I will point out in detail in the following chapter.

When central state planners conceived the land restitution laws – especially when the private and communal pastures were given back to their former owners – they never envisioned the response of villagers or of those who had to implement the land reform laws. The neoliberal vision behind private and communal pasture restitution was geared towards enabling entrepreneurial livestock owners to improve agricultural production. Privatization of pastures was the means to a more general aim: the transformation of Romanian rural society, its economy and landscape. Not only did villagers react differently to the way anticipated by central state planners, but local state officers also had their own interests and their own agenda, which conflicted with the central government's plans. Instead of being conscientious foot soldiers of land reform they turned their role as implementers of the new restitution laws to their own advantage.

Vanishing Pastures in Postsocialist Countries

Turning pastures into scrubland or built-up areas seems to be a widespread phenomenon in postsocialist Romania. The political economy of the postsocialist state has suffered a setback in all regions of Romania. Pastures have been abandoned or scarcely grazed at all in many areas where animal husbandry hitherto represented the main traditional economy. The Apuseni Mountain (Transylvania), which was historically such an area, was severely hit by the low profitability of animal husbandry. An absence of grazing can be as damaging, from an ecological point of view, as overgrazing, as shown by biologists such as Márton Enyedi and his colleagues.[22] The abandonment of semi-natural grassland in Transylvania as well as an inappropriate management approach led to the conversion of the grassland into forest. Biologists, in fact, recommend in their studies that trees growing on grassland should be cut and the grassland extensively grazed.[23]

The lack of attention paid by social scientists to such land use changes prevents me from illustrating it with more case studies. Nevertheless, the expansion of built-up areas in postsocialist Romania, especially at the edge of large cities, has usually been made at the expense of agricultural land, pastures or forests. The new hypermarkets, the new residential neighbourhoods and newly industrial areas were all constructed on land previously used for agricultural purposes.

In other parts of the postsocialist world pastures have also suffered a multitude of changes. In Russia, for instance, large areas of grassland were privatized and the new owners converted pasture into arable land. The collapse of livestock production due to the liberalization of the internal market has further reduced the area used for fodder. It is true that the huge area of natural and semi-natural fodder fields in Russia – more than 70 million hectares – has still not been affected to an alarming degree.[24]

In Slovakia, the Tatra region, the croplands and the pastures were steadily abandoned after 1989 due to the same economic problems as experienced in other parts of the postsocialist world. Some of these lands were naturally transformed into woodland scrub and then into forest.[25] Geographers working with satellite images report that the growth of urban fabric is converting the land used previously for agriculture (including pasture) into built-up areas in the Czech Republic.[26] Moreover, in this country, the historical owners and their heirs had pastures restored to them that lay in and around the Protected Landscape Area of the White Carpathians.[27] The regulations controlling the Protected Area stipulated that the new owners must follow a careful grassland management programme: the pastures had to be grazed properly in order to prevent encroachment by bushes. Needless to say, the new owners ignored the park administration's regulations and neglected to mow the meadows. Those owners who had abandoned agricultural practices did nothing to prevent the encroachment of bushes on their pastureland, while the park's administration was unable to impose sanctions on the landowners or to change the status of the pastures.

In Albania, a reverse phenomenon has taken place. The co-operatives had cultivated intensively even the most remote mountainous pastures on steep slopes, turning unproductive pastures into productive ones. Postsocialism has radically changed the land use here: new private owners have turned arable land into pastures to graze livestock intended for subsistence production.[28]

Squatting on agricultural land was a matter of national importance in Albania.[29] In particular poor villagers from the mountains of Northern Albania moved down to the plains, to work the land formerly owned by the state that remained undistributed. They built shanties on these lands that lack the benefits of electricity, running water or any other modern facility. The local and central governments took no action against these people, as in the case of the Rudari, but profited at every electoral campaign by promising to legalize their status and improve domestic facilities. The Albanian squatters, just like their peers in Dragomirești, were used as a voting machine by the politicians and state bureaucrats at all levels but were ignored for the rest of the time.

In peri-urban villages, in Eastern Europe but also in former socialist countries in Asia such as China and Vietnam, the increase in foreign investments led to an expansion of built-up areas on agricultural land.[30] The conversion of agricultural land, including though not exclusively pastureland, into residential areas was facilitated by the devaluation of agricultural production, which made agricultural land less expensive for the new investors. The city of Hanoi, after the beginning of the land reform, is an excellent example of the expansion of residential and industrial constructions on land formerly used for agriculture.[31] Between 1988 (the year when the land reform started) and 2000 the city lost an average of 268 hectares annually. The residential expansion was both legal and illegal. Whereas in some cases agricultural land was taken over by squatters during a spontaneous housing boom, in other cases new economic developers bought the agricultural land from villagers or from the state and converted it into residential, commercial or industrial areas. Again, in both cases political interests played a major role in the change in land use.[32]

The fate of the pastures in postsocialist times merits further study. Several features, though, seem to be obvious from the few cases I have presented here. One is that the changes the pastures have undergone are important but not as dramatic as those inflicted on the forest. There has been a loss of pasture through squatting and mismanagement of the land, but at the same time cropland has been converted into pasture, as Johannes Stahl (2010a) mentions in the case of Albania, or pastures were even revived as is the Estonian case, due to the international subsidies and the recognition of pastures traditional values.[33] Pastures have shrunk because of changes in the political economy of the postsocialist countries: when animal husbandry was no longer supported by the postsocialist state, villagers found other uses for their pastures. Some, as in the case of Dragova and Hanoi, have legally turned them into built-up areas, residential or industrial, thus benefitting from their inclusion in the global economy. Other pastures, especially those belonging to the state, have been taken over by squatters, poor people seeking new ways to expand their livelihood. Whether by legal or illegal means, this change in land use has primarily benefitted politicians and state bureaucrats.

Are these changes evident only in postsocialist countries? One could hardly argue for a positive answer. Losses of grassland and of semi-natural pastures seem to be characteristic of contemporary environmental history, in Europe at least. In central Spain the pastures are being steadily replaced by scrublands as a result of progressive land abandonment.[34] Due to multiple social and political factors such as the abandonment of agriculture and the transfer of rural populations into different economic sectors like construction and services (commerce, tourism etc.), pastures have been abandoned. The decline of animal husbandry and the consequent use of pastures for grazing, rapid urban development and the boom in touristic activities have resulted in a massive change in land cover: large areas of pasture in central Spain have been turned into scrubland. The outcome is that not only is a historical landscape rapidly changing but there is also a heavy loss of flora and fauna associated with grazed pastures. Romero-Calcerrada and Perry show in their study that similar changes have occurred in other parts of Spain and the Mediterranean. A similar process is unfolding in post-war Finland: pastures have shrunk because of the expansion of wood plantations or arable land.[35] After more than two hundred years of grazing livestock on the pastures in the River Rekijoki valley, in the last forty years grazing there has ceased whereas mowing stopped twenty or thirty years earlier. The same socio-economic forces, as in the case of Spain, have led to the abandonment of pastures and their conversion to forest. Deciduous trees and bushes and plantations of coniferous samplings have replaced not only the existing land cover but also the entire ecological system.

Is there then something unique about this change in the way pastures are being used in the postsocialist world? To such a question there is no simple answer. The same global economic forces prevail in both postsocialist and non-postsocialist countries: the population boom, the development of tourism, the higher demand for food and for wood leading to an expansion of residential areas, arable land and forest. At the same time, land restitution to former owners and the rapid adaptation of postsocialist rural areas to the new economic demands meant that these transformations were more rapid here than in non-postsocialist areas. In less than twenty years the postsocialist landscape has suffered dramatic changes and the waning pastures are part of that change.

Notes

1. I mean by 'built-up area' those zones that are legally designated as settlement areas. In Romania there are roughly two types of zones: *intravilan* (meaning literally, 'in the settlement'), which is the area designated for buildings and *extravilan* (literally meaning 'outside the settlement'), areas designated for agricultural cultivation (it includes also forested areas). In order to change the land use legally one needs the approval of the Ministry of Agriculture and Forestry. A formal change in the use of a plot from agriculture to residential and vice versa cannot be decided at local level.
2. The official papers of the Dragomirești mayoralty.
3. There is no established distinction between pasture and meadow. I therefore use the local distinction.
4. Thelen et al. (2011).
5. The source is FAOSTAT data from 2004. I thank Daniel Müller for offering me the data.
6. The source is the Agricultural Statistics of Dragomirești, the County Statistics Office, Pitești.
7. For instance, the average monthly inflation rate for food items was around 22 per cent in 1997 (Heidhues et al. 1998: 353).
8. Iancu and Mihăilescu (2009) use an anonymous Internet text called *How Danone Bankrupted Tante Mița from Moeciu* in order to demonstrate changes in popular food tastes in postsocialist Romania. Tante Mița is presented as a livestock owner from Moeciu, a village not far away from Dragova whose traditional economy is based on animal husbandry and dairy production as famous as those from Dragova, who was put out of business by Danone dairy production. Danone dairy products are cheaper but 'poisoned' with additives, according to the anonymous text.
9. Rausing (2002).
10. Smith and Jehlička (2007).
11. The expansion of the inhabited area was made from the main road and the dry riverbed, where the old houses are built, towards the peaks of the hills.
12. Sos (2008).
13. Ciudin (2006).
14. Silvas (2005).
15. The source is the County Department of Statistics, Pitești and official papers from Dragova mayor's office (for 2004).

16. The source is the County Department of Statistics, Pitești.
17. Constantin and Mitrut (2009: 153).
18. The consumer co-operative was part of a collective system of stores which sold different products. It was similar to the collective farm.
19. This is a state structure that enforces the environmental laws.
20. For more details on this episode see Dorondel (2011b).
21. Constantin and Mitrut (2009).
22. Enyedi et al. (2007). For a comparison between the Transylvanian traditional management of meadows and the Sweddish one and the consequences for biodiversity see Dahlström et al. (2013).
23. Cremene et al. (2005).
24. Milanova et al. (2010).
25. Kopecká and Vováček (2010).
26. Romportl et al. (2010).
27. This account is based on Sikor (2006).
28. Stahl (2010a), as well as other sources that analyse the decreasing number of cattle, does not detail the changes suffered where pastures are no longer grazed.
29. This example is based on de Waal (2004).
30. Leaf (2002).
31. The account is based on Quang and Kammeier (2002).
32. I use here the more inclusive term agricultural land simply because Quang and Kammeier do not specify the type of land previously designated as agricultural that has been changed into a built-up area.
33. Stahl (2010a); Roellig et al. (2015).
34. The argument is based on Romero-Calcerrada and Perry (2004).
35. The account is based on Luoto et al. (2003).

 CHAPTER 6

Fragmented Lands

'Let us not forget agriculture, which will always constitute a country's wealth.'
—Umberto Eco, *The Cemetery of Prague*

One of my first questions when I interviewed villagers from Dragomireşti was 'How much land do you have?' Each time I was surprised when my interviewee could not reply promptly to such a simple question and needed some time to calculate the exact size. It is not that the villagers did not know *where* their land was within the commune; it was rather that the *total area* of it had to be calculated before they could respond to my question. The explanation, I realized later, was that every landowner in Dragomireşti has several pieces of land scattered throughout the commune. In Dragova it was pretty much the same situation; villagers always needed time to calculate the total size of their land. The explanation that comes to mind is that the multitude of plots spread around mean that villagers cannot respond straightaway to a seemingly simple question. This chapter suggests that there is another reason too: villagers from both communes do not rely entirely on agriculture, as they have other means of subsistence as well; most Dragomireştens have industrial jobs while Dragovans are involved in rural tourism and in selling dairy products. As I have shown in chapter 1, this double economic engagement with both the land and non-agricultural activities is an historical feature in both villages, which shows the adaptation to local ecological features. The lack of suitable cropland, the perfect environment for orchards and the presence of the forest ready to be marketed have played a historical role in Dragomireşti. The rugged geography of Dragova, which lends itself chiefly to animal husbandry and forestry, and the location of the village at the border of two provinces have given rise to involvement in commercial activities since medieval times. The political economy of the socialist state – the expansion of the industrial sector and the state's involvement in agricultural production and trade – has played a part in the area's history. The postsocialist political economy has furthered the involvement of villagers in both agricultural and non-agricultural sectors as a way of surviving the tremendous and rapid economic changes. Thus, villagers are not exclusively tied to the land, nor do they think of land as their only means of subsistence.

Their link to the land does not purport a total identification as an ultimate livelihood – hence their falter in telling me the total size of their land.

This chapter explores the local practices adapted to both local ecology and the wider political economy of the central state, and it demonstrates villagers' strategies for coping with a period of radical transformation.

'Neither Workers, nor Peasants'

In 1965, when Nicolae Ceaușescu came to power, a new era began for Romanian industry. Ceaușescu decided to support industry, particularly heavy industry, rather than agriculture. In a Report of the Central Committee of the Romanian Communist party he wrote: 'the centre of our political party was and still is the industrialization of the country, particularly the development of heavy industry and machine industry .... Only by developing industry will we be able to overcome the historical backwardness encountered in the countryside in contrast with our cities'.[1] This was the period when mammoth industrial enterprises began: the steel factory in Galați, a city in the eastern part of Romania, is just one example of a gigantic construction meant to industrialize the country. In 1968, the automobile factory Dacia was built in Mioveni, a small town just 10 kilometres away from Dragomirești. Dacia represented the jewel in the crown of Romanian industry: the country's first 'national car' was built with the assistance of the French car factory Renault and the very first model of a Dacia car was in fact a copy of the Renault 8.[2] This policy changed, at national level, the size of the labour force working in agriculture. While in the late 1940s 74 per cent of population worked in the agricultural sector, in 1989 only 28 per cent did so.[3] The rest of the population was employed in industry and services. The outcome of this change in the national economic strategy was that much of the labour force was withdrawn from agriculture for the benefit of heavy industry.

Argeș County is representative of the evolution of Romania's socialist economy. While before World War II the entire area relied mostly on agriculture, from the1960s onwards it became one of the most industrialized counties in Romania.[4] The massive socialist investment in the car plants, one in Câmpulung – which built the first off-road Romanian car – and one in Mioveni (where the Dacia plant is located) have changed the economy and social structure of the county. Young men from Argeș County had the chance to escape agriculture and became workers in the industrial sector. The high salaries – even by national standards – better work conditions than those in agriculture and a radical improvement in social status were very attractive, especially for the young generation.[5] Young people from Dragomirești were no exception. The statistics speak for themselves: while in 1970 there were 1,150 members of the collective farm, in 1989 only 442 remained.[6] All others were employed mainly in industry and services. As the Dacia plant was so close to the village, some 15 kilometres away, most young villagers were employed there. The inhabited area's landscape changed radically in the 1970s and 1980s. Renovated houses that had been rebuilt using new construction materials such as brick replaced old wooden houses in the commune. Most houses added new rooms to the one or two rooms they traditionally had.

The fact that young villagers worked for Dacia does not mean they were not involved in agriculture at all. Although there was doubtless a 'feminization of agriculture' under socialism as Michael Cernea has put it – mostly women worked for the collective farm – men also gave a hand.[7] After the shift ended at Dacia, industrial workers came back home to their villages and turned into peasants. They would then help their parents or their wife to tend both the cropland that had to be worked for the collective farm as well as the subsidiary land.[8] The traditional men's work mowing the hay or hoeing the maize was still carried out by the young industrial workers, in their free time. From spring to autumn the period from 17:00 to 20:00 was dedicated to agricultural work whereas in the morning they worked for Dacia. 'It was not easy, but at least we never lacked food as was the case with urban people. We always had pigs, a cow and chickens,' one worker-peasant remembers. In a shortage economy, when food access was a national problem, having a secure food supply was important for the family.

In 1998 Renault decided to buy the plant, which it abandoned in the middle of 1970s for political reasons. The French company bought the plant after long and thorough negotiations with the Romanian neoliberal government (1996–2000). Immediately after, Renault started the restructuring of the labour force. More and more villagers from the Valley were dismissed. Nevertheless, a significant number of the villagers, all of them Romanians, escaped the restructuring net and continued to work for Renault. Thus, Dragomireştens' household economy still rests on two pillars: subsistence agriculture and the industrial wage. The worker-peasant economy is based on a perpetual fragile equilibrium and any disruption in either of the two economic domains can unbalance the household's livelihoods. In contrast with the farmer as presented in most postsocialist studies, the worker-peasant's agricultural practices, in response to wider economic changes and plans to reorganize the agrarian landscape, are different.[9]

A farmer, whether he or she produces for subsistence only or for the market, will concentrate all his or her working time on the land. The worker-peasant simply cannot afford such a luxury since his or her time is split between an industrial job and agricultural work.[10] The spouse who works in industry is a part-time agricultural worker. The heading of this section is a quotation from such a worker-peasant from Dragomirești, which condenses into one sentence his social identity, way of life and the dual economy of his household. He used to say: 'We are neither one hundred per cent peasants nor fully workers.' The worker-peasant can only do the work that is not socially acceptable for women, such as spreading dung on the field or work that requires physical strength such as mowing or building hayricks. The time he can afford to spend on agricultural work also dictates the type of crops the householders choose to grow. A worker-peasant household must diversify not only as insurance against the weather, or simply as risk mitigation but because of the lack of time available to invest in one single larger crop.[11] Cultivating then harvesting a single crop requires intensive labour for a certain period, which a worker-peasant family cannot usually spare. Diversifying the crop provides a safety net and risk avoidance, and means that agricultural work can be carried out over a longer time span.[12]

The worker-peasant cannot manage too large a plot of land either. Buying or selling land is not a viable option. Therefore it makes more sense to a worker-peasant to invest less money in a smaller plot rather than make bigger investments in larger plots as from the outset his agricultural production is meant for household consumption only. He is only interested in working a plot large enough to cover the household's needs. It is a simple calculation based on the capital the family has to invest in the next harvest and the available labour force. Part of the worker's wage is invested in agricultural overheads, such as ploughing. The labour force is provided both by members of the household and through work-exchange with neighbours, friends or siblings. Thus, rural ties remain essential for one who wants to be involved in a work-exchange network.[13]

I explore further worker-peasants' agricultural practices, focusing on the adaptation of these practices to local ecological conditions. Worker-peasants have returned to their traditional practices, which once helped them to respond to economic incertitude. Today, the same practices help them to respond to the central governments' plans for reorganizing society and landscape.

Agricultural Practices of Worker-Peasants

Hertha Müller, a German-Romanian novelist and Nobel Prize winner, once wrote: 'the past comes back as soon as one pays greater attention to the present.'[14] One could hardly find better words to describe the decollectivization process in former socialist countries. Land restitution has recreated, mostly independent of the legislators' intentions, the pre-socialist patchwork landscape. Although central governmental planners were looking to the present and the future when they issued the land reform laws, the past came back in unexpected ways. One of the features of the pre-socialist agricultural landscape was a fragmented land ownership structure. Land restitution to historical owners of the same plots as they had before collectivization reconstituted a historic property structure, only more fragmented. The long strips running across the commune from east to west, described in more detail in chapter 1, reappeared after decollectivization. Comprising all types of land cover, from forests, orchards and pastures on the eastern hills to cropland along the river, meadows and forests on the western hills, the land strips (*chingi*, 'belt' in Romanian) play the same role as in the pre-collectivization period: they ensure owners' access to various types of land. A map from 1906 representing the distribution of land ownership on one of the largest land holdings in the commune, belonging to an extended family from Vâlceni, shows the long strips crossing the river and continuing up onto the hilltops. Different land strips were owned by different members of the family but the practice of equal inheritance sustained over the generations led to a different situation after 1989: one single strip is now owned by two, three or even four members of the family. Thus, the interwar landscape became even more fragmented after the land reform. A bird's-eye view immediately reveals the drastic changes in the landscape: the consolidated land of the collective farm was split into myriads of small parcels, as the satellite image shows.

Illustration 6.1. Postsocialist Land Fragmentation in Dragomirești

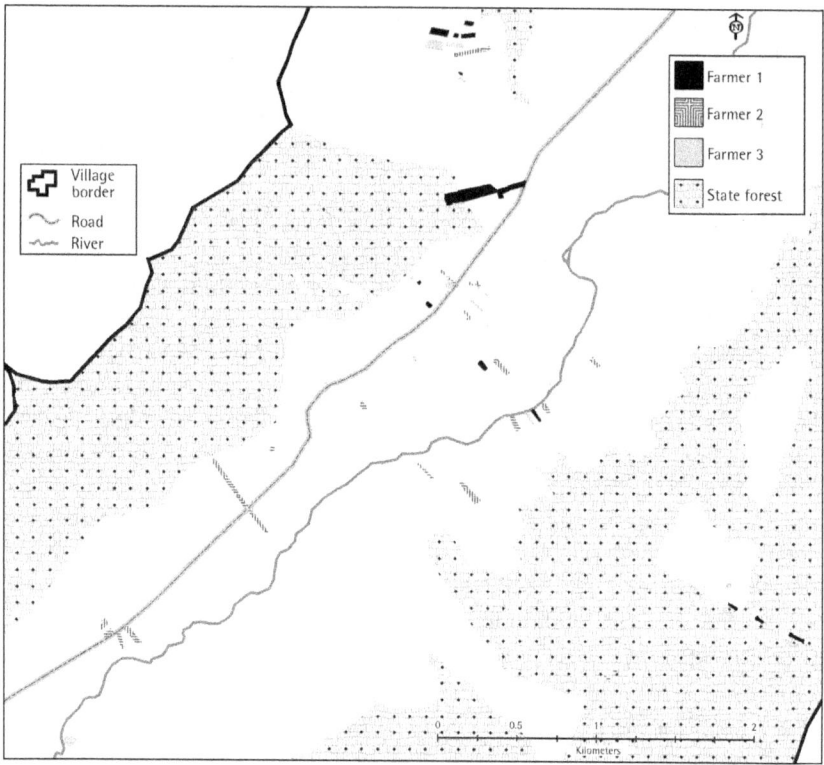

Figure 6.1. Participatory Map Showing Land Fragmentation in Dragomirești

The participatory mapping (see figure 6.1) also points up the structure of land property in Dragomirești. The map shows the land owned by three villagers, indicated by a colour (green, red and black). The map shows that one of the most fragmented patterns of land ownership in the commune belongs to the villager who owns the most land – represented in green: 7 hectares fragmented into twenty-one plots spread throughout the village's territory. From a legal point of view this villager is not the only owner of the land; his two sisters are co-owners as they inherited the land from their father jointly. Nevertheless, as our villager is the only one living in the commune, the two sisters decided to let him manage the land; they require only some produce every autumn (cheese, meat and potatoes). Statistically, villagers own on average 0.8 hectares in Dragomirești village, and in Costești village 1 hectare while in Vâlceni it is 1.7 hectares; the land is distributed relatively evenly among the households. From this point of view the statement of Chris Hann that 'few ruptures in the history of human land tenure have matched the disruption caused by collectivization and decollectivization' is true for Dragomirești, up to a point.[15] Decollectivization has recreated a patchwork landscape, which though messy is useful for a community which makes a living from both farm and off-farm jobs.

The relatively equal land ownership in postsocialist times is due partly though not exclusively to the historical pattern of land distribution. History recurs in unexpected ways and shapes present actions. Before collectivization, not all plots were officially registered at the mayor's office, especially when one bought land from another member of one's family. In this case, no official papers were issued although everyone in the village knew about the transaction. Such transactions, which avoid paperwork and fees to the notary, seem to have been quite numerous and were eased by the absence of a cadastral map.[16] Inheritance by verbal agreement was also quite common until the beginning of the twentieth century, again avoiding the intrusion of official laws and state offices. *Cu limbă de moarte*, meaning literally 'the last words before dying' was a widespread practice of assigning land to one's children.[17] Thus, during collectivization it was easier for Walachian villagers to 'hide land', that is to declare less land than one owned. In those turbulent times, this was a way of getting out of political trouble. Nevertheless, in 1991 all villagers claimed the land they knew their parents owned, regardless of whether the records were official or unofficial. The LLC and the mayor's office received several written complaints which had as common ground those plots of land that were not given back because of the lack of official papers to prove ownership. In fact, precisely because those few well-off peasants did not have all their lands restored to them, the postsocialist land ownership distribution in Dragomirești is relatively even.

The messy aspect of land ownership and land fragmentation created fluid boundaries between plots. Most land conflicts in the commune stem from allegations of trespassing. The boundary between two plots of arable land is a small ditch 10 centimetres wide and 10 centimetres deep, called *răzor*. One plot is separated from the next plot by a wooden stick thrust in the soil at the edge of the răzor. When the tractors plough the land, the răzor is easily destroyed and the wooden stick disappears. Often, the tractor cannot stay within the boundary of each plot simply because some plots are narrower than the tractor's harrow. The real problem arises when the two neighbours plant different crops: inevitably one plot holder would lose at least part of his crop if he or she has sown seed before the other plot holder ploughs his or her land. Sometimes, if a villager considers that his or her neighbour owns more land than he or she is entitled to, he or she will simply move the stick a few centimetres onto his or her neighbour's land. In a few seconds the plot expands by half a metre along the entire land strip.

Fluid boundaries are also an issue concerning pastures, even if some of them are fenced. In one case, a villager called Arsene moved a wooden fence a few metres over onto his neighbour's pasture. Arsene was the new owner of the pasture, which he had recently received from his grandmother. The property title indicated he owned more land than he had actually received. He argued that because his grandmother is old she had not been able to attend when the decollectivized land was being measured and given back to entitled owners. Thus, his grandmother was tricked by her neighbour, who now owns more land than is stated on her property title. Arsene's neighbour – Lucia – argued that she knows very well where her land's boundaries lie as she remembers that her parents planted three rows of plum trees in order to separate the two pastures. The plum trees, Lucia argued, were uprooted by the collective farms; 'But look,' she indicated to me, 'you can still see the holes left by the three plum tree rows.' Lucia agreed that Arsene's grandmother was not present when the agricultural engineer measured the land but this was because they had good relations and the old lady trusted Lucia's honesty. The quarrel took place amid shoving, screaming and threats to each other with the police officer, agricultural officer and the agricultural engineer passively attending. I should say that the plot under dispute was just merely 10 square metres of pasture of rather poor quality. The quarrel was concluded by both parties agreeing on two things: that no one knows exactly where the boundary between the two plots lies and that recalculating the two plots is absolutely necessary. This type of conflict for insignificant land plots is quite common in Dragomireşti; similar conflict was observed in a Transylvanian village by Verdery.[18] Such quarrels over small pieces of land with no significant market value are motivated by multiple factors – from kinship ties to personal identity.[19] In addition to these considerations, relevant to landownership in Dragomireşti, is the importance of agricultural land for maintaining the household economic balance. A worker-peasant household can better survive the turmoil of postsocialist economic changes if their food supply is secured by working small plots of land.

The central governments conceived land reform as an avenue to a future improved economy and landscape. Private land ownership had to be the engine of the capitalist transformations in Romanian agriculture whereas the new landowners had to be the transmission belt of these changes. Faced with economic uncertainties, villagers have rediscovered old agricultural practices such as intercropping, ploughing the land with interwar iron ploughs, replacing the chemical fertilizer with manure and the plantation of non-hybrid seeds.

In the early 1990s, land fragmentation was already a visible physical feature of the cropland in Dragomireşti. The agricultural machines were sold off to the former state farm director who took them to the plains in the south, where there are larger arable surfaces more suitable for using the large tractors and combines than the small pieces of cropland found in hilly regions. The few old tractors that remained in the village tend to be used for ploughing the cropland and for hauling the trunks from the forest. There is no agricultural machinery in the village that could hoe the weeds, spray chemicals or harvest the crops. The intercropping practised by villagers, since decollectivization, is in any case incompatible with machinery. The villagers of Dragomireşti know from older residents that before collectivization, when they hoed with weed hooks and harvested with their hands, maize was planted together with pumpkins (*Cucurbita maxima*) and beans (*Phaseolus vulgaris*). To every two or three maize 'nests' (*cuiburi*) villagers add one or two pumpkin seeds and two or three beans.[20] Peasants keep the most 'beautiful' pumpkin seeds and beans from the previous harvest in order to sow them in subsequent years. Nobody in the village buys hybrid seeds anymore simply because such seed enterprises have been privatized and hybrid seeds are now expensive. Buying hybrid seeds would make sense for a household interested in achieving higher production levels, which would be partially intended for sale. A worker-peasant has no time to spend in a market place or the incentive to do it; the investment would in this case be higher but would not make sense in terms of the strategy of the household, which strives to maintain the balance between subsistence agriculture and industrial wage-earning.

Using a tractor has become a sort of luxury for some peasants. The tractor owner cannot afford to reduce his charges per hectare simply because the tractors are old, the spare parts are very expensive and because gasoline prices are soaring. Sometimes, tractor owners wait months after ploughing the land to get paid. There are tricks that enable them to gain more money per hectare, one of which is to set the harrow to plough 10 centimetres deep in the ground. The best depth for ploughing is around 25 centimetres. If the harrow is set for 25 centimetres then the tractor consumes more gasoline and the time spent in the field is greater. Of course, ploughing more shallowly means the furrow is incompletely turned and less well shredded, with negative consequences for the next harvest.[21] Thus, some landowners have reverted to using the old iron ploughs pulled by horses. In one particular case, a plough has had its own adventure, spanning from the precollectivization period to the postsocialist era: it was bought in the interwar period by one of the better-off peasants and it was the pinnacle of agrarian technique at that time. At the beginning of the 1950s, when it was clear that there was no escape from the collectivization steamroller, this peasant buried the iron plough in his backyard, where it stayed in the ground for forty years. The day after Ceauşescu was chased away, that peasant's son unearthed the plough. After a thorough reconditioning he sold it to one of his godsons who still uses it. Thus, it is not unusual to see villagers out in the fields in spring and autumn, ploughing with an interwar iron plough pulled by one horse.

Once the villagers regained ownership of their lands, they stopped adding chemical fertilizers, which became more expensive, especially after 1996 when the chemical factories were privatized. While the collective farms used pesticide and fertilizers for obtaining large crops villagers have neither incentive nor money to spend on such things. The price was one reason but there were other reasons as well for not buying fertilizer. Buying fertilizer means, as Donald Worster has pointed out, dependency on an outside, remote agent.[22] This is not part of the economic strategy of a peasant in general, much less of the worker-peasant with no interest in marketing his or her agricultural production. It is not just the money a household would need to spend (although this is an important issue) but the independence of the household that counts. Thus, most of the land is now fertilized with natural fertilizers (manure). The statistics speak for themselves: at the commune level the mayor's office spreads 5 tons of chemical fertilizers on 100 hectares of pasture whereas householders use 2,000 tons of manure and no chemical fertilizer at all.[23] Nevertheless, several more affluent peasants bought several bags of chemical fertilizers but they do not know how much to use or how to spread it. One day I witnessed a discussion between two villagers about how much fertilizer they ought to use per hectare. Neither of them really knew and they decided to ask people who had worked for the collective farm, hoping they would know how much and when to spread it on the field.

Intercropping does not represent just an approach to agriculture that became obsolete during the socialist period and has since been rediscovered and put into practice as a means of dealing with economic insecurities. Villagers have based their economic strategy on pre-collectivization knowledge and agricultural experiences. Intercropping has several benefits. First of all, intercropping makes sense as long as cropland is scarce in the commune. Planting a plot with pumpkins or with beans only and a separate plot with maize would make no economic sense. Not only do the three plants grow well together; mono-species plantation, if the management is suboptimal, may be subject to pests and diseases.[24] Second, maize in particular consumes a high quantity of nutrients such as phosphorus, potassium or nitrogen from the soil. Beans planted together with maize fixes the nitrogen in the soil, helping the maize to develop. Besides, intermingling growth of legume and cereals, especially maize and beans, enhances the productivity of the plants through mobilization of phosphorus in the soil.[25] The chemical reactions triggered in the soil by phosphorus mobilization feed not only the plants but enhance the soil qualities as well. Feeding the soil, not just the plants – advice often forgotten equally by farmers and policy makers – is part of the intercropping benefits.[26] Second, intercropping is a complex agricultural system that involves various types of crops, agricultural practices and animal husbandry. Maize serves as a side dish (the famous Romanian *mămăliga* –

polenta) replacing bread but it is also used for feeding pigs and chickens. Pumpkin serves as food for the pigs and chickens while bean stew is a dish much appreciated in Romania. The pig is an easy animal to keep, does not occupy too much space in the backyard, is cheap to rear and is the main source of meat for local villagers.[27] Few households do not raise pigs in their backyards. The fact that the number of pigs raised by villagers decreased only slightly from 660 heads in 1989 to 599 in 2004 attests to the importance of this animal in the villagers' diet.[28] In turn, pigs' manure, along with cows', serves as natural fertilizer for the cropland. Raw pig manure, along with urine and litter from the barns is, in fact, quite poisonous to the environment.[29] Drawing on an intimate knowledge of domestic pig biology and a very old relationship between this animal and villagers, the latter know how to transform a dangerous waste into a valuable resource. Villagers collect the soil with a shovel and get rid of the liquid. Then the soil is mixed with cow manure, in a special mixture of one-third pig manure and two-thirds cow manure, left to dry in the open and only then spread on the fields. This practice proves ecologically sustainable and economically inventive. It neutralizes poisonous natural elements, which otherwise should have been disposed of elsewhere, causing environmental pollution, and transforms them into an economic asset.[30] Crops, animals and agricultural practices are bound up together and represent a household strategy for coping with an unfriendly economic milieu.

After World War II, along with mechanization and fertilization of agriculture, the use of hybrids became part of modern agriculture in both capitalist and socialist countries. The development of a seed industry led to a genetic uniformity of crops but also to a higher predictability of production levels and a more standardized quality.[31] Industrial agriculture is practised on large tracts of land and it is based on intensive agricultural practices such as controlling pests, soil preparation and large irrigation systems. Consequently, plant breeding for this type of agriculture is directed towards maximizing yields.[32] Collective farms used hybrid maize seeds since they aimed at higher production levels – not just for economic reasons; there was also an ideological imperative to prove the superiority of the collective property regime and of the socialist organization of economy and society over the capitalist system. After 1990, the hybrid seed factories were privatized and the new plants imposed higher prices. Thus, villagers gave up investing in such items and started to use the seeds from the previous harvest. There were advantages and disadvantages of such a system. The advantages were that villagers no longer paid for the seeds as they preserved their own best seeds from one year to another; they also refused to be dependent on remote hybrid seed producers or subject to the soaring prices set by these producers. The disadvantages were that the maize cobs were smaller, with fewer maize kernels, and each plant produces only one maize cob, not two as the hybrids do.[33] The hybrid grows more uniformly than the local crop, all informants agreed. Thus, the production per hectare is now lower than in socialist times. But the most significant change is that while the hybrid maize produced a predictable quantity per hectare – if correctly managed – the maize yield from local seeds is totally unpredictable. No villager, regardless of how knowledgeable he or she is, can predict the quantity of maize per hectare in these circumstances. Finally, the hybrid maize is more sensitive to pests and needs more careful management and investment, whereas the local 'postsocialist maize' seems to be more resistant to pests and does not require much work and attention.

The genetic uniformity and the narrowing of the genetic base of modern agriculture or, on the other hand, the development of local crop varieties better suited to local soil, clime and ecosystem are all ideas unknown to Dragomireștens.[34] Their actions were motivated by the soaring prices of the hybrids and the need to maintain their household's status quo (by securing both food and an industrial wage).

Local land use has also changed significantly as well as the plants cultivated on it. The most severe changes relate to the use of arable land: while in 1989 there were 546 hectares of arable land, in 2004 there were only 409 hectares. In contrast, pastures and meadows expanded in size from 644 hectares in 1989 to 777 hectares in 1995. I have shown in the previous chapter what actually happened regarding the pastures. I only want to point out here that pastures have expanded at the expense of the arable land.

Alongside changes in land use, some plants were no longer cultivated: two-row barley (*Hordeum distichum*) and barley (*Hordeum sativum*) completely disappeared while potatoes were cultivated in a smaller area. The collective farm of Dragomirești produced 209 tons of barley and two-row barley in 1989 but villagers stopped cultivating this plant in 1993. Barley and two-row barley are especially used for making beer, an alcoholic beverage very popular in postsocialist Romania.[35] Nevertheless, the new private beer producers most likely will look to buy large amounts of barley produced by the new private farms and not to negotiate with small producers such as those in Dragomirești. Similarly, the production of potatoes, once the pride of Dragomireștens' collective farm, has dropped from 1,789 tons in 1989 to 450 tons in 2004.[36] There are multiple explanations for this massive change. Potatoes require more work and attention from the landowner than, let us say, maize. The potato plant is more vulnerable to pests and it requires the application of pesticides at certain stages of its life cycle and that of the weeds that plague it.[37] Cultivating potatoes requires more time invested in agricultural labour and more investments than does maize. It made more sense, after 1990, to cultivate potatoes on small plots just for domestic consumption as long as the worker-peasant had no time to spend in a market place selling his agricultural produce. The production of maize has also decreased from 473 tons in 1989 to 283 tons in 2004. We may easily infer that the use of local seeds, the cultivation on small plots, the use of mechanized work only for ploughing and the use of manure only as fertilizer reduced the maize production by half.[38] However, without denying all these facts and data a complementary, if not an alternative, interpretation could be that peasants simply chose a strategy that suits them better. Whereas producing for the market was not part of the worker-peasant strategy, the villagers adapted their agricultural practices to their own economic needs. Access to the market, lack of credits and support from the banks, soaring prices of agricultural inputs and the political economy of the postsocialist state must all have played an important role in changing agricultural practices. However, it cannot be denied that the villagers' household strategy, based on knowledge of local ecology, has adapted perfectly to the new economic and political milieu. All these agricultural practices led to a decrease in agricultural production – an outcome that was unexpected and undesired by central governments. Instead of transforming themselves into a capitalist machine of agricultural production, villagers from Dragomirești rediscovered old agrarian practices that were more suitable for their own economic needs. This return to the past is also evident when one turns one's attention to the local orchards.

Orchards and Țuica

As a character in Andreï Makine's book, *Once Upon a Time on the Banks of Amur,* says, alcohol can be a way to forget the past and avoid thinking about the future. This is not the reason why most Dragomireșteans grow fruit trees and produce țuica. Here, this famous alcoholic beverage has historical roots and cultural significance. As I have detailed in chapter 1, until the beginning of the twentieth century villagers from this region grew different types of plums almost exclusively for producing țuica. Just a few of them sold the fruits on the market, either dried or fresh. Under pressure from the local bureaucrats who accused villagers of alcoholism, people from the region started to plant types of fruit trees that produced fruits more suitable for eating fresh. Under socialism, orchards were extended in the county and the types of fruits also improved. Despite the fact that it was strictly forbidden to produce artisanal țuica during socialism, villagers continued to distil it at home in improvised small distilleries. It is not that locals could not survive without alcohol; țuica plays a fundamental cultural role within the community.[39] For all religious celebrations as well as family events such as baptisms, weddings and funerals, țuica is a customary beverage. Whereas in other parts of Romania wine is the main beverage used for these religious feasts, in this area țuica plays a central role. It is common for a family organizing *pomana* (meaning literally charity), a meal with the purpose of offering food and drinks to the dead souls, to have extra attendees as the țuica they would provide on such an occasion is of superior quality.[40] Similarly, those who are well known for having good quality țuica are always invited to parties; such people are admired for the fine quality of their beverage, and their țuica is prized.

But what is meant by a 'good țuica'? It is surely a matter of technique and knowledge, judging how long to distil the marc, how hot to make the fire burn and when to refresh the marc. The difference between a fruity țuica and a sour one can depend on a few drops of alcohol poured in the vessel which collects the beverage: refreshing the marc too soon could mean a waste of good quality marc; distilling the marc too much could mean that a few drops of sour alcohol poured into the collecting vessel results in the whole quantity being spoiled and having to be thrown away. It also has to do with the quantity and quality of marc one has at one's disposal.[41] A villager owing half a hectare of plum trees only uses the fruits which are harvested directly from the tree, ignoring the fruits which have fallen on the ground, some of them already rotten. A villager owning few trees would first pick up the fallen fruits, regardless of whether they are rotten or not, then harvest the fruits in the trees. More fruits mean more marc, thus more țuica produced. The quality of the marc in these two cases is significantly different; thus the quality of the țuica will be different. It is not thus accidental that those villagers owning the largest orchards produce the best quality țuica whereas poorer villagers produce țuica of a more modest quality. Knowing all these points, after a few months in the village I was able to say in advance if a villager I was going to interview would offer me a good or a poor quality țuica (they always offered me țuica). I was rarely mistaken.

Moreover, there was a radical change in the types of plum trees cultivated after 1990. At decollectivization, the real prize was not, as in other parts of rural Romania, the cropland but the orchards. The collective farms made large investments in their orchards a few years before 1989. Therefore, the first years after decollectivization were very good for producing țuica. The collective farm planted high quality plums (*Prunus domestica*), mostly for export. For instance, the types called Tuleu Gras, Renclod Althan or Stanley were perfectly suited for fresh consumption as they have large fruits (over 40 grams each) with small stones that are easy to remove.[42] These plum types were very demanding in terms of work and investment, though: the collective farm had to use fertilizers and pesticides at least four to five times per year and thoroughly clean and maintain the trees.[43] A few years after decollectivization the plum trees started to dry out as a consequence of poor maintenance and virtually no investment in these high quality orchards. Villagers planted new trees but this time, new types were preferred. Instead of high quality plums, suitable for fresh consumption but also for industrial processing, villagers replanted old species that are more robust but of poorer quality. The fruit is smaller and not as tasty but does not need to be sprayed with pesticides and fertilizers, which after 1989 became too expensive for the villagers' pockets. Production levels before and after decollectivization, also differ significantly. Before, every single year the orchards produced virtually the same amount of fruit; after, the trees bore fruits every two or three years. There were years, after 1989, when there was no fruit produced at all. As one informant told me, referring to the apple harvest, 'In 2003 we had so many apples that we could feed the cows with them. This year [2004] we won't taste apple at all.' It is a similar situation with plums. The villagers' strategy, once again, makes sense. They do not produce fruits for the market but only for țuica and their personal consumption (for making jam). In order to produce for the market they would need to make large investments in storage facilities – the fruits are easily damaged if not stored correctly – and in transport; besides, one member of the family would need to remain in the market place for days, which a worker-peasant family could not afford. Thus, returning to a tradition that predates the World War I period made perfect sense for villagers of Dragomirești.

Market at the Front Door

Land fragmentation in Dragova has historical roots as I have shown in chapter 1 and current land ownership distribution reflects the *status quo*. Out of 160 households only 20 households do not own any land at all while 150 households own between 1.5 and 4 hectares. Only 10 households own between 4 and 6.2 hectares. Compared to land ownership in Dragomirești, land ownership distribution in Dragova is quite different. The spread of parcels per landowner is not as drastic as in Dragomirești but there is virtually no landowner with fewer than three parcels. Nevertheless, one should take into account that the local economy is based on animal husbandry and rural tourism and land means almost exclusively pasture or meadow. Besides, the rugged geography of Dragova makes some plots hardly usable.

I have presented in the previous chapter quite a pessimistic view of the fate of the pastures during postsocialism. Although Dragova has lost pastures that have been transformed into built up areas for tourism purposes, the pastures that remained were quite well maintained. While in Dragomirești it is mostly Rudari who contribute to pasture maintenance, in Dragova the villagers take a turn working the pastures. Many of them have animals so they have a direct interest in maintaining high quality communal pastures. Whereas sheep are sent to high altitude pastures, up on the mountain, the cows are grazed on the islaz. The figures prove locals' interest in animal husbandry. Milk production increased from 15,290 hectolitres in 1989 to 17,375 hectolitres in 1995, although the number of cows decreased from 1,230 heads in 1989 to 832 in 2004. In turn, the number of sheep and goats increased from 540 to 1,790 in the same time span.[44]

There are at least four reasons for the increase in milk production: the affluence of tourists visiting the commune has created a market right on the villagers' doorstep. Indeed, tourists do not visit Dragova just for the scenery but also to consume some of the famous smoked cheese, fermented cheese kept in oak bark or local sheep pastrami. Some guesthouse owners are not involved at all in keeping animals, so they buy these products from those who rear animals. Tourists themselves also buy these products to take home while some people come from the nearby cities just to buy them. A second reason for keeping animals and increasing the production is that villagers do not pay any taxes to the state for this activity. Except for those who sell dairy products officially in their own guesthouses or those who provide these products to the guesthouses – in which case the guesthouse owner has to have documentation to prove the origin of the products served to his or her guests – all others sell their produce without having any official documents. This means that the entire income remains in the household. It is not unusual to see people standing right in front of their own door selling cheese and asking visitors if they are interested in buying other dairy products. They prefer this type of commerce to the alternative – selling their products in the marketplaces in Rucăr (a larger village 5 kilometres away from Dragova) or in Câmpulung, a town 33 kilometres away from their village. If they do so, they need to pay taxes to the marketplace administration and further taxes to the state. Instead of searching for their customers they wait for the customers to come to them.

A third reason for increasing milk production is that this is an important source of their income, along with having guests in their private rooms. Almost all villagers I talked to kept animals during socialism but few of them had an industrial wage. In contrast to Dragomirești where most villagers have a pension from Dacia, villagers from Dragova do not have a regular pension. Thus, in order to survive, villagers need to keep animals and sell dairy products. Finally, a fourth reason has to do with the fact that villagers in Dragova are ensnared in a barter system. The ecological conditions they live in make growing cereals or vegetables impossible. Instead of buying them from the market, they developed an exchange commodity barter system with the lowland villagers from southern Romania, which continued throughout the communist period and survived it. Bartering has historical roots in the commune. Every autumn, cars (which replaced the old horse-drawn wagons from the interwar period) full of maize, potatoes and sometimes wheat flour are unloaded in Dragovans' backyards in exchange for firewood and dairy products. Dragovans thus have to produce enough dairy for barter and for selling to tourists.

Earning a living from selling dairy products is neither an easy task nor an inexpensive one. During socialism villagers earned a lot of money from selling sheep wool and lambs, mainly because the state was involved in buying these products. The postsocialist state has withdrawn from any economic participation in agriculture, so every shepherd has to get by as best he or she can. A shepherd from Dragova outlined the following calculations to me:

> Wool is where you should make a profit from sheep. Think a bit! A sheep produces lamb and milk. But selling lambs once a year [for Easter] and some kilograms of cheese just cover the costs of the sheep. From September to April (here the winter is very tough and very long) I just feed the animal without any gain. Let's count it up: you feed the sheep 300 grams of maize and around 2 kilograms of hay in one day. That means, 2,000 lei for the maize, and 10,000 lei for the hay.[45] That means 12,000 lei per day. If you take into account the fact that I keep the sheep in the village for 100 days during winter, then I spend about 1,200,000 lei for one sheep. How can I get this money back? Not to mention the hazards of disease or miscarriage. In the last case you could lose 20 per cent of the lambs. Having sheep is not like having a cow, which gives you milk during winter so that you still cover some of your expenses. Then, selling a lamb is a tricky business. If Easter[46] falls in early April, then you are screwed! The lamb is very young and weighs around 2 kilograms. But if Easter is in May then you can earn good money. One living lamb (*in viu*) fetched 700,000 lei [around €20] last year.

This excerpt shows not only the difficulty for animal keepers seeking to ensure their livelihood but the thorough calculations a shepherd has to make in order to earn a living. Easter is so important for shepherds because this is the only time when Romanians eat lamb, which is a ritual meal. It is thus a perfect opportunity for shepherds to cash in, as this is their only chance in the year to sell lambs.

In addition to the economic difficulties, animal keepers have to comply with state bureaucracy governing food safety. Under EU requirements new environmental and food safety provisions and norms have been introduced in Romania.[47] Until 2000, when the Romanian government started negotiations to join the EU, shepherds from throughout Romania sold their lambs in ad hoc marketplaces on the bare land at the margins of the large cities.

Often, they also slaughtered the animals there so the customers – living in apartment buildings and totally inexperienced in such activities – would be more easily convinced to buy. After the negotiations on agriculture had begun, Romanian state bureaucrats established laws banning shepherds from selling their products in open and informal spaces. They have to take their animals to a slaughterhouse and need written approval from a veterinarian in order to prove the animal is healthy and not a carrier of a transmissible disease. This means the sheep owner needs to pay a significant amount of money before knowing how many animals he or she will sell. Further, the meat seller has to acquire a producer's certificate (which costs one million lei – around €30), which gives him the right to sell on the market. While local authorities usually turned a blind eye to such 'traditional' practices, the national government and the national police proved to be more vigilant in catching shepherds who break the new laws. It is thus understandable that animal keepers prefer the market on their own doorstep to the city marketplace for selling their products.

However, animal keepers cannot totally escape the scrutiny of the state. Unlike in Dragomirești, in Dragova all animals are ear tagged – a first sign of the commoditization of animal products. In Dragomirești, the milk produced by cows is either turned into cheese or partially consumed in the house, whereas another small portion is sold in the village. There is no taxation system nor is the milk registered with a state office, so tags are pointless: meat and dairy products are consumed locally with no involvement – or acknowledgement – by a state office. By contrast, Dragovans sell animal products to tourists and people outside the commune, hence the need to obey at least some of the national rules governing food safety. The tag contains vital information about the animal and registers it, making it possible to track a potentially sick animal and to control potential diseases. Ear tags are absolutely compulsory for any animal keeper who intends to sell dairy products outside the commune. While local bureaucrats from the mayor's office may refrain from levying taxes for informal tourism or for selling dairy products in front of the house, they would not dare disregard European rules on food security.

There are several big players in the commune who produce dairy mostly for the national market. Those few who own large flocks of sheep do not keep their animals in the village but up in the mountain in custom-built facilities. Thus, their animals are not registered with the Dragova mayor's office as being on the commune's territory. One of them is the former secretary of the mayor's office; let us call him Severin. He comes from an old, rich family from the village; through land reform laws he received back 9 hectares of forest and ten hectares of pasture. Together with his sister he owns 2,000 sheep and 14 cows and produces 1.5 tons of cheese per week. Severin has six shepherds who take care of the flock and hires seasonal workers to mow the pasture. He sells 75 per cent of his cheese to a middleman who offers him a decent price. It is not a good price, Severin emphasized, but it is a predictable income. A certain quantity of cheese is sold in the Rucăr marketplace for a much better price but he is stuck there for days. Trying to diversify his dairy production sales, Severin made a good deal with several Saudi firms that import rams. Finally, a small quantity of cheese is sold to guests at his guesthouse. It is important to note that he obeys the national regulations on food safety which specify that a guesthouse owner can sell to his or her guests animal products he or she produces. If he or she owned a restaurant only, he or she would not have been able to sell these products. This regulation, issued under EU pressure as well, is meant to increase the accountability of small meat and dairy producers to the veterinary doctor. It is easier for the veterinarian, the only representative of the state at local level concerning food safety, to check guesthouses than the many small local restaurants spread all over the area.

Needless to say, most villagers systematically avoid these rules and regulations. Only those few sheep owners such as Severin, who are involved in long-distance commerce, respect the state rules concerning food safety. Small-scale animal keepers consider these norms and regulations abusive and an intrusion of the state into their business. These regulations are set without consulting the producers and are introduced by a state that does not support them in any way. They therefore feel perfectly entitled to dodge the state laws and taxes. Cheating the state by avoiding taxes and regulations that try to control their economic activity is a customary practice in this area. The socialist state with its well-organized control apparatus, which was more prone to using violence of any kind, nevertheless failed to impose strict control over shepherds' commerce. Shepherds' marginality within the socialist system conferred on them power and enabled them to develop special skills in avoiding the state control over their products.[48] The postsocialist state, with its inefficient and often corrupt bureaucracy, is even more unlikely to be able to impose its rules on the shepherds.

Comparing the two groups of villagers in Dragova, one can see that the animal keepers do not adhere to the projected plan of development devised by the postsocialist state to modernize the economy and make the environment more accountable to the national state. They avoid paying taxes to the state and eschew norms of food safety regulations. Those few sheep owners who have big flocks are the only persons who follow the plans of the national state and justify the belief of central planners in a successful reorganization of society and the natural environment.

Fragmented Landscapes

Even if land fragmentation is not as drastic as in Dragomirești, it still leaves a visible mark on the Dragovan landscape. There are though several differences between the two villages, which could mostly be accounted for by their ecological differences. In Dragomirești, the cropland is highly fragmented both in terms of ownership and land use, which means that each owner, or group of owners, have to make decisions about which plants to cultivate.[49] The decision is dictated by the household's economic needs and depends on the available workforce in the family, the available capital and the household strategy for the immediate future. This is one of the main reasons for the patchwork appearance of the cropland in Dragomirești: a strip of land cultivated with maize lies between one cultivated with wheat and another one cultivated with alfalfa (*Medicago sativa*). By contrast, the ecology of Dragova does not permit many choices of land use other than pasture. This difference has repercussions on the value of the land as well. Whereas it does not make sense to buy or to sell a narrow strip of cropland so that the land value significantly decreases in Dragomirești, land fragmentation in Dragova increases the value of those plots with good access to the main roads. If an owner of a well-situated plot wants to sell it to someone who intends to build a guesthouse, fragmented ownership works *in favour* of both the seller and the buyer. Someone who buys land to build a guesthouse does not need more than one-half hectare; 1 hectare would be too much. Imagine the following scenario. There are two sellers, one offering 1 hectare – a consolidated plot of land – and another one who owns 1 hectare split into two plots. A buyer who only wants half of a hectare will most probably make a transaction with the seller who has two plots. Having 1 hectare of land for sale implies first the cost of employing a cadastre expert. The cadastre expert measures the plot and makes two cadastral maps, one for each half hectare. Without a map the transaction would not be possible – and one should remember that there is no cadastral map of the countryside in Walachia and Moldova. If there are several owners of that plot, the seller has first to individualize his or her plot, which means extra costs.[50] Only after all these multiple legal actions would a landowner be able to sell his or her share of the hectare of land. His or her profit would be, in this case, smaller than that of an owner with two plots. In Dragova, land fragmentation is a blessing rather than a curse.

The land market in the two villages supports this interpretation. In Dragomirești, a commune with a population of 2,852 and 819 households, 111 transactions were registered between 2001 and 2004. Of this number, 45 sales concerned land within the village, mostly houses and their courtyards, and only 66 concerned agricultural lands, including cropland, pastures, meadows and orchards. In Dragova, a commune with a population of 1,057 and 743 buildings (this includes the guesthouses), there were 185 transactions registered at the mayor's office (in the same period of time) relating to agricultural land, residential houses and their backyards. The fact that the land market is more buoyant in Dragova is due to the value of the land. Only land of some value is traded; no transactions in land with little value can be made, as there are no buyers. The land is valuable because one can buy it and build a guesthouse, a lucrative enterprise. This is a correct interpretation but there is more to it than this. A fragmented cropland such as the one in Dragomireşti, with several plots spread out across the village, is not very attractive to the two potential categories of buyer: locals, most of them worker-peasants, and outsiders. A worker-peasant generally has enough land to work with his family so he is not necessarily interested in buying new lands. An outsider would be interested in acquiring land only for doing business. At any rate, the fragmented cropland cannot be used for cash crops. In contrast, owning three to four plots – pasture or meadow – spread around Dragova's territory is not an unattractive proposition. Despite the rugged geography, a buyer will be able to mow the hay on one plot at a time. Besides, the ultimate product for a Dragovan peasant, dairy produce, is more likely to be sold quickly and advantageously, thus repaying the efforts of the landowner. A fragmented cropland cannot be used for anything else but subsistence farming; a fragmented pasture can still be used for raising animals and selling dairy products.

Fragmentation and Its Effects in Postsocialist Europe

Sabates-Wheeler's general picture of Romanian land reform shows that one of its main outcomes was land fragmentation. Far from being exceptions, Dragomireşti and Dragova represent just two examples among many that could be provided if exploring the agricultural situation in Romania. Forty per cent of Romanian landowners have less than 1 hectare of land, while 48.5 per cent have between 1 and 5 hectares. She presents more detailed statistics on land fragmentation: the average farm size in Romania is 2.3 hectares, while the average plot size is 0.43 hectare. On average, a farm has 4.5 parcels of land. There are 4.7 million farms and 40 million parcels in Romania.[51]

There are few things on which scholars of postsocialism are agreed but land fragmentation is definitely one of them. Land fragmentation is a problem encountered by most postsocialist countries in Eastern Europe. Of the various forms of land ownership, such as co-operatives, state farms and private, this last category is the one I refer to in this section. However, despite the variability of legal forms of land ownership throughout Eastern

Europe a common feature exists throughout this area: the coexistence of a large group of small landowners with a small group of large landowners.[52] According to van Dijk, Romania and Bulgaria are the countries with the most severe land fragmentation; more than half of all agricultural land is divided into units smaller than 2 hectares. The Republic of Moldova is another striking case: the average size of peasant farms is 0.65 hectare and many landowners use hand tools to farm. Land fragmentation is usually linked to subsistence farming. The case of Moldova is a fairly classic one: one-third of landowners reported that they never sold agricultural products in the market.[53] Albania is a strikingly similar case: through land reform 700,000 hectares of land was distributed to 470,000 households, which resulted in a highly fragmented agricultural landscape. More than 90 per cent of the holdings are divided into several parcels.[54] Thomas Sikor and his colleagues have calculated that the average holding consists of four to five parcels, each parcel measuring an average of 0.3 hectare. The authors show the consequences of land fragmentation in Albania: agricultural production has collapsed in this country contributing, along with other economic phenomena, to widespread poverty.[55]

In Russia, the reorganization of agriculture from 1992 to 1994 triggered the distribution of equal shares of land to rural dwellers.[56] One of the outcomes of land reform was that in 2003 there were 16 million household plots on 6.5 million hectares. The average size of a Russian plot is 0.4 hectare. The hope of central reformers that private farmers would become significant food producers for the country was not fulfilled: the disparities between the price of agricultural products and the agricultural inputs, the lack of any credit for small landholders, and problems accessing a market – even when there was something to sell – led to increased poverty in rural areas. The benefits of land reform have not convinced people, especially the young and skilled ones, to remain in rural areas. According to Stephen Wegren, an agricultural economist, Russian rural areas are plagued by the demographic decline as many settlements become deserted, and by poverty – 60 per cent of the rural population of Russia have an income below the official minimum subsistence level.[57]

Postsocialist Vietnam experiences land fragmentation as well.[58] The whole country is split into 75 million land plots with an average of seven to eight parcels per farming household. Hung et al. shows that this extreme fragmentation started with the *Doi Moi* land reform in 1986, although other causes such as population growth, the inheritance system or state policies could also be responsible. Setting aside many details of the Vietnamese case, land fragmentation is equally a product of land reform and the free choice exercised by villagers, and carries heavy costs. Land fragmentation seems to explain, at least partially, the misfortune that has befallen that country's agriculture: it impedes higher productivity, increases family labour inputs and requires financial investment.[59]

Looking from the perspective of the central state and its attempts to transform the socialist approach to agriculture into a capitalist one, land fragmentation is perceived as a reformer's worst nightmare. It is considered as one of the main causes of land degradation and a major impediment to agricultural innovation and increasing productivity. Other authors have shown the positive aspects of land fragmentation.[60] In Albania, for instance, due to the microclimatic variation, soil type, moisture, wind and the like even within one single village, land fragmentation allows farmers to spread the risk. When pests strike on one plot, the other plots belonging to the same farmer but located at a safe distance and cultivated with different crops remain untouched. A fragmented land holding distribution also allows farmers to use a variety of eco-zones and secure various types of agro-cultures from vineyards to meadows, and from cereals to orchards and forest.[61] A similar explanation works well for the Vietnamese case as well: land fragmentation may also be the villagers' preferred choice, as it allows them to spread the risks of floods, droughts and diseases. Besides, owning fragmented parcels of land allows villagers to reduce the peak-time season and thus use the available labour force more effectively by diversifying crops on different plots.[62]

A similar situation applies to animal keepers. The state policies, issued under the supervision of international institutions with neoliberal policies and ideologies, were most favourable to large farms but totally hostile to practitioners of small-scale agriculture.[63] The milk production from the Albanian state farms dropped dramatically immediately after the fall of the communist regime.[64] In 1992, the milk supply totally ceased due to the collapse of the state system of collection and distribution but also to the land reform, which brought about the dissolution of large state enterprises and changes in the land use. Nevertheless, managing to avoid malfunctioning state institutions and dodge taxes, the newly privatized peasant farms started to supply the cities with milk, guaranteeing urbanites a basic staple food. A similar strategy was adopted both by Bulgarian animal keepers (as I was able to notice myself in the marketplaces from Sofia)[65] and Lithuanian ones. In Lithuania, for instance, a single farmer living in a settlement 15 to 20 kilometres away from a city delivers dairy to about 50 to 70 urban households.[66] The urbanites, especially those old and poorer ones, rarely rely on supermarkets for buying dairy products but instead rely on established networks which include at least one animal keeper, as Mincyte shows in her paper. Not only are these products cheaper, but small-scale agriculture is also more likely to be free from chemicals, fertilizers, hormones and antibiotics as their price is prohibitive for smallholders, an argument used by Lithuanian and Romanian buyers.[67]

The above arguments that support the benefits of land fragmentation and the agriculture on small sized plots work, in my view, for all postsocialist countries and may represent not only a way of responding to wider economic transformations but also smallholders' strategy for coping with the harshness of life. Instead of becoming obedient foot soldiers of capitalist agriculture, postsocialist villagers first attempted to secure food for the family by practising subsistence agriculture; instead of turning into large herd owners as expected by the central reformers and their advisors, animal keepers continued to rely on door-to-door milk selling, avoiding paying taxes and staying beyond the reach of the state. It is true that some of them, such as the peasants of Dragova, have a long history of dodging state interference in their business. If they managed to deal with the socialist state, hostile ideologically and politically to entrepreneurial peasants, and to sell their goods successfully on the market, they will also find ways to avoid norms, laws and institutions of the postsocialist state.

Land fragmentation – a blessing or a curse? The question might well be asked with regard to postcolonial countries as well. Reviewing the literature on land fragmentation in Africa, Blarel et al. shows that there are basically two explanations advanced by scholars dealing with this social and biophysical process. One explanation sees land fragmentation as an exogenous imposition on African farmers – caused by egalitarian inheritance and population pressure leading to the breakdown of common property systems. Different law systems in Africa, the authors continue, restrict land transactions or impose egalitarian objectives. A second explanation for land fragmentation in Africa considers it a strategy adopted by farmers that brings more benefits than economic costs. Scattering parcels of land over a wide area would, according to the literature reviewed by Benoit Blarel and his colleagues, reduce the risk associated with loss of crops from drought, floods or pests. Their conclusion is that land fragmentation does not necessarily impede land productivity in the case of Ghana and Rwanda, the two countries they take as examples in this work. Consequently, it is not an economic issue.[68]

South Asia seems also to have experienced land fragmentation. Heston and Kumar have shown that the small paddy fields of 1 to 2 acres in India are scattered into 4.4 parcels each with an average size of 0.37 acres. Larger land holdings, those between 15 and 20 acres, are broken up into 7.9 fragments each with an average size of 2.10 acres. The two authors further point to the highly fragmented land on the Northwest coast of Malaysia: the co-ownership system imposed by land registration law led to the case in which several persons co-owned an average of 2.61 acres. Many of the parcels of land, the authors assure us, are less than 1 acre, which makes them difficult to farm.[69]

Remaining in South Asia, the average per capita landholding in Nepal is 0.14 hectare whereas in Bangladesh a peasant possesses on average 0.06 hectare.[70] In Sri Lanka there is a similar situation, with an average landholding size of 0.7 hectare with an average of 2.5 parcels per landholding. Over time landholdings became fragmented into several plots. Niroula and Thapa ask the same question as other authors working on land fragmentation: is this a positive factor or does it have a negative effect on agricultural productivity. By blaming the same factors producing fragmentation such as population growth, inheritance systems and institutional policies, the authors' answer tends to give credit to the negative aspects of land fragmentation. Fragmented land, they argue, incurs high production costs, impedes efficient land management and the implementation of location-specific use of land, all detrimental to sustainable land conservation.[71]

More examples intended to convince the reader that land fragmentation is not exclusively a postsocialist phenomenon and that concerns over its causes and consequences are globally spread would be redundant. While I do not intend to subvert this conclusion, I would add that the causes of land fragmentation in postsocialist countries seem to stem equally from the past and the present. Land fragmentation is a social and economic reality of the modern period as I have outlined in chapter 1. The patchwork landscape, in terms of land use and land ownership, was part of the pre-collectivization reality. Collectivization and land nationalization put an end to fragmentation and consolidated the land. Land reform and its emphasis on restitution to legitimate historical owners and on private property ownership have reshuffled lands, ownership rights and land use, giving rise to a new economic reality and a new landscape.

Notes

1. See excerpts from the *Raportul CC al PCR cu privire la activitatea partidului în perioada dintre Congresul al VIII-lea și Congresul al IX-lea, 19 iulie 1965* in Hamelet (1971).
2. The name of the car recalls the ancient kingdom of the Dacians (Dacia), the local population which was conquered by the Roman Empire in 106 AD. The Romanian people are descended from Dacians and Romans; later the Slavs and other migratory people contributed to the mix.
3. Verdery (2003: 85).
4. Barco and Nedelcu (1974).
5. Sampson (1976).
6. The County Department of Statistics, Pitești.
7. Cernea (1978).
8. After 1981, the collective farms had introduced working norms per day (Matei and Mihăilescu 1985). These were compulsory for every member of the co-operative. Sometimes a person, especially a woman, could not fulfil the norms and she needed

to be assisted by someone from the family. Each collective farm member could also receive up to 15 ari (1,500m^2) to work the co-operative's land. Those families with more members, whether engaged in the industrial sector or not, could receive more land to work. Thirty per cent of the products from this land were retained for the household. The household had no ownership rights over this land, only the right to use it (Cernea 1974). As Cernea mentions, in 1973 at the national level 12.3 per cent of the co-operatives' cropland, 22.5 per cent of orchards and 63.8 per cent of vineyards were worked in this system. This land was so thoroughly worked that in 1973, for instance, less than 50 per cent from the potato production was made on the co-operatives and state land; the rest was produced on leased and private land. In the same year, less than 33 per cent of the national plum production was made on co-operative and state farms; the rest was produced on leased and private land (Cernea 1974).
9. Cartwright (2001); Hann (2002); Verdery (2003); von Hirschhausen (1997).
10. Usually the worker-peasants are males. There are several explanations for this. One is that the first available jobs, mainly in heavy industry, required male force. Second, it was easier for a man to travel back and forth and to spend a great amount of time on frequently wretched public transportation such as regional trains or buses than for a woman. Third, it was socially unacceptable for a woman to spend so much time away from the household, as in the 1960s, when the phenomenon of the worker-peasant exploded, women still had a strong domestic status.
11. See Scott (1976).
12. On the same issue, see Dorondel (2012).
13. Kaneff (2002).
14. Müller (2005: 136).
15. Hann (2007: 309).
16. This situation is specific to Walachia and Moldavia. In Transylvania, until 1918 under Hungarian rule and Austrian influence, the cadastre was introduced in the nineteenth century (Prosterman and Rolfes 1999).
17. There was also a *foaie de zestre* (dowry sheet) – a document that declared the land and goods a married girl would receive as dowry from her parents. However, this was a peasant upper strata practice, less important for the middle-class peasantry.
18. Verdery (2003).
19. Verdery (2005).
20. The collective farm had agricultural machines to plant maize. Thus, the distance between the rows was 70 to 80 centimetres and the quantity of planted seeds was also established mechanically: 15 to 30 kilogrames of seeds to 1 hectare of land (Petre 2005). Since planting is now done manually, people would not observe these standards anymore.
21. Petre (2005); Vătămanu (2012).
22. Worster (1990).
23. AGR2B/2004 – the mayor's office report for the County Department of Statistics in Pitești for the year 2004. AGR is a statistical report for agriculture.
24. Wiersum (2004).
25. Li et al. (2007).
26. Müller (2012).
27. Pig was a cheap source of meat in many parts of the world. See, for instance, Cronon (1983: 201).

28. AGR/2003 and the County Department of Statistics, Pitești.
29. Biolan et al. (2006).
30. The agronomists show that the waste water containing pig excrement cannot be used naturally because it burns the plants. Only after fermentation, along with other vegetable remains such as dry leaves, straws, maize stalks and creeping stalks is it transformed into manure (Dinu et al. 1992).
31. Demeulenaere (2012).
32. Soleri and Smith (2003).
33. The agronomists are quite against this practice, though. For instance, Grecu and Haș (2001: 3) shows that the production of maize in Romania has dropped by at least 25 per cent due to the 'usage of an improper biological material [i.e. seeds from the previous production]' on 30 to 40 per cent of the maize cultivated surface in Romania. Petre (2005) is equally against such a practice, considering that the seed needs to be treated against soil bugs and other pests. Hybrids, it claims, have better resistance against weeds. The agronomists' perspective is dominated by their chosen model of modern, efficient agriculture.
34. Ethnoecologists preach the local breeding of seeds for purposes linked to conservation of the variety of local seeds. See for details Soleri and Smith (2003).
35. The beer producers, most of them large Western beer companies, base their beer production almost exclusively on the Romanian production of barley and two-row barley. Nevertheless, the whole production of the two cereals dropped significantly after 1989: the acreage on which these cereals were cultivated decreased from 646,000 hectares to 218,000 hectares; the entire production thus dropped from 3.437 million tons per year to 1.016 million tons per year. The agronomists' explanations are the same as for maize: decreasing the amount of fertilizer used by farmers but also a deterioration of scientific agricultural practices including poor preparation of the soil for the new cultivation, the decreasing quantity of fertilizer and poor quality harvesting work. The data and explanations come from Vasilescu (2006).
36. Data about agricultural production comes from the County Department of Statistics, Pitești.
37. The agronomists show that potato cultivation requires a more precise chemical treatment than other crops. The proportion of chemicals is vital: too many chemicals would adversely affect the soil and the potato plants; too little would create an animal or vegetal parasite immune to chemicals. The quantity of sprayed chemicals must be uniform (around 20 drops per square centimetre). The herbicide must also be spread at the optimal moment, when the weeds are just sprouting – this is the moment of maximum vulnerability of the undesired plant when chemicals prove most efficient. The collective farms had machines to carry out all these tasks whereas peasants use a portable pump to spray the potatoes (Berindei and Bria 1982; Nicola 2007).
38. A similar explanation for a massive drop in crop production is given by Mungiu-Pippidi (2010) and Hann (2006).
39. A similar situation is to be found in a neighbouring valley where Fox has worked (Fox 2011).
40. For more details on *pomana* rituals and religious meanings, see Dorondel (2004).
41. Distilling țuica is strictly a male job.
42. Butac et al. (2011).
43. As specialists showed, *Prunus domestica* is prone to viral attacks, especially Plum pox, one of the most widespread and virulent viruses in the area. This virus was

responsible for massive destruction of orchards. Production can drop by as much as 70 per cent after this virus attacks an orchard. Nevertheless, the local species such as Scoldus – extensively cultivated after orchard restitution in Dragomirești – are immune to the virus (Butac et al. 2009). Thus, this type of plum tree does not need to be sprayed with chemicals.

44. County Department of Statistics and the Agricultural register of the commune. The figure for the socialist period may well be incorrect as villagers usually declared fewer animals than they had and lower dairy production.
45. His calculation is based on the 2003 cost of maize (9,000 lei per kilogram) and hay (5,000 lei per kilogram).
46. There is a very complicated system of establishing the date of Easter in the Orthodox tradition. It is based on some ancient calculation taking into account the phases of the moon and some theological considerations. Therefore, Easter could fall (*a cade*) one year in early April and the following year in mid May. The vast majority of the Romanian population is Orthodox (86 per cent).
47. Fox (2011).
48. For a similar conclusion, see Kligman and Verdery (2011) and Stewart (1998).
49. Sabates-Wheeler (2005) defines the multiple understandings of land fragmentation: physical, social and activity (operational) fragmentation.
50. Individualization of a plot presupposes the recognition of property rights by the court for every individual and, based on this decision, the drawing of a cadastral map. Only then can the owner takeover his or her plot.
51. Sabates-Wheeler (2005: 26).
52. Van Dijk (2003).
53. Patterson (2009).
54. Data come from Sikor et al. (2009). See also Stahl (2010a).
55. Sikor et al. (2009).
56. The data and the case study is based on Wegren (2004; 2009).
57. Wegren (2009: 71).
58. This example is based on analysis in Hung et al. (2007).
59. Hung et al. (2007).
60. Sikor et al. (2009); Stahl (2010a).
61. Stahl (2010a).
62. Hung et al. (2007).
63. Fox (2011); Mincyte (2011).
64. The case is based on Nicholson (2003).
65. Also Petko Hristov, personal communication.
66. Mincyte (2011).
67. Ibid.; Bogdan and Mihăilescu (2009).
68. Blarel et al. (1992).
69. Heston and Kumar (1983).
70. The following sets of data come from Niroula and Thapa (2005).
71. Ibid.

 CHAPTER 7

Wasted Rivers

> '... poisoned and burned waters, over these no creature can fly.'
> —G. Bogza, *Țări de piatră, de foc și de pământ*
> *(Countries of Stone, Fire, and Earth)*

This last chapter before the conclusion is one of a kind. Whereas land and forest are topics that are fiercely debated in the literature on postsocialism transformation, water resources – also subject to tremendous political and economic pressure – have been largely neglected. As several authors have pointed out, water as a topic of social and humanities research has been less researched on a global scale.¹ This chapter attempts to fill the void by analysing the environmental changes taking place in water in postsocialist Romania. Two lessons are to be drawn from this chapter. One is that not only land and forest are considered a valuable resource by the local political and administrative elite and are thus subjected to economic and political pressures, but water as well. In fact waters and rivers, together with forests, are the most precious natural resources to have been turned into significant amounts of cash. Thus, water is more than just the natural element that erodes cropland or moves property boundaries from one bank of the river to the other by simply changing its course – as Mureș River did in a Transylvanian village.² Waters – rivers, lakes, ponds and water sources – were the very target of the political elite that, once commoditized, brought wealth to the owner.³ A second lesson to be drawn from this chapter is that water is part of the landscape and, where it exists, must be seen in close relationship with cropland, pasture and forest. As I will show in this chapter, rivers, ponds and rivers' sources are part of the story of landscape disruption in postsocialist times. To leave rivers out of the picture would be to tell an incomplete story.

A Dying River

One afternoon in late July 2004, *nenea* Paul announced to me: 'Tonight we are going to the river to fish with the fork. It's a suitable time as it will be full moon.' I knew about 'fishing with the fork' being illegal.[4] Several villagers had told me about it and I had seen in their backyard wooden forks that seemed not to have been used for quite a while. The fork has two sharp teeth and a metre-long handle. This is a rather simple instrument adapted for fishing in shallow waters. The rest of the afternoon we spent the time preparing the light, a lantern whose flame is based on calcium carbide. It is important to have this type of pale light because only in such a light is the fish visible to the eye: a spark in the dark waters of the river, which disappears in a second. This type of fishing is practised during summer nights at full moon. The moonlight and the calcium carbide flame ensure the perfect light for fishing in rapid rivers. The fisherman needs speed and precision in order to stick the fork into the fish but he also has to learn how to walk slowly upstream through the river.[5] After a couple of hours of fishing in the cold waters we had caught little more than one kilo of small fish – just enough to feed a family for dinner. Of course, among the three of us I was the clumsiest, so my catch was next to nothing. Nevertheless, this experience showed me that the quantity of fish caught is actually very small. A few decades ago, that was a way of supplementing food for locals.

The history of the river has shaped its architecture. Although local documents do not mention fishing as an important economic source for the villagers, Argeşelu River must once have been an additional source of food for the villagers. Out of its total length of 76 kilometres the river runs beside the commune for 12 kilometres. Local oral history mentions the large fishes that once populated the river. The traditional fishing tool throughout the whole area was the wooden fork, an instrument perfectly adapted to the shallow and rapid rivers of the hills. The water flow was always small, except in the spring, when the snow was melting and the level of the river rose significantly. The changes in the river architecture apparently rendered this fishing style obsolete. The growing number of water mills in the nineteenth century created a special architecture of the river. Artificial lakes and ponds helped to run the twenty-eight water mills, sixty-eight distilleries and three water-powered stamps along the river.[6] These places with rather deep water sheltered chab (*Leuciscus cephalus*), barbell (*Barbus fluviatilis*), eel (*Anguilla*) and crayfish (*Astachidae sp.*).[7] Most probably the wooden fork was not very helpful in such waters and different kinds of fishing tools were required. In the early 1950s, the last water mill in Dragomireşti commune was dismantled, probably as a consequence of changes in crop cultivation and national economic demands. Flax and hemp were no longer interesting crops for the socialist regime. Besides, the collectivized cropland, which lies along the river, was used to grow cereals. In order to protect the cropland the collective farm planted trees along the river and regularized the river flow. As a consequence, the lakes and ponds disappeared. The river's waters were shallow but rapid, with a small but steady debit during the winter or the summer. In these waters the fork became, once again, a helpful tool.

Our failure to catch more fish should not be put down (only) to the fact that two out of three fishermen – nenea Paul's son and me – were inexperienced. It was clear from our short escapade that the fish were in short supply in those waters. The lack of fish is actually the outcome of the constant degradation of the river since 1989. Villagers used to take the pebbles, which constitute the bank of the river, for their construction work. The sand from the riverbed was targeted as well. Pebbles and sand mixed with cement produces concrete. Basically all private constructions erected in the area after 1989, be they houses, garages or small shops, have in their foundations and structural pillars, sand and pebbles from the river. This made construction cheaper as pebbles and sand bought from specialized shops are quite expensive. For instance, for a 150-square-metre house one requires around 20 cubic metres of pebbles and sand. One cubic metre of sand costs around 500,000 lei (some €15) whereas 1 cubic metre of pebbles costs around 450,000 lei (€12).[8] Taking sand and pebbles for free from the river saves the constructor around 10 million lei (more than €300). Villagers do not perceive the two items as part of the natural environment but as free commodities indispensable for construction. Looting the river of two of its natural components seemed to be a socially acceptable behaviour as long as nobody perceived it as damaging to the environment. After years of merciless exploitation of the river's bed and banks, the river's bank was degraded and lost its shape.

The riverbank also became the favourite place to throw away garbage for both the mayor's office and villagers. For instance, those villagers who receive social benefits, most of them Rudari, have to work a certain number of days for the mayor's office. They are usually asked to clean the ditches or to help on different construction sites within the commune.[9] They have no other place to throw away waste but the river's bank. A short trip along the river reveals mountains of garbage – a mixture of debris, domestic rubbish and maize stalks – guarding both banks. Plastic bottles, scrap paper, iron, cans and tyres thrown there by the local population mingle with maize stalks and weeds offloaded by the social benefit workers from their horse carts. According to the local officials, Rudari have 'to manage' garbage somehow. There is no designated place in the commune to dump the garbage, nor any company, private or public, to collect it.

This is a long-standing tradition in rural areas. Before socialism the amount of garbage produced by villagers was smaller and it was usually biodegradable. Every month, men used to collect the family garbage, transfer it to the field and burn it. The ash was then spread around. During socialism everything changed, especially after the 1970s: when the economic shortages became more acute, the socialist state turned green; glass, iron and scrap paper were collected in schools and then passed to the collecting points. Every single student had to bring a certain quantity of these items, while schools had quotas to meet. According to these practices, new ideological discourses were displayed publicly, in which any wastage was severely criticized and punished.[10] Thus, these items were considered a resource and rarely turned into garbage. The situation has changed again since 1989 as the obligation to recycle ceased. A new garbage policy, or rather the lack of any policy, characterized the beginning of the new political regime.[11] Besides, the opening of Romania to the global markets brought a flow of various new goods wrapped in diverse packages. These goods also meant the arrival of new disposable materials such as plastic bottles or aluminium cans, which never existed before in Romania. After consuming the goods people simply throw away the packaging, the cans or the bottles without any concern for the environment. It is not just the Dragovans who do so but most people in Romania. Often, Rudari complain about the number of plastic bottles, cans and other items thrown away by drivers travelling along the national road that crosses Dragomirești, which they endlessly and pointlessly have to collect. A similar quantity of garbage accumulates every week.

The emergence of new non-recyclable disposable materials was concomitant with the state steadily privatizing its functions, among them the garbage collection services.[12] Local administrations now have to pay private firms to collect the domestic garbage out of their budgets. Although the municipalities are legally obliged to ensure waste disposal is properly managed, the lack of funds means that these legal requirements are not carried out in practice.[13] As the mayor's office in Dragomirești has a tight budget, garbage collection is simply not on the agenda. Villagers have to find their own ways to dispose of domestic waste, and the river's bank seems a good solution to them.

These items are not without an inherent market value. If recycled, as usually happens in Western Europe, they would be turned into cash. Recycling requires specific technology, adequate legislation, waste management systems and socially accepted practices of separating waste. Although part of the accession negotiations with the EU, waste management has taken small steps in Romania and the process is confined to the large cities.[14] The lack of all these determinants in rural areas not only impedes effective waste disposal but turns the potential economic value of waste into a social and environmental liability.

In the village of Dragomirești there is still a functioning distillery located conveniently on the river's bank. The distillery belongs to Marian, the state forester already known to the reader from chapter 3. This is one of the three distilleries in the commune but the only one located next to the river. It was privately owned before collectivization: located on this spot since the beginning of the twentieth century, it belonged to the local co-operative during the socialist era and after decollectivization it was bought, in 1991, by Marian's father. Quite a lot of villagers come to distil țuica there: for this service they leave for Marian 10 per cent of the final product. I do not have data for the whole quantity of țuica produced there but considering that Marian sells around 2,000 litres annually we may assume that the total quantity produced is over 20,000 litres each year. For 2 and a half litres of țuica one needs around 10 kilos of marc. The residue left after distillation is always thrown onto the river's bank. The marc could be used as fodder for the bulls, pigs and sheep but only in limited quantities and mixed with other ingredients.[15] However, since there is no longer an agro-industrial complex in the commune and selling a few kilos of marc to individual farmers would be economically inefficient Marian prefers to discharge the marc quickly. In the autumn and winter especially, when țuica is distilled, a walk along the river is accompanied by the smells of alcohol and rotten plums and apples from marc. The river water is polluted by alcohol and cyanide, contained in the plum stones. This gives rise to an undesirable rise in organic matter in the water – an ecological process called euthrophication – as a result of the marc's chemical decomposition. The river thus provides a perfect ecosystem for microorganisms to grow rapidly, causing dramatic change in the microbiological composition of the water and contributing to the elimination of plants and fish from the river.[16]

Besides debris, domestic garbage and marc residue, the river is also infested with maize stalks. At the end of the maize harvest villagers cut the crop and discard the stalks at the end of their plot, which happens to be the river's bank.

Again, the status of this type of garbage has changed over time, influenced by different political regimes and property rights. Before collectivization, the stalk was used as fodder for bovines and horses and as a source of heating. The animal eats the leaves and the soft parts of the plant, which in itself does not represent a rich diet. Maize stalk is rather poor in minerals and vitamins and only when mixed with beet (*Beta vulgaris*) and pumpkin does it represent a better diet for the bovines.[17] The stalk was therefore added to other types of fodder richer in protein, vitamins and minerals and was used for economic reasons rather than for nutritive ones. The remaining woody stalk was then used for heating. During the socialist era, the stalk belonged to the collective farm – because the cropland and its production belonged to the collective – and was used for fodder. The stalk was chopped into small pieces and given to the bovines and horses. The Romanian agronomist Gheorghe Băia notes that the maize stalk represented up to 20 per cent of the total fodder for the collective farms' animals.[18] Those who worked the small plots given by the collective also used maize stalks for fodder.

176   *Disrupted Landscapes*

Illustrations 7.1 and 7.2.   Garbage on the River's Bank

Again, the economic value of the stalk was rather more important than its nutritive capacities. Nevertheless, most households had little involvement in maize stalk management. After decollectivization, villagers had to make agricultural production decisions – and what to do with the stalks was part of those decisions. Since after decollectivization the number of cattle steadily decreased, as I have shown in chapter 5, and the restitution of pasture ensured that villagers had access to adequate fodder, maize stalk was no longer needed. Concomitantly, as the forest was given back to its former owners, obtaining firewood became easier than it had been during socialism. The cheapest means of disposal was dumping the stalks on the river's bank, at the end of the cropland.

Different periods produce different types of garbage, which in turn require a different waste management approach. The material composition of the garbage in a rural setting in socialist Romania differs significantly from that of postsocialist times. The emergence of Romania's national market onto the global market has brought new disposable materials that in turn require new waste management approaches. Although the composition of waste material is important, the political economy is crucial in turning a disposable item from a resource into garbage. The historical shifts in waste production and disposal, as well as the involvement or, to the contrary, the disengagement of the state, directly affects the environment.

Finally, the most damaging source of pollution in Dragomirești is the private chicken complex.[19] What needs to be mentioned here is that the weekly disposal of chicken droppings is equally bothersome to villagers and damaging to the environment. Villagers living next to the complex complain forcefully about the strong smell infesting the air after droppings disposal. On hot days especially, as I myself experienced several times, the smell becomes unbearable. Chemical elements contained by the droppings such as azoth, phosphorus and potassium represent a direct threat to any creature living in the river. These chemical components lead, again, to the process of euthrophication: the fast growing of plankton that, once dead, will end up poisoning the waters. The microbiological equilibrium of the water is dramatically changed and eliminates any life forms from those waters.[20] Even if the droppings are not dumped directly into the river but on the field next to the complex (close to the bank), rainwater transports these toxic substances from the surface to a deeper level, also carrying them into the river. The mayor's office never bothered the chicken complex owner with official complaints because the complex provides the greatest share of the local administrative budget. If it relied only on the taxes raised from villagers and other small economic actors like shop owners, the mayor's office would barely survive financially. For local officials economic concerns outweigh those of environmental damage.

Argeșelu River is not the only water in the commune that has had its architecture and entire ecosystem radically altered. A small lake called Barca, 120 metres in length and 8 metres wide, located on the top of one of the surrounding hills, was the villagers' favourite place to water their animals. This lake seems to play a significant role in the villagers' imagination, as many of them believe that the lake is bottomless. A myth circulating in the village, which I heard in the first days after arriving in the village, tells that a bride and her entire cortege drowned in that lake. No swimming is possible because the lake is cursed. In a not so distant past the lake was surrounded by alders and willow trees (*Salix triandra*), from which only a few stumps remain, common reed (*Phragmites communis*), mace reed (*Typha angustfolia*), water fern (*Azolla*) and duckweed (*Lemma minor*). The lake, now a muddy pond of a few square metres, sheltered wild ducks, stork (*Ciconia*) and herons (*Ardea*) that hatched there. A whole humid ecosystem had formed here. The lake was destroyed by human activity – the collective farms drained the lake in order to gain more pasture for the animals. Uncontrolled animal excrement containing nitrates and azotites also contributed to the degradation of the ecosystem.[21] A small pond surrounded by bushes and the few cows that graze the pasture, drinking from its muddy waters, is all that remains of that ecosystem.

When I returned to the village in 2009, Argeșelu River was actually dead: no fish had been seen for the past couple of years. Its dark and shallow waters no longer shelter life forms. Its dirty and muddy waters attest to the fact that other communes located downstream act in the same way as villagers from Dragomirești. The dying river is the outcome of at least two intertwined social processes: one is the change in property rights and the other is a reckless decentralization policy.

The cropland lies along the river; thus it was always part of the river's ecosystem. The riverbank is the nearest place for villagers working their cropland to dispose of the vegetal remains. It is simply convenient to dump the undesired maize stalks at the margins of their plot. Decollectivization not only brought the cropland into private hands but also passed the responsibilities for clearing post-harvest fields from the co-operative to householders. From a relatively valuable resource in socialist times, the maize stalk turned into a liability. This change in value is due to the evolution of the local economy and the national political economy. The weight of local economy has shifted from agriculture, including animal husbandry, and industrial activities in socialist times, to mainly industrial activity in the postsocialist era. I have described in chapter 5 the new political economy that drove the dramatic decrease in the number of cattle. Keeping cattle was no longer economically viable for the household. Fewer cattle meant no need for maize stalks as fodder.

The reconfiguration of property rights at national level made the river's bank a no man's land. Officially, the river and its banks are managed by the state through a public company (The National Institute of Hydrology and Water Management). However, there is no clear demarcation in the field between the cropland and the river's banks; thus no clear property rights can be asserted by the public company. Villagers therefore perceive this place as being unclaimed by the owner, a no man's land – a perfect place for their waste disposal. Villagers' behaviour reflects a de facto reality. This also constitutes the main reason villagers recklessly exploit the sand and pebbles from the riverbed. The fact that no one in the village has ever seen a state officer imposing controls on the status of the river reinforces this feeling.[22] The no man's land de facto status of the river invites villagers to abuse it. When balancing the economic savings villagers can make against the environmental damages produced in the river, the economic concerns inevitably prevail.

Enclosure of a Water Source

The river at Dragova has met with a different fate. It was not directly targeted as Argeşelu River has been but its sources have been subject to debate, claim, and enclosure. The river is fed by seven sources, all of them located outside the village, on a pasture found at the bottom of a steep slope. Dragova commune was never collectivized, so the local land reform policies addressed only the restitution of the forest and, in some cases, pastures. This small pasture was claimed by the Murgescu family to belong to them. As capturing a water source could be an extremely lucrative business, the mayor became interested in that humble plot. As a head of the LLC he arranged for this land to be acquired by his mother-in-law, while Murgescu received in exchange a small forest plot in an accessible place. In fact, the pasture belonged with the forest on the top of the hill, an inaccessible and thus unclaimed forestland. The Murgescus were very happy *not* to receive that particular forest. Who needs dozens of trees on an inaccessible peak, which are therefore impossible to exploit? Of course, the Murgescus knew that the small pasture at the bottom of the hill shelters the seven water sources but they never intended to exploit the sources, nor had they the financial capacity to do it. In any case, a water source is not owned by the landowner but is the property of the Romanian state and managed under special regulations. The institution that licences the private exploitation of a water source is the National Agency for the Natural Resources (NANR). In order to exploit a water source one needs to be able to penetrate a dense bureaucracy in order to obtain the innumerable permissions, pay the relevant taxes and have the industrial facility to exploit it. Or, at least that person should have enough money to invest in such a big enterprise. The Murgescu family was in no position to fulfil any of these requirements.

The mayor was ready to pay the modest cost of acquiring a forest plot in an inaccessible spot in exchange for owning the land above the water sources. I should say here that there were several investors, including foreign companies, interested in capturing the sources. Investors came to the village in an attempt to evaluate the source and its financial value. Every time the mayor lobbied the members of the Local Council, whose official approval was legally requested, to refuse applications from the foreigners. Besides, some investors seemed reluctant to invest simply because the land belonged to the state but was due to be restored to private ownership through land reform. Until the new Constitution was established in 2003, foreign citizens and companies were not allowed to buy land in Romania. Thus, they would have had to lease the land, which at the time had uncertain ownership status: not yet private but claimed by a family. The mayor raised further obstacles for potential investors. The water had to be bottled somewhere but obviously not on site, which is a few kilometres away from the village, with no electricity or any other facility. In order to do this, the firm would have to dig a long ditch for the adduction pipes; again, this would have required the mayor's approval. The rumours in the village were that the mayor impeded any investor until he himself had acquired the land above the sources and the money to start the business.

Shortly after the mayor's family had acquired the land, they enclosed the plot and his wife's firm started preparations to exploit the source. In order to do so this firm, along with others, had to attend an auction. Winning an auction for the exploitation of natural resources such as underground water means the winner has significant political relations at national level. It seems that the mayor has powerful connections, as it was his wife's firm that won the auction. But he made enemies as well. In an informal conversation with him he told me that several SDP colleagues argued that this business was 'a hat too large for his head'. Indeed, in order to start the enterprise he needed to borrow 4 billion lei (around €98,000) from a bank. He also had to employ people to lay the 9 kilometres of pipes required, to lease or buy trucks and digging machines, and to build an extraction facility up in the mountains. All these requirements have not scared the mayor off. As for his political influence the visit from the president of the Senate described thoroughly in chapter 5 proves it beyond any doubt. Finally, the firm started to exploit the water source, after digging the long ditch for the adduction pipes up to a new construction next to the main road in Podu Dragovei, his native village. Again, despite the resulting partial destruction of the main road, undermined anyway by the logging firms' trucks, his power remained undisputed in the village. Moreover, he portrayed himself as a benefactor of the community because the water exploitation firm will pay taxes to the local government, which can be further invested 'to do good to the people'.

Although his power remained unchallenged, the mayor's intention to capture the water source triggered huge dissatisfaction in the village. Firstly because this land had never been enclosed as it lies en route to the communal pasture. For centuries, villagers have taken their cows there, crossing the land that now belongs to the mayor's family. Secondly, the water source will have an impact on Dragova River's flow. In summer, when it is pretty dry, the river will dry up. As this river is the only water source for the villagers' animals the local concern is understandable. Animal husbandry and rural tourism represent the main sources of income for the villagers. Drying up the river poses a direct threat to the cattle; they would become harder to husband, resulting in an important loss of revenue for most villagers. The mayor tried to calm fears by giving his word that the sources would not be exploited in the summer when the flow is lower anyway. When I came back to the village, in the summer of 2007, the water flow was tiny. The reality was a stark contrast with the bucolic image of the mighty river found on the bottle distributor's website.

Dragova River has to cope with two other challenges. The growing number of tourists, some of whom camp on the narrow land strip between the gorges on the way to Podu Dragovei village, has led to an increasing quantity of

Illustration 7.3. A Vanishing River

garbage: plastic bottles, cans, plastic sheets and papers are discarded periodically on the river's bank. Although the National Park administration installed garbage bins – most of them bought with EU grants – they are still rare and too few to serve the number of tourists. Another challenge the river has to face is deforestation. Both legal and illegal logging contribute to the river's devastation. The branches of felled trees found next to the river impede the waters and form unintended barriers. The water then takes multiple paths before regaining its natural track. Illegal loggers have no machines to carry the logs away from the forest. Instead, they slide them down the steep slopes onto the main road. When logging happens on slopes on the opposite side of the river, logs do not affect the river track. But when the logging takes place on the slopes bordering the river then sliding heavy logs leaves deep ditches in the banks. The branches left in the river rot, contributing further to degradation of the river.

An economist would argue that while the mayor and his family earn a fortune other members of the community pay for the externalities.[23] A private firm takes action but does not bear the costs of damage caused to the environment. The negative externalities – to continue in the same direction – rest mainly on the shoulders of the community: those who earn a living from keeping animals suffer because the source has been enclosed and exploited privately. It thus makes sense for the private firms to externalize their production costs and to be 'ecologically irrational' as Noel Castree puts it.[24] The firms' gains represent the community's loss. The degradation of Argeşelu River and the privatization of Dragova water sources cannot be understood outside postsocialist economic and political restructuring. Liberalization of the market, the ideology of private property as the milestone of the new society and economy and the privatization of state functions, to name only a few postsocialist changes, largely contributed to the devastation of the two rivers. Commodification of natural resources for a sustainable exploitation – a global claim, not just a postsocialist one – leads not only to depletion of the resources but also to the resources' dispossession of villagers' ownership by powerful local people.[25] In the name of economic efficiency and of the financial contribution brought to local communities, private companies are allowed to dump toxic garbage, despite the harm caused to the environment, or to enclose a water source. At the same time, valuable natural resources become an important stake in local politics. As Mungiu-Pippidi puts it, the fierce competition for power positions and for bureaucratic offices is motivated by unlimited access to valuable state-owned resources.[26] The most direct route to making money from uncontrolled exploitation of natural resources crosses through a state office.

The tale of the two rivers teaches us another lesson: human exploitation of one single natural resource such as land or forest has consequences for all types of natural resources. We need to see the intimate connections between agricultural practices, animal husbandry, logging and the consequences for the river. A decreasing number of cattle transformed the maize stalks into garbage to be dumped next to the river. Preparing țuica is part of the local economy and social relations but disposal of the marc harms the river. Logging is part of the local revenue but shortcutting technical procedures or completely ignoring them have direct consequences for the river. Waters, rivers, ponds and lakes were all under the same social, economic and political pressure as the forest and land.

When land reform was devised in the central offices of Bucharest, one can reasonably imagine that destruction of the rivers was not part of the master plan. Under the conditions of the EU accession the Romanian state had issued laws and norms to protect the environment.[27] As I showed in chapter 4, the land reform unfolded alongside the attempt by the central state to organize nature protection. For instance, in order to adapt the national regulations to the *acquis communautaire*, the Romanian state adopted the Framework Cadre for Water (FCW) 2000/60 of the Parliament and of the European Commission. This corpus of norms seeks to offer a legislative framework for sustainable water management and of the water ecosystems among the EU and accession countries. The FCW was translated into a master plan to manage the waters on national territory sustainably.[28] Among other things, the FCW encourages citizens of these states to take active part in water management. Villagers of Dragomirești seem to be little concerned about the health of their river. In fact, the fierce exploitation of the sand and pebbles as well as the garbage dumped in the river should be read as a local reaction to the wider economic constraints they have to bear and to the changes in state functions. They see the natural resources of the river as an ownerless free commodity to be used in a harsh economic environment in which they struggle to survive. They react to the state privatization functions by discarding their garbage in a place considered as belonging to anyone or to no one. By muddling through, they behave in a very different way to that expected by the central government.

It is not just the people-versus-state relationship that deeply affects waters. Local bureaucrats and local political elite, as implementers of the environmental norms and laws, had their own plans. Privatization of the Dragova River's sources serves a personal interest that is opposed to the master plan adopted by central government. The mayor of Dragomirești does not take any action against the private chicken farm that spills excreta on a field close to the river because the taxes paid by the complex owner to the local government enable the local government to function. The owner of the distillery that dumps marc on the river's banks is an important political and economic actor in the commune and a state forester, a representative of the state at local level paid to watch over the environment. The struggle for the environment it is not between the state and local people but between different levels of state offices that have divergent economic interests opposing each other.

Depleting Postsocialist Waters

Regarding rivers, postsocialist changes should have brought relief from pollution. Due to the restructuring of heavy industry and the introduction of the legal principle 'the polluter pays', the postsocialist waters are supposedly under less stress than during socialist times.[29] Nevertheless, at national level rivers, lakes, ponds and creeks are not doing so well. The large cities of Romania are full of small advertisements announcing: 'We sell sand and pebbles at a good price' followed by a mobile phone number. This is the sign of an illegal exploitation of rivers by private individuals muddling through. A national report identifies four major categories of problems the postsocialist waters face: pollution with organic nutrients, the type I have ethnographically described in this chapter; pollution with nutrients; pollution with dangerous substances; and the hydromorphological changes.[30] The following few examples show that rivers would be worried, if they were conscious beings.

On 30 January 2000, a dam holding tailings breached and released some 100,000 cubic metres of infested waters containing heavy metals that spilled into two rivers from northern Transylvania.[31] The toxic water containing high levels of cyanide was the outcome of an Australian-Romanian gold mine operation. Within a few days the toxic waters reached the Tisza, a tributary of the Danube. Described by the chairman of the Hungarian Parliament as the largest ecological disaster after Chernobyl, the incident affected 2,000 kilometres of the Danube basin, killing thousands of fish, poisoning waterfowls and affecting thousands of people living on the riverbanks. In the spring of the same year catastrophic floods sent more contaminated waters downstream to the Tisza and the Danube.

The privatization of one of the largest fish enterprises after 1989 has been a curse for the villagers of Jurilovca (Southeast Romania). By tradition, almost all of them were fishermen whereas agriculture was just an additional source of revenue.[32] This is not surprising if one considers that over 60 per cent of the commune's territory lies underwater and includes Razelm, the largest lake in Romania. The lake is part of the Danube Delta reserve, one of the most important wetlands in Europe. Privatization of the state fish enterprise came together with the private administration of the lake. The private administrator, one of the most powerful men in the country in economic and political terms, has excluded villagers from fishing in the lake. His firm hired bodyguards to watch over the lake's resources. As there is no other important source of revenue in this part of the country other than fishing, fishermen were turned overnight into poachers. As a consequence, there was a rush for fish that, within few years, led to the depletion of several types of valuable fish.

Powerful economic actors, with strong connections in Parliament and the central government, have leased thousands of hectares of cropland in the dammed areas along the Danube Valley.[33] Once a wetland, crossed by myriads of water channels, ponds and lakes, with a population of fishermen, this land was separated from the Danube in the 1960s by large dams. The damming of the Danube during socialism represented one of the most brutal transformations of an ecosystem throughout Europe. The mini-deltas and wetlands along the river were transformed in several years, through state actions, into cropland. After 1990, this land was leased to powerful investors who earned significant amounts of cash from EU subsidies. Although the area is not appropriate for cereal cultivation, the subsidies these investors received turned them into untamed enemies of nature restoration. They wield their position, power and fortune in order to maintain a status quo that serves their interests against the economic interests of the inhabitants living there and at the expense of the degraded environment of that area. Ecological restoration of the area would bring important benefits not only to the environment, heavily damaged by the propensity for agriculture and the brutal ecological intervention of the socialist state, but to the residents as well. As it is now, rural inhabitants depend on the benevolence of the few large landowners who make the rules in the agricultural domain in this part of the country. A neo-feudal economic and political relationship enslaves both people and nature.

Rivers, lakes, ponds and other sources of water suffered damage throughout the postsocialist world. The scarcity of studies is to be blamed for the few reports we have on the fate of waters during profound postsocialist change, rather than that they were exempted from political and economic pressures.

In Bulgaria, rivers also suffer from the careless exploitation of sand and pebbles. Petar Petrov reports the damages caused to the river crossing the village of Biser (Southern Bulgaria).[34] The river is exploited by villagers and by private companies from neighbouring cities. Construction companies bring digging machines and lorries and exploit the river industrially, on a large scale, on the principle of 'dig and run'. As Petrov mentions, this seems to be a common practice among construction companies in Bulgaria. Villagers do the same thing, though they do not use machines but domestic tools such as shovels and horse carts. Not only is the riverbed deeply affected by these actions but also the dams and dikes initially constructed for mitigating the flood. The reasons are the same as in Romania: pebbles and sand are perceived as free commodities with uncertain ownership while local authorities passively assist in the rivers' destruction.

The population of the Republic of Moldova is in an awful situation: both surface and groundwaters are polluted with nitrates, sulphates and iron, but also with bacteria and faecal coliforms, mainly due to the lack of a sewage system.[35] Rivers seem to be the favourite spot for dumping garbage in Moldova as well. The language illuminates, in this particular case, the categorization of such spaces. People do not say they throw garbage into the river (*râu*, in Moldavian) but into the *râpă*, a word translated by Amy Samuelson as ravine or ditch. In both Romanian and Moldavian languages râpă also suggests a deserted, bad place, a rift in the land. Thus, as the language that people use in this particular case shows us that the river is not classified as a component of nature but as an un-useful place that now has found its use as a dumping spot.[36] The situation Samuelson describes is identical to the one in Romania: there is no waste disposal service for rural inhabitants and they have to muddle through somehow. The national government has issued laws and norms to protect the waters but they remain largely on paper because of the lack of funds.[37]

Moldavian agriculture still uses banned pesticides remaining from the Soviet period such as DDT, further contributing to the contamination of groundwater. What the Soviet farming system began has been completed by the postsocialist private agricultural system with the support of Western development agencies: the contamination of groundwater with pesticides and fertilizers used for an intensive agriculture.[38] Besides, pit latrines, widespread in Moldova, are another source of groundwater contamination.[39]

Further east, in Kazakhstan, the lakes just outside the city capital of Alma-Ata were polluted by the untreated wastewaters from a neighbouring town.[40] Industrial waters mixed with household wastewaters poisoned the fish, which was, allegedly, sold in the city markets, endangering the population's health. The lack of any facility for sorting and treating the garbage in a neighbourhood in Alma-Ata led to the groundwater being infiltrated with chemicals leaking from garbage dumped in a pit from 1970s onwards. Alexander coined the phrase 'official-yet-illegal' to define these pits, which not only echoes the passivity of the state officials regarding the environmental issues described throughout the chapter but also describes the involvement of different institutions and people in producing these wounds on the body of their localities.[41]

Both ground and surface waters are under extreme pressure throughout Southeast Europe. The magnitude of changes postsocialist waters are experiencing is at least equal to the changes that forests, pastures and the cropland have suffered. The privatization of state functions, the commoditization of rivers, lakes and ponds, and changes in property rights are only a few causes of the dramatic depletion of waters. Nevertheless, the picture I have drawn here is not specific to the postsocialist world. Toxic spills, contaminated rivers, privatized lakes and enclosed watersheds are common to the postcolonial world as well.[42] The rush for water and the political struggles over preferential access to water is as fierce in many other parts of the world as in the postsocialist states. What characterizes postsocialist countries is that the rush for water unfolds concurrently with land reform, changes in property rights over natural resources and the decentralization policies required by the new 'face' of the postsocialist state. Newly empowered by land reform, local bureaucrats and local officials advance where the central state's influence has receded. Whereas reports protest at the increasing commodification of waters in the postcolonial world, emphasizing the involvement of global neoliberal forces, in postsocialist countries the lack of central state involvement and the local bureaucrats' pursuit of their own private interests have played a crucial role in depleting the nation's rivers.

Notes

1. See for instance Worster (1985) on technological control of water in building the American West; White (1995) on the transformation of the natural river Columbia from the nineteenth century onward into a technological entity; and Cioc (2002) on the attempts of 'disciplining' the Rhine since the nineteenth century and the environmental consequences. More recent literature includes Mauch and Zeller (2008); Barca (2010); Wohl (2011); Kneitz and Landry (2012), and Zeisler-Vrasted (2015). For a socio-anthropological approach, see Strang (2004).
2. Verdery (1996).
3. Dorondel (2005); Mitroi (2013).
4. The government decision modifying Law 192/2001, Art. 56(c) reads: 'Fishing with spears, forks, stakes or any other stinging or clinging tool and fishing through raking or harpooning is forbidden.' The punishment is a fine between 300 million and 800 million lei (€800 to €2000) – a fortune by Romanian standards.
5. I use the masculine form of fisherman here because this is a strictly male occupation.
6. The penetration of capitalist relations after 1830 in Romania encouraged the development of the mills that brought important income. The large number of distilleries is explained by the local economy based on orchards and the production of țuica (see also chapter 2).
7. Pârnuță et al. (2003: 13).
8. The prices are for 2005. I have taken the technical details from the calculations of an engineer who built two houses in that period.
9. Thelen et al. (2011).
10. For a discussion of the politics of garbage under communism, see Gille (2007).
11. For an excellent analysis of the waste regimes, a concept which I do not openly engage with here but which I find extremely useful for further analysis, see Gille (2010).
12. Not just postsocialist state functions but those of the Western states have also been privatized. See, for instance, Hibou (2004 [1999]).

13. Law no. 515/2012 approving Governmental Ordinance no. 21/2002 regarding public services.
14. Brăilescu (2005).
15. Băia (1972: 224).
16. Duncan et al. (2012). The organic pollution of rivers is one of the most important types of pollution at the national level (Planuri de management 2007). I thank Professor Ioan Țibru for explaining to me the biological mechanisms of this process.
17. Băia (1972).
18. Ibid.
19. The chicken complex belonged to the collective farm and it was privatized in early 2000.
20. For details, see Duncan et al. (2012).
21. Alexiu et al. (2011).
22. In other parts of Europe water management is under thorough regulations, as in the United Kingdom. These regulations are not only 'on paper' but are enforced in the field. See, for instance, Strang (2004).
23. About externalities, see Kaul, Grunberg and Stern (1999).
24. Castree (2008a: 145).
25. There is a large geographical and political ecology literature, exploring the commodification of nature in the postcolonial world, which supports this statement. For an excellent review, see Castree (2008a; 2008b).
26. Mungiu-Pippidi (2006).
27. Börzel and Buzogány (2010).
28. Planuri de management (2007).
29. Ibid.: 6.
30. Raport de mediu (2013: 62 et seq.).
31. This example is based on the excellent analysis in Harper (2007).
32. This example is based on Dorondel (2005b) and on Mitroi (2013).
33. This account is based on Șerban (2013).
34. Petrov (2013).
35. Samuelson (2013); World Bank (2008).
36. Samuelson (2013: 108).
37. World Bank (2008).
38. Samuelson (2013: 78).
39. Hogosson and Larnholt (2010).
40. This example draws on Alexander (2009).
41. Alexander (2009).
42. Singh (1997); Tsuma (2010); Whiteford and Whiteford (2005).

Conclusion: A Disrupted Landscape

'There are no stories without meaning.'
—Umberto Eco, *Baudolino*

I returned to Dragomirești in 2009, after Romania had become a member of the European Union, burning with curiosity to see how deep the changes in the landscape were. Although expected, the changes astonished me. The hills, still patchily covered with clusters of trees in 2004, were now completely bare land. The eastern hill pasture, which was still just half covered with huts when I left the village, had now completely disappeared under the new huts built there. The river is dead and the muddy waters cannot sustain life anymore. Fishing, even for pleasure as we did in 2004 (as recounted in chapter 7) had disappeared. The cropland was as fragmented as in 2004 but several strips had been left idle. Their owners, I was told, were too old to work the land, or they had died or migrated to Western Europe. The EU's Common Agricultural Policies financial support, with its emphasis on large scale farms and its explicit aim of either making villagers specialize in agriculture or turning them away from agricultural livelihoods also seems to have played a role in this process.[1]

Small farmers, like most Dragomireștens, are exempted from EU subsidies. Thus, the land market is still depressed in Dragomirești. My visit to Dragova also brought surprises. Wood exploitation within the National Park was busier than ever. The same mayor, re-elected in 2008, plays the same significant role within the commune, pursuing his wood business and continuing to exploit the Dragova Creek.[2] Animal keepers still sell dairy products from the small tables in front of their houses. Tourism is increasing as well as the number of guesthouses. The new noisy ATVs (All Terrain Vehicles) acquired by several village investors haunt the small, unpaved roads of the village and the narrow paths into the forest, contributing to forestland destruction and biodiversity disturbance.[3] This is another sign of an influx of tourists.

As a visitor to these places for almost a decade I am a witness to the marks – and scars – inflicted on the landscape. The landscape has been devastated both by local state bureaucrats and their followers, with the tacit assistance of villagers, in a very short time. This book tells the story of a disrupted landscape, reveals the political, social and economic mechanisms behind the change and identifies the main players involved. Through these mechanisms a new landscape has been produced which is very different from the previous socialist landscape. The context and setting of these biophysical changes are the fall of the socialist regime and the emergence of an anticipated 'brand new' society. The economic and political changes that followed the fall of Ceaușescu's regime are part of a greater plan to transform the socialist society, economy and natural landscape into something different in terms of their scope, shape and function. Central government issued laws governing property restitution to historical owners under the supervision of econo-lobbyists, Western experts paid by international economic institutions to advise on which *path* the new society, economy and landscape should take.[4] The econo-lobbyists must have been from the same team as those development experts who worked in Lesotho, among other developing countries, having a standardized, context-independent formula to be applied to any given situation.[5] Under their supervision, the Romanian central government has privatized agricultural land and industry connected with agriculture, withdrawn state support from all agricultural business and cut state subsidies for farmers. The intended outcome was a transformation of the collective farm peasant into a capitalist farmer, and of animal keepers into farmers with tens, if not hundreds of animals. The restitution of forest to its former private owners – the Shibboleth of neoliberal ideology – was meant to ensure sustainable forestry practices and the preservation of biodiversity.

The assumption behind these economic and political measures was that socialist agriculture had to be rationalized once again and rendered efficient, this time in a neoliberal context. In short, land reform was an ideological and political program intended to reverse collectivization and forest nationalization that unfolded at the end World War II, which was an earlier ideological and political program seeking to engineer society, the economy and the natural landscape. The high modernist state, wonderfully analysed by James C. Scott, planned to impose a grid system on the messy realities of socio-economic life at local level, in order to make them easily observable, controllable and taxable.[6] The postsocialist state had similar aims though, as I have pointed out throughout this book, with different results. The plans of central government had to fit the new economy, social relations and landscape management to the new political and economic framework, namely the neoliberal one. The implementation of these plans has encountered two types of reaction, both of which have had profound consequences for the natural landscape. One concerns the reaction of local state bureaucrats, those who were responsible for the implementation of land reform. The second type of reaction, which has had an equal impact on the natural landscape, is that of villagers who have refused to become foot soldiers of the new capitalist agriculture.

State Versus Local Bureaucrats

In his critique of Scott's analysis of the state, Herzfeld points to some of the sources of his discontent with Scott's approach: 'the absence of an ethnographic sensibility toward the state functionaries' and the surprisingly monochromatic treatment of local state bureaucrats.[7] Local bureaucrats, continued Herzfeld, should be seen in all their diversity as human beings sometimes trying to mitigate the harshness of the laws for their clients or on the contrary, as manipulative individuals hijacking the law for selfish interests.[8] Tania Li contributes to Herzfeld's critique by preaching the importance of empirical investigation into the official state apparatus, a necessity fully acknowledged by Scott.[9] Taking up these theoretical stances, this book has examined the role of street-level bureaucracy – namely those bureaucrats who are called upon to implement land reform – in changing the agrarian landscape. Deforestation in particular but also the waning pastures and river enclosure are to a great extent the result of the actions of local state office holders such as the policeman, the state forest guard, the agricultural officer or the mayor and the vice-mayor and of the elected members of the local council. In one case, state bureaucrats have taken advantage of their powerful position as implementers of land reform laws in order to build a patron–client relationship with Rudari, a disadvantaged ethnic group, with the clear aim of illegally exploiting private forest.

The clear patron–client relationship between bureaucrats and this poor ethnic group that has historically specialized in wood exploitation is based on two factors: first, this ethnic group has been totally disadvantaged by forest restitution to its historical owners; second, is their need to survive in a harsh economic climate. Emphasizing the benefits of private property and the importance of historical legitimacy the legislators completely left out those ethnic groups such as Rudari and Roma, which never owned forest. These ethnic groups were the perfect tool in the hands of a powerful local bureaucracy who had the opportunity, the capability and the will to misappropriate the forest restitution process to serve their own private interest. It is however important to say that both parties were clear that they could only achieve their goals together. Local bureaucrats would not be successful in exploiting forest without the Rudari's labour, tools and knowledge. For this excluded group, involvement in forest exploitation is the only means of survival outside the meagre social assistance available to them. The waning of the communal pasture is partly a result of the exchange of services and goods between patrons, alias local bureaucrats, and their clients, the Rudari, which characterizes this type of relationship. This relationship was mutually advantageous despite the obvious imbalance in power between the two parties, allowing poor Rudari to survive and to build new huts on land that was never theirs by law or custom. In this way, local bureaucrats have fulfilled part of their duty to support their clients' livelihood. The patron–client relationship is not a dyadic relationship but entails a variety of social connections.[10] The fierce exploitation of private forest that has taken place has also involved a third party – the forest's new private owners. Although we cannot suggest that local bureaucrats colluded with private forest owners, they had at the very beginning common interests: forest owners wanted to exploit the newly acquired forest without state interference, and so refused to guard their forest as they were required to do by law. Forest owners never trusted the state agencies, be they local or central, nor the services of a professional forester (a state representative empowered to enforce state rules). This attitude provided an excellent opportunity for local bureaucrats to involve Rudari in illegally chopping down the unattended forests.

In the case of Dragova, the mayor, who is the channel through which the commune is connected to the wider political scene and the main centres of state power but who is also elected by villagers to represent the local community, is the main actor contributing to deforestation. As head of the local administration, and therefore part of the state apparatus, the mayor had the opportunity, knowledge and skills to profit from the forest restitution process. Acquiring standing trees (but no forestland, as I explained in chapter 4) he served his private wood exploitation firm with cheap raw material. Furthermore, he knew how to play other state office holders, as the head of the PCNP, in order to get access to the forest within the national park.

The special position enjoyed by local state bureaucrats and officials in rural Romania has a long history, which goes back to the beginning of the modern Romanian state in the nineteenth century. Since 1864, when the institution of the mayor's office was created, the mayor represented, in the words of one informant, 'the chief, the policeman and the judge of the commune'. Although he is elected and is formally accountable to his constituency, he has immense and, sometimes, undisputed power. The socialist state changed that in some respects: the mayor had authority but had to share it with the local Communist Party elite and with other state officials; sometimes, decisions he or she had to take were out of his/her hands. More importantly, the resources were out of his/her hands as well. Postsocialist society and especially land reform have restored considerable powers to the mayor.[11]

These political relations that so deeply affected the forest would have not been possible without the discreet support of higher state offices, even from Parliament, accorded to local state office holders. These high officials offer immunity to local state bureaucrats and channel certain types of resources only through them. The visit of the president of the Romanian Senate in Dragova, to which I have alluded throughout the book, is an obvious example of the support accorded by high state officials to local bureaucrats. This support consolidated the mayor's power at local and regional level and, at the same time, has helped to confirm him as the only political broker within the commune who has connections with the outside world. In this context, it was easy for the mayor first to enclose and then to privatize a water source despite opposition from the villagers. It was equally easy to convince the manager of the national park, also a politically appointed state office holder, to allow him to exploit wood on the park's territory. Thus, the relationship between different office holders is equally important if we want to understand the privileged access to natural resources enjoyed by local bureaucrats. These political relationships have not only reconfigured the power structures within the commune but also had a strong impact on forests, waters and pastures that have been equally affected and depleted.

All these examples show that the imposition of the master plan to modernize the socialist economy, society and landscape and change them according to neoliberal principles have met with opposition from local state bureaucrats – those same officials required to implement the reforms on the ground. This is not the only difference between the analysis this book provides and the view Scott's book takes.[12] Political mechanisms for implementing change in the socialist agricultural landscape and the social relationships that characterize it have in fact had consequences diametrically opposed to the plans of the high modernist state, to make society and the natural environment more legible from the centre. In the view of Scott and his followers (such as Paul Robbins for instance) the state has tried to modernize the natural world by introducing new species and organizing land use and property rights to produce more sustainable revenue.[13] In the postsocialist case, land reformers have also tried to impose a new rationalization of agriculture, according to neoliberal ideology, but the quiet opposition of local bureaucrats who act in their own interests has undermined the central governments' plans. It a true that 'officials of the modern state are, of necessity, at least one step – and often several steps – removed from the society they are charged with governing,' but only up to a point.[14] While central and regional officials are not part of the local community, those responsible for implementing land reform are almost always part of the local society. Precisely because they are locals and well informed about local realities, such as property rights or the location and value of a certain forest, they have been able to use the restitution laws to serve their private interests.

The primary reason for the failure of postsocialist plans to reorganize the rural economy and the natural world is not peasant resistance but that of local state employees. It is a case of the state against the state, not the state against the people.

Strategies to Cope with the Reforms

There was a second type of reaction to the neoliberal changes imposed by central government, this time from the villagers. They resisted the great plans to transform the local economy and agricultural landscape according to capitalist principles. When they received back their cropland, orchards and pastures they were expected instantly to transform themselves into capitalist farmers. Instead, they started to practise intercropping, a time-honoured agricultural practice in Dragomirești, continued to raise animals, but for household consumption only, and to rely on their industrial wages. Instead of becoming farmers with large numbers of cows or sheep, the villagers of Dragova maintained a status quo or moved into rural tourism. At any rate, they continue their practice of avoiding taxes and state regulations concerning food safety. In both cases agriculture has not been transformed, except in rare cases, into a commercial business but has continued at subsistence level. If we accept that the characteristics of industrialized agriculture are the intensive production and commercialization of farm products, crop specialization through cash cropping, high yield per hectare and dependency on machinery, as Walter Goldschmidt taught us, we may well refer to socialist agriculture as an example but not to agriculture in the postsocialist era[15] – at least, not the way agriculture is practised in these two hilly communes. Intercropping for instance proves that villagers have a good knowledge of local ecology – soil and plants – but this agricultural system can hardly bring high yields per hectare. The practice of replacing hybrid maize seeds with local types may be good for the environment and for soil but it makes it more difficult to predict crop yields.

One of the features of modern agriculture is the predictability and reliability of crop yields.[16] In Romanian hilly areas agricultural work is based on family labour and on labour exchange among friends or neighbours. If there are several people involved in such a network they each have to take turns when they have free time. What prevails is not economic efficiency but social relationships. In other words, completion of agricultural work relies on family, friends and neighbourhood relationships rather than economic considerations as would be in the case with a contractual relationship. Even those few peasants who could afford to pay people refrain from doing so because of the impossibility of predicting the work achieved by the end of the day. A day of work in agriculture is measured not in how much work has been done, measured in metres, hectares or acres, but in the time spent in the field. A *conac*, an old measurement of a working day, means half a day's work. Clearly much depends on the aptitude of the workers: some progress more slowly than others, some work faster. Some can finish mowing the entire field while others can manage only half. It is not only the quantity but the quality of work as well: some workers may be faster than others but they do lousy work; others can be slower but they are thorough. All these considerations lead to uncertainty around agricultural production. Moreover, this system shows that villagers have not seriously considered organizing production in such a way as to produce for the market as well.

Bringing back old agricultural practices or maintaining a status quo is not just a reaction on the part of the villagers to wider economic and political changes. They do their own thing, sometimes ignoring laws, norms and state regulations or just using them for their own advantage, sometimes breaking them when they consider them to be obstructing their livelihood. In other words, villagers not only have agency, as other scholars have pointed out; but they have also imposed on local bureaucrats their own way of understanding economics.[17] For instance, local bureaucrats should impose food security laws on the animal keepers who sell their products in front of their houses. Although it is strictly forbidden to set fire to the fields after harvesting, peasants still do this without any restriction from local bureaucrats. Local bureaucrats do not impose these laws on villagers simply because they understand their way of life and have no wish to enter into conflict with the community.

Thus, villagers oppose the greater plans to modernize agriculture with their own strategies, based on past experiences and on excellent knowledge of local ecology. History, more recent or more distant, has been recalled and employed in the villagers' strategy for coping with profound and sudden changes. Nevertheless, what I suggest in this book is only partially consistent with the view proposed in Scott's work.[18] The great plans of the high modernist state attempted to create a legible and simplified landscape and in some regards succeeded. The imposition of scientific principles of modern forestry and their outcome, the shape and tree composition of the modern forest, the organization of modern cities and such like attest to this success. The great plans of the postsocialist state were to re-organize an efficient and sustainable approach to agriculture according to neoliberal ideology. The outcome was subsistence agriculture, a landscape fragmented into myriads of parcels, with property rights that are often unclear.[19] Instead of transforming the landscape into a simplified and legible one, the land reform has transformed the socialist landscape (which was a system with contested property rights and debatable efficiency but nevertheless legible and rather modern) into an 'opaque' landscape. The postsocialist landscape is more illegible, to use Scott's terminology, than the socialist one.[20]

All these having been said, I do not want to imply that the neoliberal plans to reorganize agriculture have entirely failed. The ethnography I provided in chapters 3 and 4, for instance, show the enormous interest villagers take in their privately owned forest. However, they are not particularly interested in encouraging biodiversity in their forest, but simply in turning the wood into cash. Their emphasis on private property and their attempts to avoid state intervention in wood business and forest protection represent an *avant la lettre* neoliberal lens through which to read the natural landscape. Only those villagers having a guesthouse, and thus a direct economic interest in protecting the forest, militate in favour of the environment. Another example of a partially successful transformation of postsocialist agriculture is the emergence of a few shepherds who own large flocks and make a business from this traditional occupation. Whereas other villagers muddle through, the shepherds managed to build national and international connections in order to trade their products. They hire external labour, establish strategies to expand their business, have diversified their activity by selling dairy on multiple markets and have built guesthouses. They have fulfilled the dreams of the Romanian reformers. Finally, one should not forget that the first land reform law was passed through the Romanian Parliament after villagers in many parts of Romania had already claimed their cropland from the collective farms. Again, villagers' emphasis on private property, although it had strikingly different connotations for the villagers than for the neoliberal ideologists, has travelled in the same direction.

Nature's Agency

Socio-political and economic dynamics in Romania have doubtless affected the country's natural resources and the landscape. However, this is not a unilateral process but a circular one. Components of the natural landscape such as forest, land, water and animals have played a crucial role in enriching and empowering local state bureaucrats. Forest has its own history, which travels alongside human history a long way back – these two intertwined histories complicate the postsocialist forest restitution process. Forest attracted local bureaucrats because it is a valuable resource with potential for being marketed rapidly, and it has directly contributed to empowering some people and disempowering others. Forest exploitation was the aim of local politics and has sometimes actively contributed to shifts in property relations. Young trees growing wild on private pastures became the outposts of the forest and enabled state foresters to mark the land beneath as state forestland. Forest has its own life, its history and its agency upon villagers as well.

Animals such as the wild boar or the Carpathian bear have played a role as agents of the state and of the economic changes at the local level. These animals are not only tools in the hands of the state agencies; their own feeding ecology has had an impact too. The wild boar, which became so hated by Dragova villagers and triggered the change in the local economy from animal husbandry to rural tourism, did nothing but feed on the pasture that is part of its habitat. In Jurilovca, a fishing and farming village in the southeast of Romania, the postsocialist enemy is the blind mole rat (*Spalax typhlus*).[21] Agriculture became more important after 1990 as fishing brought less money than during socialism after the privatization of the state fishing enterprise and the concession of nearby lakes to private actors. The mole always existed in this area but it was kept under control by the socialist collective farm. Now that food is more difficult to find in the field because the owners of newly privatized farms gave up their vegetable gardens and started to cultivate cash crops (rape, wheat) the rodent feeds on the vegetable gardens close to villagers' backyards. Villagers tried several techniques in their attempts to kill the animal: they observed the activity of the rodent at the end of the underground passage, trying to hit it with a shovel when it emerged or flooding the underground passages or simply using poison. Having failed to kill the rodent, some villagers harvested the potatoes earlier than they should, as they feared they would lose the whole crop. Other villagers simply gave up and changed crops. They also started to cultivate maize. Although the type of soil in that area is not particularly suitable for cereals – unless a significant quantity of fertilizers is spread on the crop field – they continue to grow them because they fear that the mole will destroy their vegetable gardens (of potatoes, carrots or similar vegetables). These examples show us that animal ecology and human ecology intermingle and conflict, as is so often the case around the world. For instance, in Kerala, India, elephants in their search for food cross the landscapes inhabited by humans and destroy their crops, sometimes killing people.[22] The farmers' opposition to the elephants' raids is equal to their fury at the local forest departments responsible for protecting wildlife. Half the world's distance from Kerala, in the city of Brasov, Romania, the Carpathian bear annually kills several people in its search for food in the city garbage bins.

When animals do not play a direct role in changing local economy and agricultural practices they are still viewed as symbols of political and social power. The bear is regarded by the locals in Dragova as an active political weapon of the state against private forest owners. In a way, villagers think, the bear serves the state in the same manner that rangers watch the forest; the bear serves to keep people out of their forests. Humans and animals compete for the same territory but luckily without any human injuries as yet. The snake in Dragomirești plays a socio-political role: since poor Rudari cannot engage openly in a critical social discourse against local state bureaucrats, they use the snake as a metaphor for their economic marginality and political exclusion. Losers of the land and forest restitution policy, they use the snake as a way of attracting attention to their poor living standards.

Nature's agency has the merit of stressing an idea often overlooked by social scientists: we need to pay attention to the materiality of the landscape. Forest, animals, waters, crops, pastures and land have their own internal dynamics, their life, which we should take into account when trying to understand human culture and society. As social scientists we are poorly equipped to consider the materiality of the landscape; often, we do not know how to deal with it and focus instead exclusively on state, market, social or political relations. Market mechanisms, political economy or the analysis of local relations are important for understanding the deep and rapid changes that postsocialist societies have undergone. But in order to gain a more complete picture we need to look at the biophysical features of the landscape as well. Too often, anthropologists, sociologists and economists have talked about the lack of access to market, lack of credits and other economic impediments – all real of course. It is time though to look at the type of crops and fruits people cultivate and their advantages, the agricultural practices they engage in, such as intercropping, and understand this as a household strategy and as a form of freedom. Using local resources, from manure to seeds, may not bring economic efficiency but in this way villagers avoid dependency on economic actors located outside the village. Thus, in keeping an eye on the materiality of the landscape and its metamorphosis we may discover new ways of understanding the deepest transformation of our time. Sometimes, social and political processes are mediated through or conditioned by the materiality of plants, seeds, forest, rivers or animals. The materiality of a forest, for instance, its value as a commodity as well as its agency when encroaching on pasture, reflect wider social, economic and political processes of the postsocialist society. The materiality of forest is the intersection where the power of local bureaucrats to hijack state policy meets the economic needs of an impoverished population. Nature agency concerns a different type of materiality in which state power, manifested through its local bureaucrats, changes the ownership of the newly forested land. The intrinsically characteristics of the plums, their perishability, which requires certain conditions of storage – a certain light, temperature and humidity – and transport conditions dictate what one can do with them. To grow certain plum trees is more demanding in terms of knowledge of its biology and ecology, technical skills and funds invested than, say, in maize. It is, again, about the materiality of the plum tree itself, its biological resistance to pests which intersects with market access, availability of investments and the economic needs of a household. Villagers themselves reflect to the materiality of the plum trees and its fruits, generally to the materiality of agricultural produces and we should do it too. Looking through the lenses of nature agency and the materiality of the landscape we understand the processes of valuation, contestation and appropriation, which mark the relations between state, local bureaucrats, villagers, market and the natural landscape.

What Lessons for the World?

At this juncture it is the reader's legitimate right to ask the question, what do we learn from the story of transforming the socialist landscape into a postsocialist one? Is there anything specifically postsocialist about the political and economic mechanisms of deforestation as described in this book, or is this a general account about deforestation everywhere? How different is the struggle between postsocialist villagers and the administration of national parks as compared to similar struggles in postcolonial settings? Detailed answers to these questions require a separate book. Yet, I dare to outline a few suggestions.

The reactions of Dragovan villagers to the attempts by national park officials to control the forests restituted through land reform are similar to reactions of villagers in similar circumstances around the world. Establishing a protected area in Tanzania meant the criminalization of customary practices of local people such us hunting and wood extraction. What constitutes a place of biodiversity conservation for the state agencies or international agencies for nature protection is the hunting, cultivation or wood extraction ground for local villagers.[23] The African centralized park authorities established control over nature through laws and the imposition of a system of ideas – the conservationist ideology – that is alien to locals. A similar struggle between competing ideologies, which triggers a struggle for resources, is also common to Indonesian national parks and protected areas. Evicted locals, violence, a ban on hunting, grazing and logging are outcomes of conflicting attitudes to the natural environment.[24] Classifying a certain area as having a protected regime, creation of boundaries and exclusion of local people from using the natural resources from that territory are part of the state's tools of forest appropriation.[25] Local villagers' rights are dismissed in favour of the greater good that the forest generally, and protected areas in particular, provide. In reaction, villagers re-appropriate forestland for cultivation, sabotage the newly planted species and generally disobey the state imposed rules concerning forest activity.[26] In short, the competition for forest resources between villagers and the state takes the form of each party building an ideology that justifies its access to land, trees and labour in the forest. Despite local aspects which surely differ from one setting to another, from one continent to another, all these developments, such as the state attempt to control forest and villagers' various forms of resistance would seem familiar to postsocialist villagers.

Nevertheless, a wind of change is blowing. Several authors have noticed that the new trend in natural resources management that promotes decentralization policies and encourages community participation in conservation may lead to a more sustainable exploitation of natural resources.[27] The emergence of a property rights agenda in forestry at the global level, supported strongly by activists, international institutions and national governments, has started to give not only a voice but also tenure rights over the forest to people who live in the forest. Rights activists advocate the recognition of forest people's group identities and rights over their natural environment.[28] Nature restoration, another new conservation trend in which local users of a natural resource are called to contribute to renewing and maintain the health of an ecosystem, offers new ways to restructure human–nature relationships according to more sustainable principles.[29] Instead of projecting nature protection as a top-down action, an exogenous project imposed on locals, the new trends attempt to engage local people in preserving natural landscape and the animals that populate it. Instead of keeping villagers out of the national parks and protected areas the new trend is to offer them property rights over forests so they are transformed from potential perpetrators into conscious guardians.

Two particular points seems to differentiate between practices under postsocialism and those of the postcolonial states. In the process of land reform, one state institution grants people forestland, based on undisputed historical rights, while other institutions impose a stronger control over them. The intricate policies of the postsocialist state, acknowledging private rights over forest and denying them at the same time, may be a feature of the postsocialist transformation. Whereas the postcolonial states try hard to deny customary laws over forest, the postsocialist state has acknowledged and sanctioned the historical rights, only to thwart them. A second possible postsocialist characteristic concerns the position of local state office holders. Land reform as a vast political program of changing the agricultural landscape has also conferred a special position on local bureaucrats. As I have shown throughout the book, local state office holders were able to hijack central state policies and take advantage of their particularly powerful position at local level. Although in postcolonial settings the local elite also has its own private interests, it seems more eager to promote central state policies than its postsocialist peers. In the postcolonial context, resources are channelled along political party lines. Being on the 'right side' of the political line could ease access to resources offered by the state. In exchange for this favour, the local rural elite becomes the political and economic agent of the central state in the countryside.[30] In a postsocialist context the state bureaucrats *are* the local political and economic elite. In the two communes few villagers could be considered important economic actors and still be outside the state apparatus. The explanation lies in the sudden and often violent transformation the postsocialist states went through in 1989 and the magnitude of these changes. This break restructured the state at all levels and created new policies and political practices. In the process of new state formation, the old and new political elite have occupied the new centres of power, creating new institutions and structures in which they have a central role.

The two 'posts' – postcolonialism and postsocialism – have few things that set them apart and plenty in common. Among commonalities I include the same fierce struggle for natural resources among different actors and the catastrophic consequences for the natural environment. As in most postcolonial settings, a vast geographic area – former socialist countries – has suffered profound environmental changes. Depletion of forest and waters, land degradation and loss of biodiversity is part of the present-day human–environment relationship. Disrupted landscapes are a sad reality of our world and a significant part of the grand narrative of our times.

Notes

1. Fox (2011).
2. The mayor and his businesses were the subject of several newspapers' coverage. Nevertheless, he remains undisputedly one of the richest and most powerful people in Argeş County.
3. Although explicitly banned under the Law 265/2006 in protected areas as a major source of noise pollution, the ATV is very popular in mountainous areas.
4. Wandel (1998).
5. Ferguson (1994: 258).
6. Scott (1998).
7. Ibid.; Herzfeld (2005: 372–73).
8. Other scholars speak about the double embeddedness of local officials. They are embedded in both hierarchical administrative and political structures but also as members of the local community. See, for instance, von Benda-Beckmann and von Benda-Beckmann (1998) and Dorondel and Popa (2014).
9. Li (2005); Scott (2005).
10. Eisenstadt and Roniger (1980).
11. For the particularly important position of mayors 'as avatars who "embody" abstract concepts of ideologies of place, community and politics that are both territorial and relational', see Jayne (2011: 805). Although Jayne's study refers to urban spaces I find

it useful for understanding the complex position of the mayor within the web of relations constituted by the upstream/downstream politics, conflicts and agendas – all linked to spatial restructuring and access to resources.
12. Scott (1998).
13. Robbins (2001).
14. Scott (1998: 76).
15. Goldschmidt (1947 [1978]).
16. Scott (1998); Robbins (2001).
17. See, for instance, Sikor et al. (2009).
18. Scott (1998).
19. Verdery (1999).
20. Scott (1998).
21. This example is provided by Mihai Popa (personal communication).
22. Münster and Münster (2012).
23. Neumann (1998).
24. Peluso (1993).
25. Vandeergest and Peluso (1995).
26. Peluso (1992).
27. Agrawal (2005); Leave (2014); Ribot et al. (2008).
28. For more details on this approach, see Sikor and Stahl (2011).
29. For an overview of this emergent field, see Cairns and Heckman (1996); Choi et al. (2008) or Hall (2014).
30. Hart (1989); von Benda-Beckmann and von Benda-Beckmann (1998).

References

Achim, V. 1998. *Țiganii în istoria României* [The Place of Gypsies in the Romanian History]. București: Editura Enciclopedică.
Agrawal, A. 2005. *Environmentality. Technologies of Government and the Making of Subjects*. Durham and London: Duke University Press.
Alexander, C. 2009. 'Waste Under Socialism and After: A Case-Study from Almaty'. In *Enduring Socialism. Explorations of Revolution and Transformation, Restoration and Continuation*, edited by H. G. West and P. Raman, 148–68. New York and Oxford: Berghahn Books.
Alexiu, V., D. Stancu and M. Chirițoiu. 2011. *Arii protejate din Judetul Argeș* [Protected Areas from Argeș County]. Pitești: Editura Universității din Pitești.
ANES. 2007. 'Cercetarea etnografică privind discriminarea multiplă' [Ethnographic Research Concerning Multiple Discrimination]. Report Elaborated by the National Agency for the Equality of Chances Between Women and Men (ANES). București.
Băcanu, S. I. 1999. *Monografia comunei Davidești jud. Argeș* [The Monograph of Davidești Commune, Argeș County]. Pitești: Cultura.
Băia, G. 1972. *Alimentația animalelor domestice* [Fodder for Domestic Animals]. București: Editura Didactică și Pedagogică.
Baiski, D. 2005. 'Cândva înfloritoare, sericicultura românească se află în agonie' [Sometimes Ago Flourishing, the Romanian Sericulture is Now Dying]. *Agenda* 16 (16 April 2005). Accessed 6 April 2014. http://www.dusanbaiski.eu/node/52.
Bandelj, N. 2008. *From Communists to Foreign Capitalists. The Social Foundations of Foreign Direct Investment in Postsocialist Europe*. Princeton, NJ: Princeton University Press.
Barca, S. 2010. *Enclosing Water. Nature and Political Economy in a Mediterranean Valley, 1796–1916*. Cambridge, UK: White Horse Press.
Barco, A. and E. Nedelcu 1974. *Județul Argeș* [Argeș County]. București: Editura Academiei RSR.
Berindei, M. and N. Bria, eds. 1982. *Mecanizarea lucrărilor în producția de cartofi* [The Mechanical Work for the Potatoes Production]. București: Ceres.
Bierschenk, T. and J.-P. Olivier de Serdan. 1997. 'Local Powers and a Distant State in Rural Central African Republic'. *The Journal of Modern African Studies* 35 (3): 441–68.
Bierschenk, T. and J.-P. Olivier de Serdan, eds. 2014. *States at Work: Dynamics of African Bureaucracies*. Leiden: Brill.

Biolan, I. et al. 2006. 'Tehnica de colectare, prelucrare ecologică, stocare și valorificare a îngrășămintelor de origine animală pentru prevenirea poluării mediului înconjurător' [The Technique of Collecting, Storage and Development of the Manure for Preventing the Damaging of the Environment]. *International Conference and Exhibition of Hydraulics, Pneumatics, Sealing Elements, Fine Mechanics, Tools, Specific Electronic Equipment and Mechatronics*, 16th ed., November 2006. Râmnicu-Vâlcea.

Blarel, B. et al. 1992. 'The Economics of Farm Fragmentation: Evidence from Ghana and Rwanda'. *The World Bank Economic Review* 6 (2): 233–54.

Bogza, G. 2011. *Țări de piatră, de foc și de pământ* [Countries of Stone, Fire, and Dust]. București: Jurnalul National.

Börzel, T. and A. Buzogány. 2010. 'Environmental Organisation and the Europenisation of Public Policy in Central and Eastern Europe: The Case of Biodiversity Governance'. *Environmental Politics* 19 (5): 708–35.

Bouriaud, L. 2005. 'Causes of Illegal Logging in Central and Eastern Europe'. *Small-scale Forest Economics. Management and Policy* 4 (3): 269–91.

Bouriaud, L. and M. Marzano. 2013. 'Conservation, Extraction and Corruption: Will Sustainable Forest Management Be Possible in Romania?'. In *Natural Resource Extraction and Indigenous Livelihoods: Development Challenges in an Era of Globalization*, edited by E. Gilberthorpe and G. Hilson, 221–39. London: Ashgate.

Brăilescu, C. E. 2005. 'Towards Separate Waste Collection in Bucharest, Romania. A Social Acceptability Approach'. MA dissertation. Rotterdam: University of Rotterdam.

Brearley, M. 2001. 'The Persecution of Gypsies in Europe'. *American Behavioral Scientist* 45: 588–99.

Brubaker, R. 1996. *Nationalism Reframed. Nationhood and the National Question in the New Europe*. Cambridge and New York: Cambridge University Press.

Büscher, B. 2012. 'Inverted Commons: Africa's Nature in the Global Imagination'. In *Forests and Fields: Global Environments in Ethnographic Perspective*. Special issue of *RCC Perspectives* 5, edited by D. Münster, U. Münster and S. Dorondel, 31–37.

Busuiocescu, N. D. 2000. 'Monografia satului Conțești' [The Monograph of Conțești Village]. Unpublished manuscript.

Butac, M., C. Popa and M. Militaru. 2009. 'Identification of Some Genetic Resistant Sources to Plum Pox for Obtaining Initial Material Needed in Plum Breeding'. *Acta Horticulturae* 825: 177–80.

Butac, M. et al. 2011. 'Romanian Germplasm Fund and its Use in Plum Breeding Program'. *Scientific Papers of the Research Institute for Fruit Growing Pitești* XVII: 17–22.

Cairns, J. Jr. and J. R. Heckman 1996. 'Restoration Ecology: The State of an Emerging Field'. *Annual Review of Energy and Environment* 21: 167–89.

Carrithers, M., J. Bracken and S. Emery. 2011. 'Can a Species Be a Person? A Trope and Its Entanglements in the Anthropocene Era'. *Current Anthropology* 52 (5): 661–85.

Cartwright, A. L. 2001. *The Return of the Peasant. Land Reform in Post-Communist Romania*. Aldershot: Ashgate.

Castree, N. 2008a. 'Neoliberalising Nature: The Logics of Deregulation and Reregulation'. *Environment and Planning A* 40 (1): 131–52.
———. 2008b. 'Neoliberalising Nature: Processes, Effects and Evaluations'. *Environment and Planning A* 40 (1): 153–73.
———. 2010. 'Neoliberalism and the Biophysical Environment 1: What "Neoliberalism" Is, and What Difference Nature Makes to It'. *Geography Compass* 4 (12): 1725–33.
———. 2011. 'Neoliberalism and the Biophysical Environment 3: Putting Theory into Practice'. *Geography Compass* 5 (1): 35–49.
Căciulă, P. and I. Căciulă. 1998. 'Monografia Satului Ciocanu Comuna Dâmbovicioara' [The Monograph of Ciocanu Village, Dâmbovicioara Commune]. Unpublished manuscript.
Cătănuș, D. and O. Roske. 2000. *Colectivizarea agriculturii în România. Dimensiunea politică 1949–1953* [The Collectivization in Romania. The Political Dimension 1949–1953]. București: Institutul Național Pentru Studiul Totalitarismului.
———. 2004. *Colectivizarea agriculturii în România. Represiunea 1949–1953* [The Collectivization in Romania. Repression 1949–1953]. București: Institutul Național Pentru Studiul Totalitarismului.
Cellarius, B. 2004. *In The Land Of Orpheus Rural Livelihoods and Nature Conservation in Post-socialist Bulgaria*. Madison: University of Wisconsin Press.
Cernea, M. 1973. 'The Co-operative Farm as an Organization: An Attempt at Conceptualization'. *Revue roumaine des sciences sociales* 17: 109–30.
———. 1974. *Sociologia cooperativei agricole* [The Sociology of the Agricultural Cooperative]. București: Editura Academiei RSR.
———. 1976. 'Co-operative Farming and Family Change in Romania'. In *The Social Structure of Eastern Europe. Transition and Process in Czechoslovakia, Hungary, Poland, Romania, and Yugoslavia*, edited by B. L. Faber, 259–72. New York, Washington and London: Praeger Publishers.
———. 1978. 'Macrosocial Change, Feminization of Agriculture and Peasant Women's Threefold Economic Role'. *Sociologia Ruralis* XVIII (82–3): 107–24.
Chari, S. and K. Verdery. 2009. 'Thinking Between the Posts: Postcolonialism, Postsocialism, and Ethnography after the Cold War'. *Comparative Studies in Society and History* 51 (1): 6–34.
Chelcea, I. 1944. *Țiganii din România. Monografie etnografică* [The Gypsies from Romania. Ethnographical Monographs]. București: Editura Institutului Central de Statistică.
Chiburte, L. 2008. 'Teoria accesului la resurse naturale și practicile sociale de exploatare a pădurilor' [The Theory of Access to Natural Resources and Social Practices of Forest Exploitation]. *Sociologie Românească* 3–4: 116–26.
Choi, Y. D. et al. 2008. 'Ecological Restoration for Future Sustainability in a Changing Environment'. *Ecoscience* 15 (1): 53–64.
Cioc, M. 2002. *The Rhine: An Eco-biography, 1851–2000*. Seattle and London: University of Washington Press.
Ciudin, E. 2006. *Șerpi și șopârle. Biologie, creștere și patologie* [Snakes and Lizards. Biology, Breeding and Pathology]. București: M.A.S.T.

Constantin, D. L. and C. Mitrut. 2009. 'Cultural Tourism, Sustainability and Regional Development: Experiences from Romania'. In *Cultural Tourism and Sustainable Local Development*, edited by L. F. Girard and P. Nijkamp, 149–66. Burlington: Ashgate.

Constantinescu, G. 2006. *Argeș Dictionar etnocultural* [Argeș – An Ethnocultural Dictionary]. Pitești: Alean.

Constantinescu, M. 1972. 'Probleme economice și sociologice ale unei comune de munte' [Sociological and Economic Issues in a Mountainous Commune]. *Viitorul social* 1 (2): 500–16.

Creed, G. 1995. 'The Politics of Agriculture: Identity and Socialist Sentiment in Bulgaria'. *Slavic Review* 54 (4): 1995: 865–68.

———. 1998. *Domesticating Revolution: From Socialist Reform to Ambivalent Transition in a Bulgarian Village*. University Park: Penn State University Press.

Creed, G. and J. R. Wedel. 1997. 'Second Thoughts from the Second World: Interpreting Aid in Post-Communist Eastern Europe'. *Human Organization* 56 (3): 253–64.

Cremene, C. et al. 2005. 'Alterations of Steppe-Like Grasslands in Eastern Europe: a Threat to Regional Biodiversity Hotspots'. *Conservation Biology* 19 (5): 1606–18.

Cronon, W. 1983. *Changes in the Land. Indian, Colonists, and the Ecology of New England*. New York: Hill & Wang.

———. 1995. 'Introduction: In Search of Nature'. In *Uncommon Ground. Towards Reinventing Nature*, edited by W. Cronon, 23–56. New York and London: W. W. Norton & Company.

Crosgrove, D. E. 1998 [1984]. *Social Formation and Symbolic Landscape*. Madison: The University of Wisconsin Press.

Csaki, C. and Z. Lerman. 1997. 'Land Reform and Land Restructuring in East Central Europe and CIS in the 1990s: Expectations and Achievements after the First Five Years'. *European Review of Agricultural Economics* 24 (3–4): 428–52.

Czepczynski, M. 2008. *Cultural Landscapes of Post-Socialist Cities. Representation of Powers and Needs*. Aldershot: Ashgate.

Dahlström, A., A. Iuga and T. Lennartsson. 2013. 'Managing Biodiversity Rich Hay Meadows in the EU: a Comparison of Swedish and Romanian Grasslands'. *Environmental Conservation* 40 (2): 194–205.

Demeulenaere, E. 2012. 'Reclaiming the Seeds, Becoming "Peasants": On-Farm Agrobiodiversity Conservation and the Making of Farmers' Collective Identity'. In *Fields and Forests. Ethnographic Perspectives on Environmental Globalization*. Special issue of *Perspectives* 5, edited by U. Münster, D. Münster and S. Dorondel, 59–66.

Dietler, M. 2006. Alcohol: Anthropological/Archaeological Perspectives. *Annual Review of Anthropology* 35: 229–49.

Dijk, van T. 2003. 'Scenarios of Central European Land Fragmentation'. *Land Use Policy* 20 (2): 149–58.

Dinu, I. et al. 1992. *Creșterea și valorificarea porcilor în gospodăriile personale* [Keeping and Selling Pigs by Small-Landholders]. București: Ceres.

Dorondel, S. 2004. *Moartea și apa. Ritualuri funerare, simbolism acvatic și structura lumii de dincolo în imaginarul țărănesc* [Death and Water. Funerary Rituals, Water Symbolism, and the Otherworld Imaginary Among the Peasants from Southern Romania]. București: Paideia.
———. 2005a. 'Land, Property, and Access in a Village from Postsocialist Romania'. In *Between East and West. Studies in Anthropology and Social History*, edited by S. Dorondel and S. Șerban, 268–307. București: Editura Institutului Cultural Român.
———. 2005b. 'The "Voices" of the Romanian Integration into EU: Land and Environmental Practices in a Village from Dobroudja'. *The Anthropology of East Europe Review* 23 (2): 30–40.
———. 2007. 'Ethnicity, State, and Natural Resources in the Southeastern Europe. The *Rudari* Case'. In *Transborder Identities. Romanian-Speaking Population in Bulgaria*, edited by S. Șerban, 215–40. Bucharest: Paideia.
———. 2011a. 'Tenure Rights, Environmental Interests, and the Politics of Local Government in Romania'. In *Forests and People. Property, Governance, and Human Rights*, edited by T. Sikor and J. Stahl, 175–86. London and New York: Earthscane.
———. 2011b. 'Contesting *Pasts*: Property Negotiation and Land Reform in a Romanian Village'. *New Europe College Yearbook* 2008/2009: 121–38.
———. 2012. 'Neoliberal Transformations of the Romanian Agrarian Landscape'. In *Fields and Forests. Ethnographic Perspectives on Environmental Globalization*. Special issue of *Perspectives* 5, edited by U. Münster, D. Münster and S. Dorondel, 13–22.
Dorondel, S. and M. Popa. 2014. 'Workings of the State: Administrative Lists, European Union Food Aid, and the Local Practices of Distribution in Rural Romania'. *Social Analysis* 58 (3): 124–40.
Dorondel, S. and T. Sikor. 2009. 'Private Property: From Postsocialism to Neoliberalism?'. *Annuaire Roumain d'Anthropologie* 49: 55–62.
Duncan, E., P. J. A. Kleinman and A. N. Sharpley. 2012. 'Euthrophication of Lakes and Rivers'. *eLS*. DOI: 10.1002/9780470015902.a0003249.pub2. http://onlinelibrary.wiley.com/doi/10.1002/9780470015902.a0003249.pub2/abstract Accessed 11 November 2013.
Eikeland, S. and L. Riabova. 2002. 'Transition in a Cold Climate. Management Regimes and Rural Marginalisation in Northwest Russia'. *Sociologia Ruralis* 42 (3): 250–66.
Eisenstadt, S. N. and L. Roniger. 1980. 'Patron–Client Relations as a Model of Structuring Social Exchange'. *Comparative Studies in Society and History* 22 (1): 42–77.
Ferguson, J. 1994. *The Anti-Politics Machine. 'Development', Depoliticization, and Bureaucratic Power of Lesotho*. Minneapolis: University of Minnesota Press.
Fox, K. 2011. *Peasants into European Farmers? EU Integration in the Carpathian Mountains of Romania*. Zürich and Berlin: LIT Verlag.
Franklin, S. 2002. 'Białowieza Forest, Poland: Representation, Myth, and the Politics of Dispossession'. *Environment and Planning A* 34 (8): 1459–85.

Gille, Z. 2007. *From the Cult of Waste to the Heap of History. The Politics of Waste in Socialist and Postsocialist Hungary*. Bloomington and Indianapolis: Indiana University Press.

———. 2009. 'From Nature as Proxy to Nature as Actor'. *Slavic Review* 68 (1): 1–9.

———. 2010. 'Actor Networks, Modes of Production, and Waste Regimes: Reassembling the Macrosocial'. *Environment and Planning A* 42 (5): 1049–64.

Gissibl, B., S. Höhler and P. Kupper, eds. 2012. *Civilizing Nature: National Parks in Global Perspective*. New York: Berghahn Books.

Godoy, R. and C. P. A. Bennett. 1991. 'The Economics of Monocropping and Intercropping by Smallholders: The Case of Coconuts in Indonesia'. *Human Ecology* 19 (1): 83–98.

Goldschmidt, W. 1978 [1947]. *As You Sow: Three Studies in the Social Consequences of Agribusiness*. Montclair, NJ: Allanheld, Osmun and Company.

Grecu, C. and I. Haş. 2001. *Hibrizi de porumb* [Corn Hybrid Seeds]. Turda: Stațiunea de Cercetări Agricole.

Grodzińskca, K. et al. 2004. 'Vegetation of the Selected Forest Stands and Land Use in the Carpathian Mountains'. *Environmental Pollution* 130 (1): 17–32.

Grzymala-Busse, A. and P. Jones Luong. 2002. 'Reconceptualizing the State: Lessons from Post-Communism'. *Politics & Society* 30 (4): 529–54.

Gulca, V. 2008. 'Opportunity of Small-scale Forestry in Moldova'. *Journal of Horticulture, Forestry, and Biotechnology* 3: 120–34.

Hall, M. 2014. 'Restoration and the Search for Counter-Narratives'. In *The Oxford Handbook of Environmental History*, edited by A. C. Isenberg, 309–31. Oxford and New York: The Oxford University Press.

Hamelet, M. P. 1971. *Nicolae Ceauşescu. Biografie și texte selectate* [Nicoale Ceauşescu. Biography and Selected Texts]. București: Editura Politică.

Hammel, E. A. 1980. 'The Comparative Method in Anthropological Perspective'. *Comparative Studies in Society and History* 22(2): 145–55.

Hann, C. 1993. 'From Production to Property: Decollectivization and the Family-Land Relationship in Contemporary Hungary'. *Man* (N.S.) 28 (2): 299–320.

———. 2001. 'Comments to Michel-Rolph Trouillot, The Anthropology of the State in the Age of Globalization. Close Encounters of the Deceptive Mind'. *Current Anthropology* 42 (1): 125–38.

———. 2006. *'Not the Horse We Wanted'. Postsocialism, Neoliberalism, and Eurasia*. Münster: LIT Verlag.

———. 2007. 'A New Double Movement? Anthropological Perspectives on Property in the Age of Neoliberalism'. *Socio-Economic Review* 5 (2): 287–318.

Hann, C., ed. 2002. *Postsocialism. Ideals, Ideologies and Practices in Eurasia*. London and New York: Routledge.

Hann, C. and K. Hart 2011. *Economic Anthropology. History, Ethnography, Critique*. Cambridge: Polity Press.

Haraway, D. J. 1985. 'A Manifesto for Cyborgs: Science, Technology, and Socialism Feminism in the 1980s'. *Socialist Review* 15 (2): 65–108.

Hardin, G. 1968. 'The Tragedy of the Commons'. *Science* 162 (3859): 1243–48.
Harper, K. 2007. '"Wild Capitalism" and "Ecocolonialism": A Tale of Two Rivers'. *American Anthropologist* 107 (2): 221–33.
Hart, G. 1989. 'Agrarian Change in the Context of State Patronage'. In *Agrarian Transformations. Local Processes and the State in Southeast Asia*, edited by G. Hart, A. Turton, and B. White, 31–49. Berkeley, Los Angeles and Oxford: University of California Press.
Hartia, S. 1963. *Să folosim cu chibzuință terenurile agricole* [To Use Wiser the Agricultural Fields]. București: Editura Politică.
———. 1983. *Economia cerealelor* [The Economy of Cereals]. București: Ceres.
Harvey, D. 2005. *A Brief History of Neoliberalism*. Oxford: Oxford University Press.
HAU. 2014. 'Book Symposium – How Forests Think: Toward an Anthropology Beyond the Human' (Eduardo Kuhn). *HAU Journal of Ethnographic Theory* 4 (2): 237–88.
Heidhues, F., J. R. Davis and G. Schrieder. 1998. 'Agricultural Transformation and Implications for Designing Rural Financial Policies in Romania'. *European Review for Agricultural Economics* 25 (3): 351–72.
Herzfeld, M. 1992. *The Social Production of Indifference. Exploring the Symbolic Roots of Western Bureaucracy*. Chicago and London: The University of Chicago Press.
———. 2005. 'Political Optics and the Occlusion of Intimate Knowledge'. *American Anthropologist* 107 (3): 369–76.
Heston, A. and D. Kumar. 1983. 'The Persistence of Land Fragmentation in Peasant Agriculture: An Analysis of South Asian Cases'. *Explorations in Economic History* 20 (2): 199–220.
Hibou, B. 2004 [1999]. Preface to the English Edition. In *Privatizing the State*, edited by B. Hibou, translated by J. Derrick, vii–xvi. London: Hurst & Co.
Hirsch, E. and M. O'Hanlon. 1995. *The Anthropology of Landscape. Perspectives on Place and Space*. Oxford: Clarendon Press.
Hogosson, A. and K. Larnholt 2010. 'Water Quality and Sanitation in Rural Moldova'. Unpublished paper. Uppsala Sweden: Uppsala University.
Horwith, B. 1985. 'A Role for Intercropping in Modern Agriculture'. *BioScience* 35 (5): 286–91.
Howarth, W. 1998. 'Property Rights, Regulation and Environmental Protection: Some Anglo-Romanian Contrasts'. In *Property relations. Renewing the anthropological tradition*, edited by C. M. Hann, 181–200. Cambridge: Cambridge University Press.
Hull, M. 2008. 'Ruled by Records: The Expropriation of Land and the Misappropriation of Lists', *American Ethnologist* 35 (4): 501–18.
Hung, V. P., T. G. MacAulay and S. P. Marsh. 2007. 'The Economics of Land Fragmentation in the North of Vietnam'. *The Australian Journal of Agricultural and Resource Economics* 51: 195–211.
Iancu, B. and V. Mihăilescu. 2009. '"Produsele de calitate" și patrimonializarea gustului în România' ['Quality Products' and Patrimonialization of Taste in Romania]. *Sociologie Românească* VII (3): 37–49.

Infoeuropa 2007. 'Aderarea României la Uniunea Europeană: capitolele de negociere' [Romania Accession to the EU: the Negotiations]. *European Issues* 20. Accessed 26 May 2012. www.infoeuropa.ro.

Ingold, T. 2000. *Perception of the Environment. Essays on Livelihood, Dwelling and Skill.* London and New York: Routledge.

———. 2008. 'When ANT Meet SPIDER: Social Theory for Anthropods'. In *Material Agency. Towards a Non-Anthropocentric Approach*, edited by C. Knappett and L. Malafouris, 209–15. New York: Springer.

Ioras, F., N. Muica, and D. Turnock. 2001. 'Approaches to Sustainable Forestry in the Piatra Craiului National Park'. *GeoJournal* 55 (2): 579–98.

Iordachi, C. and D. Dobrincu, eds. 2009. *Transforming Peasants, Property and Power. The Collectivization of Agriculture in Romania, 1949–1962.* Budapest and New York: CEU Press.

Jackson, J. B. 1994. *A Sense of Place, a Sense of Time.* New Haven and London: Yale University Press.

Jayne, M. 2011. 'From Actor to Avatar: The Place of Mayors in Theories of Urban Governance'. *Geography Compass* 5 (11): 801–10.

Kaneff, D. 1998. 'When Land Becomes "Territory". Land Privatisation and Ethnicity in Rural Bulgaria'. In *Surviving Post-socialism: Local Strategies and Regional Responses in Eastern Europe and the Former Soviet Union*, edited by S. Bridger and F. Pine, 16–32. London: Routledge.

———. 2002. 'Work, Identity and Rural-Urban Relations'. In *Post-Socialist Peasant? Rural and Urban Constructions of Identity in Eastern Europe, East Asia and the Former Soviet Union*, edited by P. Leonard and D. Kaneff, 180–99. London: Palgrave.

———. 2004. *Who Owns the Past? The Politics of Time in a 'Model' Bulgarian Village.* New York and Oxford: Berghahn Books.

Kaul, I., I. Grunberg and A. M. Stern. 1999. 'Introduction. Defining Global Public Goods'. In *Global Public Goods. International Cooperation in the 21st Century*, edited by I. Kaul, I. Grundberg, M. A. Stern, 2–19. New York and Oxford: Oxford University Press.

Kirksey, S. E. and S. Helmreich. 2010. 'The Emergence of Multispecies Ethnography'. *Cultural Anthropology* 25 (4): 545–76.

Kligman, G. and K. Verdery 2011. *Peasants Under Siege: The Collectivization of Romanian Agriculture, 1949–1962.* Princeton: Princeton University Press.

Klooster, D. 2006. 'Forest Struggles and Forest Policy. Villagers' Environmental Activism in Mexico'. In *Shades of Green. Environmental Activism Around the Globe*, edited by C. Mauch, N. Stolzfus, D. Weiner, 183–96. Lanham and Boulder: Rowman & Littlefield Publishers, Inc.

Knapp, A. 2006. 'Bear Necessities. An Analysis of Brown Bear Management and Trade in Selected Range States and the European Union's Role in the Trophy Trade'. *A TRAFFIC Europe Report for the European Commission, Brussels, Belgium.* Accessed 26 May 2012. http://www.traffic.org/species-reports/traffic_species_mammals8.pdf.

Kneitz, A. and M. Landry, eds. 2012. 'On Water. Perceptions, Politics, Perils'. Special issue of *RCC Perspectives* 2.

Kogalnitchan, M. 1837. *Esquisse sur l'historie, leurs mœurs et la langue des Cigains connus en France sur le nom de nom de Bohémiens.* Berlin 1837.
Kohn, E. 2013. *How Forests Think: Toward an Anthropology Beyond the Human.* Berkeley: University of California Press.
Kopecká, M. and J. Vováček. 2010. 'Natural Forest Fragmentation: an Example from the Tatra Region, Slovakia'. In), *Land Use/Cover Changes in Selected Regions in the World* 5, edited by I. Bičik, Y. Himiyama, J. Ferance, 51–56. Prague: IGU-LUCC.
Kuemmerle, T. et al. 2007. 'Post-socialist Forest Disturbance in the Carpathian Border Region of Poland, Slovakia and Ukraine'. *Ecological Applications* 17 (5): 1279–95.
———. 2009. 'Forest Cover Change and Illegal Logging in the Ukrainian Carpathians in the Transition Period from 1988 to 2000'. *Remote Sensing of Environment* 113 (6): 1194–1207.
Kula, W. 1984. *Les mesures et les homes.* Paris: Editions de la Maison de Science de l'Homme.
Lahovari, G. I., C. I. Bratianu and G. Tocilescu. 1898–1902. *Marele dicționar geografic al Romîniei* [The Great Geographic Dictionary of Romania] 5. București: J. V. Socecŭ.
Lampland, M. 2002. 'The Advantages of Being Collectivized. Co-operative Farm Managers in the Postsocialist Economy'. In *Postsocialism. Ideals, Ideologies and Practices in Eurasia*, edited by C. M. Hann, 31–56. London and New York: Routledge.
Latour, B. 1988. 'Mixing Humans and Nonhumans Together: The Sociology of a Door-Closer'. *Social Problems* 35 (3): 298–310.
Lave, R. 2014. 'Freedom and Constraint: Generative Expectations in the US Stream Restoration Field'. *Geoforum* 52: 236–44.
Lawrence, A. 2005. 'Sustainable Values, Sustainable Forest? The Effects of Forestry Reforms in Romania'. *Conference Global Environmental Change, Globalization and International Security: New Challenges for the 21st Century, Bonn, 9–13 October.* Bonn: University of Bonn.
Leaf, M. 2002. 'A Tale of Two Villages. Globalization and Peri-Urban Change in China and Vietnam'. *Cities* 19 (1): 23–31.
Li, L. et al. 2006. 'Root Distribution and Interactions Between Intercropped Species'. *Oecologia* 147 (2): 280–90.
Li, L. et al. 2007. 'Diversity Enhances Agricultural Productivity Via Rhizosphere Phosphorus Facilitation on Phosphorus Facilitation-Deficient Soils'. *Proceedings of the National Academy of Sciences of the United States of America* 104 (27): 11192–96.
Li, M. T. 2005. 'Beyond "the State" and Failed Schemes'. *American Anthropologists* 107 (3): 383–94.
———. 2007. *The Will to Improve. Governmentality, Development, and the Practise of Politics.* Durham & London: Duke University Press.
Lipsky, M. 1980. *Street-level Bureaucracy. Dilemmas of the Individual in Public Services.* New York: Russell Sage Foundation.

Localitățile 1971. *Localitățile județului Argeș* [The Localities of Argeș County]. Pitești: Tipografia Argeș.
Luoto, M., J. Pykälä and M. Kuussari 2003. 'Decline of Landscape-scale Habitat and Species Diversity after the End of Cattle Grazing'. *Journal for Nature Conservation* 11: 171–78.
Madgearu, V. M. 1999 [1936]. *Agrarianism, capitalism, imperialism. Contribuții la studiul evoluției sociale românești* [Agrarianism, Capitalism, Imperialism. Contributions to the Study of the Romanian Social Evolution]. București: Dacia.
Mandel, R. and C. Humphrey, eds. 2002. *Markets and Moralities. Ethnographies of Postsocialism*. Oxford and New York: Berg.
Marcus, G. E. 1983. '"Elite" as a Concept, Theory and Research Tradition'. In *Elites: Ethnographic Issues*, edited by G. E. Marcus, 7–27. Albuquerque: University of New Mexico Press.
Márton, E. Z., E. Ruprecht and M. Deak. 2008. 'Long-term Effects of the Abandonment on Steppe-like Grasslands'. *Applied Vegetation Science* 11 (1): 55–62.
Marushiakova, E. 1993. 'Relations among the Gypsy Groups in Bulgaria'. In *'Project on Ethnic Relations' Princeton, USA, The Ethnic Situation in Bulgaria (Researches in 1992)*, 7–16. Sofia: Club '90 Publishers.
Marushiakova, E. and V. Popov. 1997. *Gypsies (Roma) in Bulgaria*. Frankfurt am Main: Peter Lang.
Matei, I. and I. Mihailescu, eds. 1985. *Satul românesc. Studii* [The Romanian Village. Studies]. București: Editura Academiei RSR.
Mauch, C. and T. Zeller, eds. 2008. *Rivers in History. Perspectives on Waterways in Europe and North America*. Pittsburgh: University of Pittsburgh Press.
McCollum, C. and N. C. Schoening. 2002. 'Romania: A Case Study in Delayed Privatization'. *International Journal of Public Administration* 25 (9–10): 1221–34.
McGarry, A. 2008. 'Political Participation and Interest Articulation of Roma in Romania'. *Journal of Ethnopolitics and Minority Issues* 7 (1): 1–25.
Melville, E. G. K. 1994. *A Plague of Sheep. Environmental Consequences of the Conquest of Mexico*. Cambridge and New York: Cambridge University Press.
Metzo, K. 2009. 'The Formation of Tunka National Park: Revitalization and Autonomy in Late Socialism'. *Slavic Review* 68 (1): 50–69.
Micu, C. 2012. *From Peasants to Farmers? Agrarian Reforms and Modernization in Twentieth Century Romania*. Frankfurt am Main: Peter Lang.
Migdal, J. S. 2001. *State in Society. Studying How States and Societies Transform and Constitute One Another*. Cambridge: Cambridge University Press.
Milanova, E. V., A. P. Kirilenko and N. M. Dronin. 2010. 'Land Use and Cover Change under Agricultural Development and Climate Change in Russia'. In *Land Use/Cover Changes in Selected Regions in the World* 5, edited by I. Bičik, Y. Himiyama, J. Ferance, 25–30. Prague: IGU-LUCC.
Mincyte, D. 2009. 'Everyday Environmentalism: The Practice, Politics, and Nature of Subsidiary Farming in Stalin's Lithuania'. *Slavic Review* 68 (1): 31–49.
———. 2011. 'Subsistence and Sustainability in Post-industrial Europe: The Politics of Small-scale Farming in Europeanising Lithuania'. *Sociologia Ruralis* 51 (2): 101–18.

Mitroi, V. 2013. 'Une pratique sociale à l'épreuve de la conservation de la nature. Pour une lecture symétrique de la dégradation de la pêche dans la Réserve de la Biosphère du delta du Danube'. PhD dissertation. Paris: Université Paris Nanterre.
Moore, S. D. 1993. 'Contesting Terrain in Zimbabwe's Eastern Highlands: Political Ecology, Ethnography, and Peasant Resource Struggles'. *Economic Geography* 69 (4): 380–401.
Muica, C., I. Zavoianu. 1996. 'The Ecological Consequences of Privatization in Romanian Agriculture'. *GeoJournal* 38 (2): 207–12.
Müller, B. 2012. Farmers, Development, and the Temptation of Nitrogen: Controversies about Sustainable Farming in Nicaragua. In *Fields and Forests. Ethnographic Perspectives on Environmental Globalization*. Special issue of *RCC Perspectives* 5, edited by U. Münster, D. Münster and S. Dorondel, 23–29.
Müller, D., B. Wode, and C. Wehr 2003. 'Manual on Participatory Village Mapping Using Photomaps: A Trainer Guide'. *Social Forestry Development Project (SFDP) Song Da*. Accessed 4 December 2003. http://amor.cms.hu-berlin.de/~muelleda/publications.htm.
Müller, H. 2005. *Regele se-nclină și ucide* [The King Bows and Kills]. București: Polirom.
Mullin, H. M. 1999. 'Mirrors and Windows: Sociocultural Studies of Human-Animal Relationships'. *Annual Review of Anthropology* 28: 201–24.
Mungiu-Pippidi, A. 2006. 'Corruption: Diagnosis and Treatment'. *Journal of Democracy* 17 (3): 86–99.
——. 2010. *A Tale of Two Villages. Coerced Modernization in East European Countryside*. Budapest and New York: CEU Press.
Münster, D. and U. Münster. 2012. 'Human-Animal Conflicts in Kerala: Elephants and Ecological Modernity on the Agrarian Frontier in South India'. In *Fields and Forests. Ethnographic Perspectives on Environmental Globalization*. Special issue of *RCC Perspectives* 5, edited by U. Münster, D. Münster and S. Dorondel, 41–49.
Mușat, I. 1980. *Pădurea scut și bogăție a naturii* [Forest as Shield and as Richness of the Nature]. București: Editura Științifică și Enciclopedică.
Naidoo, R. et al. 2011. 'Effect of Diversity of Large Wildlife Species on Financial Benefits to Local Communities in Northwest Namibia'. *Environmental and Resource Economics* 48 (2): 321–35.
Neumann, R. 1998. *Imposing Wilderness. Struggle over Livelihood and Nature Preservation in Africa*. Berkeley, Los Angeles and London: University of California Press.
Nguyen, T. Q. 2005. *What Benefits and for Whom? Effects of Devolution of Forest Management in Dak Lak, Vietnam*. Aachen: Shaker Verlag.
Nicholson, B. 2003. 'From Cow to Customer: Informal Marketing of Milk in Albania'. *The Anthropology of East Europe Review* 21 (1): 148–58.
Nicola, I. 2007. 'Studii și cercetări privind combaterea integrată a buruienilor din culturile de cartof timpuriu și de vară' [Studies Concerning the Complex Control of the Weeds from the Potatoes Cultures]. PhD dissertation. București: Universitatea de Științe Agronomice și Medicină Veterinară din București.

Nijnik, M. and G. K. van Kooten. 2000. 'Forestry in the Ukraine: The Road Ahead?'. *Forest Policy and Economics* 1 (2): 139–51.
Niroula, G. S. and G. B. Thapa. 2005. 'Impacts and Causes of Land Fragmentation, and Lessons Learned from Land Consolidation in South Asia'. *Land Use Policy* 22 (4): 358–72.
Novac, V. 2008. *Județul Muscel, 1831–1939* [The County of Muscel, 1831–1939]. Pitești: Nova International.
Olwig, K. R. 1996. 'Recovering the Substantive Nature of Landscape'. *Annals of the Association of American Geographers* 86 (4): 630–53.
Owczarzak, J. 2009. 'Introduction: Postcolonial Studies and Postsocialism in Eastern Europe'. *Focaal – European Journal of Anthropology* 53 (1): 3–19.
Pamfile, T. 1913. *Agricultura la români. Studiu etnografic cu un adaus despre măsurătoarea pământului și glosar* [The Agricultural Practices Among Romanians. An Ethnographic Study about the Measurements and Glossary]. București, Leipzig, Viena: Librăriile Socec & comp., C. Sfetea și Libraria Naționala, Otto Harrassowits, Gerold & comp.
Pamfil, V. 2004. 'Country Report on Land Administration in Romania'. *Central European Land Knowledge Centre*. Accessed 19 October 2006. www.celk.org/datatrs/Budapest_GIS_2004_engl_final.ppt.
Pârnuță, G. 1972. *Rucăr monografie sociologică* [The Sociological Monograph of the Rucăr Village]. București.
Pârnuță G., M. Gorgoi and Șt. Trâmbaciu. 2003. *Monografia satelor Conțești, Davidești și Voroveni* [The Monograph of Conțești, Davidești and Voroveni Villages]. Craiova: Scrisul Românesc.
Patterson, C. 2009. 'The Paradox of Market Reform: *Pămînt* and the Vicious Circle in the Republic of Moldova'. *Annuaire Roumain d'Anthropologie* 46: 77–91.
Peluso, N. L. 1992. *Rich Forest, Poor People. Resource Control and Resistance in Java*. Berkeley, Los Angeles and Oxford: University of California Press.
———. 1993. 'Coercing Conservation? The Politics of State Resource Control'. *Global Environmental Change* June: 199–217.
———. 2007. 'Enclosure and Privatization of Neoliberal Environments'. In *Neoliberal Environments. False Promises and Unnatural Consequences*, edited by N. Heynen et al., 89–93. London and New York: Routledge.
Peterken, G. F. 1996. *Natural Woodland: Ecology and Conservation in Northern Temperate Regions*. Cambridge: Cambridge University Press.
Petre, I. E. 2005. 'Studiul agronomic și economic al obținerii unor producții de grâu și de porumb în diferite asolamente' [The Agronomic and Economic Study for Obtaining Good Wheat and Corn Production on Different Plots]. PhD dissertation. București: Universitatea de Științe Agronomice și Medicină Veterinară din București.
Petrov, P. 2013. 'What Actually Was the Disaster? Flood and Reconstruction in a Bulgarian Village in their Historical, Political and Socio-Cultural Context'. *International Conference on Nature and the Environment in East and Southeast Europe: Historical and Economic Perspectives, Regensburg, 27–29 June*. Regensburg: University of Regensburg.

Plan. 2004. *Planul de Management al Parcului National Piatra Craiului* [The Management Plan of the Piatra Craiului National Park]. Romania.
Planul National. 2010. 'Planul National de Combatere a Taierilor Ilegale de Arbori' [The National Plan for Fighting Against Illegal Logging]. *The Minister of Agriculture and Rural Development*. Accessed 16 June 2011. http://www.madr.ro/pages/page.php?sub=0206&self=02.
Planuri de management. 2007. 'Planurile de management ale bazinelor hidrografice din Romania. Probleme importante de gospodarirea apelor [The Management Plans of the Hydrographic Basins of Romania. Important Issues in Water Management]'. Accessed 10 July 2013. www.mmediu.ro/gospodarirea_apelor/cooperare_internationala/Planuri_de_management.pdf&ei=8wHdUfqEEYeH4ATiwYAY&usg=AFQjCNHLy0ue1XzGwy18nkS0htiMsrlaUA&bvm=bv.48705608,d.bGE.
Popa, F. and M. Popa. 2013. 'Diagnoza situației actuale a entităților forestiere din domeniul economiei sociale' [The Diagnosis of Forestry Current Situation in Social Economy]. In *Organizațiile colective ale proprietarilor de terenuri agricole și forestiere. Profil, evoluție, tendințe* [The Collective Organizations of Land and Forest Owners], edited by C. Petrescu, 83–113. Iași: Polirom.
Prosterman, L. R. and L. Rolfes Jr. 1999. 'Review of the Legal Basis for Agricultural Land Markets in Lithuania, Poland, and Romania'. *Second EU Accession Workshop in the Rural Sector Structural Change in the Farming Sectors of Central and Eastern Europe* (27–29 June): 110–39. Warsaw.
Quang, N. and H. D. Kammeier. 2002. 'Changes in the Political Economy of Vietnam and Their Impacts on the Built Environment of Hanoi'. *Cities* 19 (6): 373–88.
Raport de mediu. Planul național de amenajarea pe bazine/spații hidrografice 2013 [Report on Environment. The National Plan for Basins/Hydrographical Spaces Planning]. Bucharest: Ministerul Mediului. Accessed 11 July 2013. http://www.mmediu.ro/beta/wp-content/uploads/2013/03/2013-0326Raport_de_Mediu_PNABH.pdf.
Rausing, S. 2002. 'Reconstructing the "Normal": Identity and the Consumption of Western Goods in Estonia'. In *Market and Moralities. Ethnographies of Postsocialism*, edited by R. Mandel and C. Humphrey, 127–42. Oxford and New York: Berg.
Ribot, J. 1998. 'Theorizing Access: Forest Profits along Senegal's Charcoal Commodity Chain'. *Development and Change* 29 (2): 307–41.
Ribot, J. A. Chhatre and T. Lankina. 2008. 'Introduction: Institutional Choice and Recognition in the Formation and Consolidation of Local Democracy'. *Conservation and Society* 6 (1): 1–11.
Robbins, P. 2001. 'Tracking Invasive Land Covers in India, or Why Our Landscapes Have Never Been Modern'. *Annals of the Association of American Geographers* 91 (4): 637–59.
Roellig, M. et al. 2015. 'Reviving Wood-Pastures for Biodiversity and People: A Case Study from Western Estonia'. *Ambio* doi:10.1007/s13280-015-0719-8.
Romero-Calcerrada, R. and G. L. W. Perry. 2004. 'The Role of Land Abandonment in Landscape Dynamics in the SPA 'Encinares del rio Alberche y Cofio, Central Spain, 1984–1999'. *Landscape and Urban Planning* 66 (4): 217–32.

Romportl, D., T. Chuman and Z. Lipský. 2010. 'Landscape Heterogeneity Changes and Their Driving Forces in the Czech Republic After 1990'. In *Land Use/Cover Changes in Selected Regions in the World* 5, edited by I. Bičik, Y. Himiyama, J. Ferance, 41–49. Prague: IGU-LUCC.

ROMSILVA. 2011. Regia Nationala a Padurilor Romsilva [The National District of Forest]. Accessed 16 May 2011. http://www.rosilva.ro/categorie.php?id=4.

Rusu, M. and V. Pamfil. 2005. *Agricultural Land Reform and Land Consolidation in Romania*. Report prepared for FAO.

Sabates-Wheeler, R. 2005. *Cooperation in the Romanian Countryside. An Insight to the Post-Soviet Agriculture*. Lanham and Boulder: Lexington Books.

Sachs, A. 2003. 'The Ultimate "Other": Post-colonialism and Alexander von Humboldt's Ecological Relationship with Nature'. *History and Theory*, Theme Issue 42: 111–35.

Sampson, S. 1976. 'Feldioara: The City Comes to the Peasant'. *Dialectical Anthropology* 1 (4): 321–47.

Samuelson, A. 2013. 'Frustration and Creativity: Environmentalism in the Republic of Moldova'. PhD dissertation. Milwaukee: The University of Wisconsin–Milwaukee.

Saphores, D. et al. 2006. 'Detecting Collusion in Timber Auctions. An Application to Romania'. *World Bank Policy Research Working Paper* 4105.

Sarris, A. H. and D. Gavrilescu. 1997. 'Restructuring of Farms and Agricultural Systems in Romania'. In *Agricultural Privatisation, Land Reform and Farm Restructuring in Central and Eastern Europe*, edited by J. F. M. Swinnen, A. Buckwell, E. Mathijs, 189–228. Aldershot and Brookfield, VT: Ashgate.

Săvulescu, G. C. 1974. *Comuna Colibași, Județul Argeș* [Colibași Commune, Argeș County]. Colibași.

Schwartz, K. S. Z. 2006a. '"Masters in Our Native Place": The Politics of Latvian National Parks on the Road from Communism to "Europe"'. *Political Geography* 25 (1): 42–71.

———. 2006b. *Nature and National Identity after Communism: Globalizing the Ethnoscape*. Pittsburgh: University of Pittsburgh Press.

Schwegler, A. T. 2008. 'Take it From the Top (Down)? Rethinking Neoliberalism and Political Hierarchy in Mexico'. *American Ethnologist* 35 (4): 682–700.

Scott, J. C. 1976. *The Moral Economy of the Peasant. Rebellion and Subsistence in Southeast Asia*. New Haven and London: Yale University Press.

———. 1985. *Weapons of the Weak: Everyday Forms of Peasant Resistance*. New Haven and London: Yale University Press.

———. 1998. *Seeing Like a State. How Certain Schemes to Improve the Human Condition Have Failed*. New Haven and London: Yale University Press.

———. 2005. 'Afterword to "Moral Economies, State Spaces, and Categorical Violence"'. *American Anthropologist* 107 (3): 395–402.

Scurtu, I. 1995. 'Minoritățile naționale din România în anii 1918–1925' [National Minorities in Romania in 1918–1925]. In *Minoritățile naționale din România 1918–1925. Documente* [National Minorities in Romania in 1918–1925. Documents], edited by I. Scurtu, L. Boar, 7–14. București: Arhivele Statului din România.

Şerban, S. 2013. 'Divergent Approaches of Danube Damming in Romania. A Historical Perspective'. *International Conference on Nature and the Environment in East and Southeast Europe: Historical and Economic Perspectives*, Regensburg, 27–29 June. Regensburg: University of Regensburg.
Sikor, T. 2006. 'Land as Asset, Land as Liability: Property Politics in Rural Central and Eastern Europe'. In *Changing Properties of Property*, edited by F. and K. von Benda-Beckman, and M. G. Wiber, 106–25. New York and Oxford: Berghahn Books.
Sikor, T. and T. Q. Nguyen. 2007. 'Why May Forest Devolution not Benefit the Rural Poor? Forest Entitlements in Vietnam's Central Highlands'. *World Development* 35 (11): 2010–25.
Sikor, T., D. Müller and J. Stahl. 2009. 'Land Fragmentation and Cropland Abandonment in Albania: Implications for the Roles of the State and Community in Post-Socialist Albania'. *World Development* 37 (8): 1411–23.
Sikor, T., J. Stahl and S. Dorondel. 2009. 'Negotiating Post-Socialist Property *and* State: Struggle over Forests in Albania and Romania'. *Development and Change* 40 (1): 171–93.
Sikor, T. and J. Stahl, eds. 2011. *Forest and People. Property, Governance, and Human Rights*. London and New York: Earthscan.
Sikor, T. and P. X. To. 2011. 'Illegal Logging in Vietnam: Lam Tac (Forest Hijackers) in Practice and Talk'. *Society & Natural Resources* 24 (7): 688–701.
Silvas, V. 2005. *Din lumea animalelor. Mistrețul morfologie și comportament* [The Animal World. The Wild Boar Morphology and Behaviour]. Iasi: Stef.
Singh, S. 1997. *Taming the Waters. The Political Economy of Large Dams in India*. Delhi: Oxford University Press.
Smith, J. and P. Jehlička. 2007. 'Stories Around Food, Politics and Change in Poland and the Czech Republic'. *Transactions of the Institute of British Geographers* 32 (3): 395–410.
Socol, G. 1999. *Evoluție, involuție și tranziție în agricultura României* [Evolution, Involution and Transition of the Romanian Agriculture]. București : IRLI.
Sodikoff, G. 2007. 'An Exceptional Strike: A Micro-history of "People versus Park" in Madagascar'. *Journal of Political Ecology* 14: 10–33.
Soleri, D. and S. E. Smith 2003. 'Conserving Folk Crop Varieties. Different Agricultures, Different Goals'. In *Ethnoecology. Situated Knowledge/Located Lives*, edited by V. D. Nazarea, 133–54. Tucson: The University of Arizona Press.
Solnick, S. L. 1998. *Stealing the State. Control and Collapse in Soviet Institutions*. Cambridge, MA and London: Harvard University Press.
Sorescu-Marinković, A. 2013. 'The Court of the Bayash: Revising a Theory'. *Romani Studies* 23 (1): 1–27.
Sos, T. 2008. 'Review of Recent Taxonomic and Nomenclatural Changes in European Amphibian and Reptilian Related to Romanian Herpetofauna'. *Herpatologica Romanica* 2: 61–91.
Spoor, M., ed. 2009. *The Political Economy of Rural Livelihoods in Transition Economies. Land, Peasants and Rural Poverty in Transition*. Milton Park, Abingdon and Oxon: Routledge.

Staddon, C. 2001. 'Local Forest Dependence in Post Communist Bulgaria: A Case Study'. *GeoJournal* 55 (2–4): 517–27.

———. 2009a. 'The Complicity of Trees: The Socionatural Field of/for Tree Theft in Bulgaria'. *Slavic Review* 68 (1): 70–94.

———. 2009b. 'Towards a Critical Political Ecology of Human–Forest Interactions: Collecting Herbs and Mushrooms in a Bulgarian Locality'. *Transactions of the Institute of British Geographers* 34 (2): 161–76.

Staddon, C. and S. Grykień 2009. 'Local Forest Dependence in Central Eastern Europe: Bulgaria and Poland'. *Annuaire Roumain d'Anthropologie* 46: 107–19.

Stahl, H. H. 1998 [1958]. *Contribuții la studiul satelor devălmașe românești* [Contributions to the Study of Romanian Commons]. 3 volumes. București: Cartea Românească.

Stahl, J. 2010a. *Rent from the Land. The Political Ecology of Postsocialist Rural Transformation.* London, New York and Delhi: Anthem Press.

———. 2010b. 'The Rents of Illegal Logging: The Mechanisms behind the Rush on Forest Resources in Southeast Albania'. *Conservation & Society* 8 (2): 140–50.

Stahl, P. H. and L. Piasere. 1990. 'Tre insediamenti di "Rudari" in Romania' [Three Rudari Settlements in Romania]. *La Ricerca Folklorica* 22: 55–66.

Stahl, J., T. Sikor and S. Dorondel. 2009. 'The Institutionalization of Property Rights in Albanian and Romanian Biodiversity Conservation'. *International Journal of Agricultural Resources, Governance and Ecology* 8 (1): 57–73.

Stark, D. 1996. 'Recombinant Property in East European Capitalism'. *American Journal of Sociology* 101 (4): 993–1027.

Stern, W. R. 1993. 'Nitrogen Fixation and Transfer in Intercrop Systems'. *Field Crops Research* 34 (3–4): 335–56.

Stewart, M. 1998. 'The Trauma of De-collectivization in Two Romanian Villages'. In *Surviving Post-socialism. Local Strategies and Regional Responses in Eastern Europe and the Former Soviet Union*, edited by S. Bridger and F. Pine, 66–79. London and New York: Routledge.

Stoyanov, N. 1999. 'Characteristics and Analysis of Implementation of the New Forest Law in the Republic of Bulgaria'. In *Experiences with New Forest and Environmental Laws in European Countries with Economies in Transition*, edited by F. Schmithüsen, P. Herbst, D. Le Master, 69–75. Proceedings of the International Symposium organized by IUFRO Research Group and the Austrian Federal Ministry of Agriculture and Forestry, Ossiah (June 1999).

Strang, V. 2004. *The Meaning of Water*. Oxford and New York: Berg.

Sturgeon, J. and T. Sikor. 2004. 'Postsocialist Property in Asia and Europe: Variations on "Fuzziness"'. *Conservation and Society* 2 (1): 1–17.

Swinnen, J. F. M. 1997. 'The Choice of Privatization and Decollectivization Policies in Central and Eastern European Agriculture: Observations and Political Economy Hypothesis'. In *Political Economy of Agrarian Reform in Central and Eastern Europe*, edited by J. F. M. Swinnen, 363–98. Aldershot and Brookfield, VT: Ashgate.

Thelen, T. et al. 2011. '"The Sleep Has Been Rubbed from Their Eyes": Social Citizenship and the Reproduction of Local Hierarchies in Rural Hungary and Romania'. *Citizenship Studies* 15 (3–4): 513–27.

Todorova, M. 2010. 'Balkanism and Postcolonialism or the Beauty of the Airplane View'. In *In Marx's Shadow. Knowledge, Power and Intellectuals in Eastern Europe and Russia*, edited by C. Bradatan and S. A. Oushakine, 175–95. Lanham and Plymouth: Lexington Books.

Tsing, L. A. 1995. 'Empowering Nature, or: Some Gleanings in Bee Culture'. In *Naturalizing Power. Essays in Feminist Cultural Analysis*, edited by S. Yanagisako and C. Delaney, 113–43. New York and London: Routledge.

———. 2001. 'Nature in the Making'. In *New Directions in Anthropology and Environment. Intersections*, edited by C. C. Crumley, with A. E. van Deventer and Joseph J. Fletcher, 3–23. Walnut Creek and Lanham, MD: Altamira Press.

Tsuma, W. 2010. *Gold Mining in Ghana. Actors, Alliances and Power*. Münster: LIT Verlag.

Turnock, D. 2002. 'Ecoregion-based Conservation in the Carpathians and the Land-Use Implications'. *Land Use Policy* 19 (1): 47–63.

Uekoetter, F. 2011. 'The Magic of One. Reflections on the Pathologies of Monoculture'. *RCC Perspectives* 2.

Urechia, A. V. 1895. *Codex Bandinus. Memoriu asupra scrierii lui Bandinus de la 1646* [Codex Bandinus. Report on Bandinus Writings from 1646]. Analele Academiei Române II (XVI). București: Lito-Tipografia Carol Göbl.

Vandergeest, P. and N. L. Peluso. 1995. 'Territorialization and State Power in Thailand'. *Theory and Society* 24: 385–426.

———. 2006. 'Empires of Forestry: Professional Forestry and State Power in Southeast Asia'. *Environment and History* 12 (1): 31–64.

Vasile, M. 2008a. 'Un fond fără formă obștea vrânceană. Statutar și cutumiar în dinamica definirii unui sistem de proprietate colectivă' [Meanings Without Forms. The 'Obște' in Vrancea. Statutory and Customary Processes in the Dynamics of Defining a System of Collective Ownership]. *Sociologie Românească* VI (1): 56–73.

———. 2008b. 'Nature Conservation, Conflict and Discourses on Forest Management: Communities and Protected Areas in Meridional Carpathians'. *Sociologie Românească* VI (3–4): 87–100.

———. 2009. 'Corruption in Romanian Forestry – Morality and Local Practice in the Context of Privatization'. *Revista Română de Sociologie* XX (1–2): 105–20.

———. 2012. 'A Typology of Godkinship Practices in Romania'. *Annuaire Roumain d'Anthropologie* 49: 107–29.

Vasile, M. and L. Măntescu. 2009. 'Property Reforms in Rural Romania and Community-Based Forests'. *Sociologie Românească* VII (2): 95–113.

Vasilescu, L. 2006. 'Studiul sortimentului de soiuri de orz și orzoaică ca materie primă pentru producerea berii' [The Study of Types of Barley and Two-Row Barley as Raw Material for Producing Beer]. PhD Dissertation. București : Universitatea de Științe Agronomice și Medicină Veterinară din București.

Vătămanu, V. 2012. 'Arătura adâncă de toamnă: mod de executare' [Executing the Deep Plough for Autumn Tilling]. *Agrimedia* (September 2012). Accessed 11 September 2013. http://www.agrimedia.ro/5/post/2012/09/aratura-adanca-de-toamna-mod-de-executare.html.

Verdery, K. 1995. 'Notes Toward an Ethnography of a Transforming State: Romania: 1991'. In *Articulating Hidden Histories. Exploring the Influence of Eric R. Wolf*, edited by J. Schneider and R. Rapp, 228–42. Berkeley, Los Angeles and London: University of California Press.

———. 1996. 'The Elasticity of Land: Problems of Property Restitution in Transylvania'. In *What Was Socialism and What Comes Next*, edited by K. Verdery, 133–67. Princeton: Princeton University Press.

———. 1998. 'Property and Power in Transylvania's Decollectivization'. In *Property Relations. Renewing the Anthropological Tradition*, edited by C. M. Hann, 160–80. Cambridge: Cambridge University Press.

———. 1999. 'Fuzzy Property: Rights, Power, and Identity in Transylvania's Decollectivization'. In *Uncertain Transition. Ethnographies of Change in the Postsocialist World*, edited by M. Burawoy and K. Verdery, 53–81. Lanham, Boulder and New York: Rowman & Littlefield Publishers Inc.

———. 2002. 'Seeing Like a Mayor. Or How Officials Obstructed Romanian Land Restitution'. *Ethnography* 3 (1): 5–33.

———. 2003. *The Vanishing Hectare. Property and Value in Postsocialist Transylvania*. Ithaca and London: Cornell University Press.

———. 2005. '"Possessive Identities" in Post-socialist Transylvania'. In *Between East and West. Studies in Anthropology and Social History*, edite by S. Dorondel, S. Șerban, 341–66. București: Editura Institutului Cultural Român.

Verghelet, M. and M. Zotta, assisted by L. Bernard. 2003. *Parcul National Piatra Craiului. Strategia de turism durabil* [The Strategy of Sustainable Tourism in Piatra Craiului National Park]. Accessed 3 August 2010. www.pcrai.ro/pdf/Strategie_Turism.pdf.

von Benda-Beckmann, F. and K. von Benda-Beckmann. 1998. 'Where Structures Merge: State and Off-state Involvement in Rural Social Security on Ambon, Indonesia'. In *Old World Places, New World Problems: Exploring Resource Management Issues in Eastern Indonesia*, edited by S. Pannell and F. von Benda-Beckmann, 143–80. Canberra: Australian National University Press, CERES Publications.

———. 1999. 'A Functional Analysis of Property Rights, with Special Reference to Indonesia'. In *Land and Natural Resources in Southeast Asia and Oceania*, edited by T. va Meijl and F. von Benda-Beckmann, 15–54. London and New York: Kegan Paul International.

von Benda-Beckmann, F., K. von Benda-Beckmann and H. Marks., eds. 2000 [1994]. *Copying with Insecurity. An 'Underall' Perspective on Social Security in the Third World*. Yogyakrta: Pustaka Pelajar.

von Hirschhausen, B. 1997. *Les nouvelles campagnes roumaines. Paradoxes d'une 'retour' paysan*. Paris: Belin.

Waal, C. de 2004. 'Post-socialist Property Rights and Wrongs in Albania. An Ethnography of Agrarian Change'. *Conservation and Society* 2 (1): 19–50.

Walker P. and L. Fortmann. 2003. 'Whose Landscape? A Political Ecology of the "Exurban" Sierra'. *Cultural Geographies* 10 (4): 469–91.

Walker, P. and P. E. Peters. 2001. 'Maps, Metaphors and Meanings: Boundary Struggles and Village Forest Use on Private and State Land in Malawi'. *Society and Natural Resources* 14 (5): 411–24.
Weber, M. 1978. *Economy and Society. An Outline of Interpretative Sociology*. Berkeley, Los Angeles and London: University of California Press.
Wedel, J. R. 1998. *Collision and Collusion. The Strange Case of Western Aid to Eastern Europe 1989–1998*. New York: St. Martin's Press.
Wegren, S. K. 2004. 'Russian Peasant Farms and Household Plots in 2003: A Research Note'. *Eurasian Geography and Economics* 45 (3): 230–39.
———. 2009. 'Land Reform in Post-communist Russia: The Effects of Household Labour'. In *The Political Economy of Rural Livelihoods in Transition Economies. Land, Peasants and Rural Poverty in Transtion*, edited by M. Spoor, 56–75. London and New York: Routledge.
Weiner, D. R. 2005. 'A Death-Defying Attempt to Articulate a Coherent Definition of Environmental History'. *Environmental History* 10 (3): 404–20.
Weiner, R. 2001. 'Romania, the IMF, and Economic Reform Since 1996'. *Problems of Post-Communism* 40 (1): 39–47.
Wells, M. P. and M. D. Williams. 1998. 'Russia's Protected Areas in Transition: The Impacts of Perestroika, Economic Reform and the Move Towards Democracy'. *Ambio* 27 (3): 198–206.
West, P., J. Igoe and D. Brockington. 2006. 'Parks and People: The Social Impact of Protected Areas'. *Annual Review of Anthropology* 35: 251–77.
White, R. 1995. *The Organic Machine: The Remaking of the Columbia River*. New York: Hill and Wang.
———. 1996. 'Are You an Environmentalist or Do You Work for Living? Work and Nature'. In *Uncommon Ground: Rethinking the Human Place in Nature*, edited by W. Cronon, 171–85. New York: W.W. Norton & Company Inc.
Whiteford, L. and S. Whiteford, eds. 2005. *Globalization, Water, & Health. Resource Management in Times of Scarcity*. Santa Fe, NM and Oxford: School of American Research Press.
Wiersum, K. F. 2004. 'Forest Gardens as an "Intermediate" Land-Use System in the Nature–Culture Continuum: Characteristics and Future Potential'. *Agroforestry Systems* 61: 123–34.
Wohl, E. 2011. *A World of Rivers. Environmental Change on Ten of the World's Great Rivers*. Chicago and London: The University of Chicago Press.
World Bank. 2008. *Project Appraisal Document on a Proposed Credit in the Amount of SDR 8.6 million (US$ 14.0 million equivalent) to the Republic of Moldova for a National Water Supply and Sanitation Project*. Sustainable Development Department, Ukraine, Belarus and Moldova Country Unit, Europe and Central Asia Region.
Worster, D. 1985. *Rivers of Empire. Water, Aridity, and the Growth of the American West*. New York and Toronto: Pantheon Books.
———. 1990. 'Transformations of the Earth: Towards an Agrocecological Perspective in History'. *The Journal of American History* 76 (4): 1087–1106.

Zamfir, E. and C. Zamfir, eds. 1993. *Țiganii între ignorare și îngrijorare* [Gypsies – Between Passing-by and Concerns]. București: Alternative.

Zeisler-Vralsted, D. 2015. *Rivers, Memory, and Nation-Building. A History of the Volga and Mississippi Rivers*. New York and Oxford: Berghahn Books.

Zingerli, C. 2005. 'Colliding Understandings of Biodiversity Conservation in Vietnam: Global Claims, National Interests, and Local Struggles'. *Society and Natural Resources* 18 (8): 733–47.

Index

A
access to forests, 106–11
agency
    natural environment changes, 7
    of nonhuman actors, 18
    state. *See* state
    villagers breaking laws, 195
Agency of State Domains (ASD), 61
agrarian landscapes
    methods for studying, 18–21
    transformation of, 1–25
Agrarian Register, 80
agrarian relations, 2
agricultural land, 3, 11, 28, 31, 33, 42, 45, 61, 138, 139, 150, 162, 163. *See also* land
agriculture. *See also* crops; farms
    feminization of, 145
    new plans for, 55–57
agronomists, 43
Albania, 4, 139
    land fragmentation in, 165
    state officials, roles of, 14
alcohol, 155–57
alder trees, 67
alfalfa, 162. *See also* pastures
analysis of the state, 191–94
animal farms, 44
animal husbandry, 6, 8, 11, 181
animals, 5, 7. *See also* specific animals
apple trees, 32
Apple Tree Valley, 33
appropriation of forests, 100, 101
archives, 20
Argeș County, 31, 42, 144
Argeș County Police, 85
Argeșelu River, 26, 33, 171–79

Asia, 139
asphalt, 110
associations (întovărășiri), 43
ATVs (All Terrain Vehicles), 189
Austro-Hungarian Empire, 2, 38

B
băieși (mining workers), 34
banks, rivers
    degradation of, 173
    property rights, 178
barbell *(Barbus fluviatilis)*, 172
Barca (lake), 177
barley *(Hordeum sativum)*, 154
beans, 11, 32
bear, 98
    Carpathian brown bear *(Ursus arctos)*, 18, 103–04
    role in economic changes, 197
beech trees, 31
    heating houses with, 65
beet *(Beta vulgaris)*, 175
Berlin Wall, collapse of (1989), 4
Białowieża National Park, 114, 115. *See also* national parks
biodiversity, 55, 104
    preservation of, 17, 190
Birdlife International, 115
Biser (Southern Bulgaria), 185
Black King (Negru Vodă), 40
black locust trees, deforestation of, 67, 68
blind mole rat *(Spalax typhlus)*, 197
boar in pastures, 129–31. *See also* wild boar *(Sus scrofa)*
boundaries, 149, 150, 199
Box Thorn Valley, 34
bribery, 73

224 *Index*

Bridge of Dragova, 37
Bucegi Mountain, 37
Bucharest, wood business in, 30
Buila-Vanturarița Park, 114. *See also* national parks
Bulgaria, 89
bureaucracies
    local state, 12–14
    Prussian, 14
bureaucrats, 64–94
    disputes with, 104–06
    land reform and, 72–77
bushes, 125

C

cadastre experts, 162
Câmpulung, 145
Carpathian brown bear *(Ursus arctos)*, 18, 103–04
    role in economic changes, 197
Carpathian Mountains, 38
Castree, Noel, 56, 182
cattle
    Dragomirești, 27
    economy of, 8
    land reform, 29
    on pastures, 123–24
Ceaușescu, Nicolae, 144
Central Europe, 4
centralization of land management, 4
cereals, cultivation of, 31
Cernea, Michael, 42, 45, 145
charities, 156
cheese, 160, 161
chemical fertilizers, 152, 186. *See also* fertilizers
chestnut forests, 16
chickens, 153
China, 4, 139
Ciocănaș, 37, 108, 134
claimants, land, 58
clear cutting, 60, 88, 95, 109. *See also* illegal logging
climate
    change, 100
    in Dragomirești, 27

Coasta Rea (the Bad Slope), 39
coexistence of landowners, 163, 164
collective farms, 2, 45, 67
collectivization, 42–48
    abolishment of, 10
    of agriculture, 4
    goal of, 42
    intercropping, 31–32
    reactions to, 11
    reverse, 190
collectivized villages, 43–48
collusion, 45
commodification of natural resources, 182
commodity chain analysis, 85, 111
common forests, 88. *See also* forests
common reed *(Phragmites communis)*, 178
communal forests, 108
communal pasture (islaz), 35
communes. *See* Dragomirești; Dragova
communist trees, 16
conclusions, 189–202
    analysis of the state, 191–94
    lessons of transformation, 199–201
    nature's agency, 196–99
    reform strategies, 194–96
conflicts (property), 149, 150
    pastures, 134–36
Constitution (2003), 180
construction materials of housing, 126
contamination, water, 186. *See also* pollution
contested forests, 95–120
    Piatra Craiului National Park (PCNP), 96–102
co-operatives
    in Albania, 139
    farms, 45
Costești, 28, 85
    land reform, 29
    railways in, 30
    Rudari in, 36
cost of pasture maintenance, 124
country project, 56
County Department of Statistics, 19
County Land Commission (CLC), 59

crayfish (*Astachidae sp.*), 172
crime prevention, 75
Cronon, William, 7, 18
crops. *See also* farms
    disappearance of, 33
    diversification of, 11
    economy of, 8
Crosgrove, Denis E., 7
cu limbă de moarte (last words before dying), 149
cultivation
    plum trees, 156
    practices, 154
Cuza, Ioan Alexandru, 29
Czechoslovakia, 4
Czech Republic, 138

D
Dacia car plant, 34, 144, 145, 158
Dacia-Renault car plant, 6, 144, 145
dairy products, 124. *See also* cattle; milk production
dams, 184. *See also* rivers
Danube River, 184
Danube Valley, 185
decentralization, 15
declaration of adherence, 44
decollectivization, 2, 7, 149
    distilleries after, 174
    policies of, 4
deforestation, 67–69, 191
    in Dragova, 192
    effect on Dragova River, 182
    forest loss mechanisms, 78–80
    hills without forests, 69–71
    local power relations and, 65
    mapping, 87–90
    practices, 112–14
    in private forests, 72
    Rudari role in, 65, 66
    Vietnam, 90
dialectical model of interaction, 15
dictators, collapse of regime, 1
diets for livestock animals, 175
disputes with bureaucrats, 104–06
distilleries, 155, 172, 174. *See also* rivers

draft animals, 29. *See also* horses; oxen
Dragomirești, 6, 25–34
    cattle, 27
    climate in, 27
    collectivization in, 43
    commodity chain analysis, 111
    deforestation in, 69–71, 112–14
    economies, 26, 48–49
    firewood used for cooking, 65
    forest holdings distribution, 81
    fragmented landscape of, 123
    land fragmentation in, 147, 148. *See also* fragmentation of land
    land ownership in, 143
    land reform in, 29
    landscape of, 26
    laws, land reform, 69
    local history of, 28–34
    occupations in, 31
    pastures, 121. *See also* pastures
    population of, 26
    Rudari, 34–36
    taxation, 28
    trees in, 28
    water mills, 172
    wild boar in, 129
Dragova, 6
    bears in, 103–04
    collectivization of, 45
    deforestation in, 192, 112–14
    economies, 48–49
    housing in, 40
    landscape of, 37–41
    ownership of forests, 39. 40
    pastures, 121. *See also* pastures
    population of, 37
    saw mills, 47
    wild boar in, 129
Dragova Creek, 189
Dragova River, 109, 179–83
    effect of deforestation of, 182
    flow of, 181
drinking water, 178. *See also* water resources
ducks, 178
duckweed (*Lemma minor*), 178

E

Eastern Europe, 4, 139
Eastern Romania, deforestation in, 88
economics
    damage to by wild boar, 130
    Dragomirești, 26, 48–49
    Dragova, 48–49
    effect of rivers on, 172
    evolution of, 144
    forest roles in, 80–86
    of forests, 111–12
    moderization of, 9
    planned, 54
    politics relationship to, 7
    transformation of state-controlled, 5
    transformations, 8, 56
eel *(Anguilla)*, 172
elite, postsocialist, 12–14
endangered species, poaching, 116
environment, 7–12, 20, 37, 42, 58, 62, 97, 101, 104
Environmental Guard, 134
Enyedi, Marton, 138
erosion of land, 55
ethnic groups, 26. *See also* population
ethnicity and postsocialist transformations, 65–67
Europe, 4
European Union (EU), 189
    government negotiations with, 101
euthrophication, 177

F

factories, privatization of, 66
farms
    animal, 44
    collective, 2, 45, 67
    co-operatives, 45
    state, 2
    subsidies (EU), 189
feminization of agriculture, 45, 145
fertilizers, 44, 116, 152
    after World War II, 153
    plum trees, 157
    public pastures, 123
Finland, 140

fir bark bugs *(Ips typographus)*, 99
firearms, ability to carry, 60
firewood, 84
flax, 44
flooding, 99
flora and fauna, 97–98
    loss of, 140
flow of Dragova River, 181
fodder
    destruction by wild boar, 130
    storage, 46
    types of, 121
food safety, 159
forest exploitation, 30, 84, 88
forest guards, 13, 73, 74, 89
    Rudari relationship with, 36
forest loss mechanisms, 78–80
forest nationalization, 25
forest people, 34–36
Forestry and Rural Development, 58, 61
Forestry Code (1996), 59, 68, 113, 126
forestry research, 48
forests
    access to, 66, 106–11
    appropriation, 100, 101
    chestnut, 16
    communal, 108
    contested, 95–120. *See also* contested forests
    disappearance of, 6
    in Dragova, 39
    economies of, 111–12
    hills without, 69–71
    outcomes over restitution, 8
    ownership of, 17
    patronage, 80
    political significance of, 86–87, 111–12
    property right claims, 17
    restitution laws, 1
    roles in economies, 80–86
    state control over, 103–04
    thinning, 60
    value of, 86
fragmentation of land, 10, 42, 143–70
    benefits of, 166

effects in postsocialist Europe, 163–67
impact on markets, 157–61
labour force and, 144–46
landscapes, 162–63
orchards and țuica, 155–57
practices of worker-peasants, 146–55
Fragrant Orchid *(Gymnadenia conopsea)*, 97
Framework Cadre for Water (FCW) 2000/60, 183
Franklin, Stuart, 115
free landholders, 2
  Dragomirești, 27
fruit trees, 32
furniture makers, 35. *See also* Rudari

G
Galicia, 31
garbage disposal, 173, 174
  bear deaths, 197
gardens, definition of, 122
gastarbeiters, 4
genetic uniformity, 154
geography (rugged), 134–36
German Agency for Cooperation, 116
Germany, collapse of Berlin Wall (1989), 4
globalization, 42, 140, 141
goal of collectivization, 42
goats
  deforestation, grazing in, 113
  land reform, 29
  in national parks, 116
Goldschmidt, Walter, 194
Gorovei, Mihai, 101
  re-nationalization of forest, 105
gradualism, 5
grass snake *(Natrix natrix),* 128
grazing, 99. *See also* cattle; goats; sheep
  in deforested areas, 113
  in national parks, 115, 118
  taxation, 122
great Kaldarara invasion, the, 35

Great Yellow Gentian *(Gentiana lutea),* 97
Greece, 102
Grzymala-Busse, 16
guesthouses, 131, 132, 136, 158. *See also* tourism
guidelines (IUCN), 97

H
Hann, Chris, 56, 148
Hardin, Garrett, 9
hemp, 33, 44
herons, 178
Hertha Müller, 146
Herzfeld, Michael, 77, 102
hierarchies, state, 13
hills without forests, 69–71
historical justice restitution policy, 66
history, 25
  of Dragomirești, 28–34
horse carts, importance of, 80
horse-drawn ploughs, 151
horses and land reform, 29
housing
  building of new, 122–27
  construction materials of, 126
  in Dragova, 40
  guesthouses, 131, 132
  illegal construction of, 125, 127
Humboldt University, 19
Hungarian kingdom, 2
Hungary, 4
hybrid seeds, 151, 153
hypermarkets, 138

I
ideologies
  of landscape, 98
  mark of, 16
illegal housing, 125, 127
illegal logging, 64–94, 73, 78, 81–82, 88
  deforestation, 87–90. *See also* deforestation
  National Plan for Fighting Against Illegal Logging, 88
  prevention of, 87

228 *Index*

impact studies, 99
Independence from Ottoman Empire (1878), 29
inheritance practices, 33, 149
Institute of Mathematics of the Romanian Academy, 75
intercropping, 31–32, 152, 153
International Monetary Fund (IMF), 9, 54, 61
interwar landscapes, 147
întovărășiri (associations), 43
irrigation systems, 153
islaz (communal pasture), 35
IUCN guidelines, 97

K
Kazakhstan, 186
Klooster, Daniel, 104
Kopanari, 89

L
labour force, 144–46
lakes, Barca, 177. *See also* water resources
lambs, wool from, 159
land
    boundaries, 149, 150
    chingi (belt), 28
    collectivization, 25
    erosion of, 55
    fragmentation, 143–70. *See also* fragmentation of land
    laws, 58. *See also* laws
    marketization of, 56
    ownership of, 57
    privatization of, 9
    restitution, 1, 146, 147
Land Commissions, 1
land fragmentation, 10, 33, 42. *See also* fragmentation of land
landholders, 2
land management, centralization of, 4
landowners, coexistence of, 163, 164
land ownership, Rudari and, 66
land reform, 7, 195
    implementation, 16
    Ioan Alexandru Cuza, 29
    laws, 65, 69
    Local Land Commission (LLC), 15
    national policies, 9
    outcome of, 12
    political economy of, 54–63
    postsocialist, 3
    reorganization of landscape, 9–12
land reform law (1991), 1
landscape
    agrarian. *See* agrarian landscapes
    consequences of privatization, 15–18
    contribution to relationships, 16
    Dragomirești, 26
    Dragova, 37–41
    fragmentation of, 162–63
    ideologies of, 98
    interwar, 147
    methods for studying, 18–21
    reorganization of, 9–12
    transformations of, 1–25
land use practices, 28–34
last words before dying (*cu limbă de moarte*), 149
laws
    land reform, 65, 69
    Law 1/2000, 61, 108
    Law 18, 59, 61, 68
    Law 544/2001, 19
    Property Law (18/1991), 57
    shepherds selling products, 160
legislative changes, 56
legitimacy of the state, 57
lessons of transformation, 199–201
lichens, 97
LIF (Ocolul Silvic), 60
Lipsky, Michael, 13
Liquidation Commission, 58
Local Council, 180
local history, 25
    of Dragomirești, 28–34
Local Inspectorate of Forest (LIF), 3
Local Land Commission (LLC), 15
local state bureaucracy, 12–14

logging
    illegal, 64–94
    without permission, 99
Luong, Pauline Jones, 16
lynx, 98

M
mace reed *(Typha angustfolia),* 178
mafia, wood and, 89
maize, 11, 175
    hybrid seeds, 153
Makine, Andreï, 155
Management Plan, 116
mapping deforestation, 87–90
maps, disappearance of, 15
marc residue, 175. *See also* rivers
marigold *(Ligularia sibirica),* 101
marketization of land, 56
markets, 4–15, 26, 30, 222
martens, 98
Marushiakova, Elena, 66
mayors, 87. *See also* politics
    access to forests, 106–11
    disputes with, 104–06
    employees of, 13
mayor's office, 39, 40, 60, 67, 68, 73, 74. *See also* bureaucracies; mayors
meadows, 122. *See also* grazing; pastures
measurements, 195
mechanization, 44
Metzo, Katherine, 117
Mexico, 104
Migdal, Joel S., 12
Military Orchid *(Orchis militaris),* 97–98
milk, 29. *See also* cattle
milk production, 158, 159, 161, 165
mining workers (băieşi), 34
Ministry of Agriculture and Forestry, 15, 58, 61, 95, 109, 125
models, dialectical model of interaction, 15
modernization, 42, 44
Moldavia. *See* Republic of Moldova
Monastery Valley, 33
mono cropping, 41

multispecies ethnography, 18
Mungiu-Pippidi, Alina, 13
Mureș River, 172

N
National Agency for the Natural Resources (NANR), 179
National Inspectorate of Forest (NIF), 59
National Institute of Hydrology and Water Management, 178
nationalization, 101
National Liberal Party, 110
National Office of Cadastre, Geodesy, and Cartography (NOCGC), 61
national parks
    conclusions, 193
    cutting trees in, 95
    relationships with villagers, 114–18
    tourism, 131
National Plan for Fighting Against Illegal Logging, 88
National Police, 85
national policies, 9
National Railway Company, 34
National Society Romanian Waters, 67
natural protected areas, 17
natural resources, commodification of, 182
nature
    human transformation of, 16
    natural protected areas, 17
nature's agency, 196–99
Negru Vodă (the Black King), 40
neoliberalism
    new plans for agriculture, 55–57
    new rights and new duties, 58–62
    postsocialism as, 54–63
new plans for agriculture, 55–57
Nicolescu, Vasile, 107
non-farm jobs, 43
non-governmental organizations (NGOs), 17, 115, 117
nonhuman, 7, 8, 18, 135
non-recyclable disposable materials, 174
Nut Tree Valley, 34

O

oak trees, 31, 65
    illegal logging, 82
    uses of, 69
Obștea Mare (the large collective forest), 105
Obștea Mică (the small collective forest), 105, 106
Ocolul Silvic (LIF), 60
officials, state, 13
Once Upon a Time on the Banks of Amur, 155
orchards, 6
    in Argeș County, 42
    and țuica, 155–157
orchids, 97–98
Ottoman Empire
    independence from, 29
    products of Dragova, 37
    wood shipped to, 40
outcomes
    of land reform, 12
    over forest restitution, 8
overgrazing, 138. *See also* grazing
ownership. *See also* property rights
    of Dragova forests, 39, 40
    of forest, 17
    of land, 57
    in national parks, 97
    neoliberal language of, 69
    Rudari and, 66
oxen, 88. *See also* transportation
    land reform, 29

P

pălincă (plum/apple/pear/maize brandy), 32
Parliament, land reform laws, 69
pastures, 121–142
    communal pasture (islaz), 35
    Dragomirești, 26
    Dragova, 38, 39
    economy of, 8
    maintenance of, 123
    and politics, 137–38
    politics and, 131–34
    property conflicts, 135–37
    property rights, 136
    snakes in, 127–29
    tourism, 131–34
    transformation of, 125
    vanishing, 122–27, 138–41
    wild boar in, 129–31
patronage, 64–94
    forests, 80
    land reform and, 72–77
    relations, 17
patron–client relationships, 191, 192
pear trees, 32
Periețeanu, 29
pesticides, 44, 116
Petrov, Peter, 185
PHARE funds, 135
Piatra Craiului National Park (PCNP), 96–102
pigs, 153
Pitești, 25
planned economies, 54
Plan of Management, 96
plantations, 48
ploughs, 151
plum/apple/pear/maize brandy (*pălincă*), 32
plum brandy (țuica), 31
plums, 6, 7
    production of, 32
plum trees, 42
    cultivation, 156
    fertilization, 157
poaching endangered species, 116
Podu Dragovei, 37, 40
Podu Dragovei village, 181
Poland, 4, 114, 115
policemen, 13
Police Special Forces, 75
policies
    decollectivization, 4
    of forest regulation, 98
    framework for creation of, 16
    historical justice restitution, 66
    national, 9
political changes, 56

political regimes, changes in, 2
political significance of forests, 111–12
political transformations, 8
politics
    access to forests, 106–11
    access to local resources, 102
    of aggression, 41
    and pastures, 131–34, 137–38
    political economy of land reform, 54–63
    relationships to economies, 7
    significance of forests, 86–87
pollution, 55, 176
    postsocialism effect on rivers, 184–87
    in rivers, 173, 174
population
    of Dragomirești, 26
    of Dragova, 37
    ethnic makeup of, 2–3
    Roma, 3
    Rudari, 34–36
    of Transylvania, 3
postcolonialism, 201
postsocialism, 201
    definition of, 4
    deforestation, mapping, 87–90
    effect on Rudari, 67
    elite, 12–14
    ethnicity (transformations), 65–67
    land reform, 3
    as neoliberalism, 54–63
    new plans for agriculture, 55–57
    new rights and new duties, 58–62
postsocialist changes to rivers, 184–87
potatoes, cultivation of, 154, 155
power, competition for, 13
preservation, biodiversity, 17, 104
Prespa National Park, 116. *See also* national parks
pristine forests, myth of, 100
private forests, deforestation in, 72. *See also* forests
private land owners, 2
private pastures, 122. *See also* pastures

private property rights, 7. *See also* property rights
    restoration of, 55
privatization
    of factories, 66
    of land, 9
    of states, 1–25, 15–18
profits from wood, 84, 85
property conflicts, 149, 150
    pastures, 134–36
Property Law (18/1991), 57
property regulations, rejection of, 68
property rights, 2
    changes in, 62
    claims, 17
    Constitution (2003), 180
    elimination of, 3
    laws, 58
    in national parks, 97
    over natural resources, 20
    pastures, 136
    private, 7
    restoration of, 55, 61
    riverbanks, 178
protected areas, 199
Protected Landscape Area Bile Karpati (Czech Republic), 117
Protected Landscape Area of the White Carpathians, 139
protected species, 18
protests, 68
Prussian bureaucracy, 14
public pastures, 122. *See also* pastures
    maintenance of, 123
pumpkins, 11, 175

Q
Quince Tree Valley, 34
quotas, 84

R
rachiu (brandy), 36
railways
    construction of, 31
    in Costești, 30
Razlog Basin (Bulgaria), 89

reform strategies, 194–96
Regional Agency for Environmental Protection (RAEP), 101
registers, disappearance of, 15
regulations, 13, 84, 194
    avoiding, 161
    rejection of, 68
relationships
    between humans and environments, 7
    landscape's contribution to, 16
    patron–client, 191, 192
    with villagers, national parks, 114–18
Renault, 145. *See also* Dacia-Renault factory
reorganization of landscape, 9–12
reptiles, 128
Republic of Moldova, 3, 164, 185
    land reform in, 29
research, forestry, 48
resources, water, 171. *See also* rivers
restaurants, 133, 134. *See also* tourism
restitution
    historical justice restitution policy, 66
    in national parks, 97
reverse collectivization, 190
revolutions, 4
re-Westernization, 124
rights, property. *See* property rights
River Dragova, 37
River Rekijoki valley, 140
rivers, 171–89
    Argeşelu River, 33, 171–79
    Danube River, 184
    degradation of banks, 173
    Dragova River, 179–83
    euthrophication, 177
    garbage disposal, 173, 174
    Mureş River, 171
    pollution, 55
    postsocialist changes to, 184–87
    Tisza River, 184
Roma fiddlers, 26
Romania, 4
Romanian Communist party, 144
Romanian Parliament, land reform laws, 69
Romanian Principalities, 2
Roma population, 3
ROMSILVA, 96
Rudari, 34–36, 65
    cutting trees, 64
    deforestation practices, 112
    effect of postsocialist transformation on, 67
    forest loss mechanisms, 78–80
    garbage disposal, 173, 174
    horse carts, importance of, 80
    housing, 126, 127
    illegal deforestation, 65
    land reform and, 72–77
    patron–client relationships, 191, 192
    as scapegoats, 73
    work on public pastures, 123
rules, 13
Russia. *See also* Soviet Union
    pastures, vanishing, 138
    population in, 2
    size of plots in, 164

S
sale of trees, 79
Sandrea, 37
saw mills, 30
    Dragova, 47
Scott, James C., 9, 10, 12, 41, 45, 99, 193
Second World War. *See* World War II
seeds, 151, 153
serfs, 27, 28–34, 32
    benefit of land reform, 29
Severin, 161
sheep, 99
    land reform, 29
    wool, selling, 159
sheltered crab *(Leuciscus cephalus)*, 172
shock therapy philosophy, 5
Siberian tiger, 116
Sikor, Thomas, 117, 164
silk worms, 44
    production of, 33
skills, agricultural, 11

slaughter of animals, banning of, 46
slavery, 28, 32
Slitere Reserve (Latvia), 115
Slovakia, 138
small landholders, 28–34
smooth snake *(Coronella austriaca),* 128
snakes in pastures, 127–129
Social Democrat Party (SDP), 86, 88, 129
social engineering, 41
socialist governments, collapse of, 1
socialist societies, transformations of, 57
social players, forests as, 80–86
soil protection, 58
Soviet Union, 2
    collapse of Berlin Wall (1989), 4
    cuius region eius religio, 41
Spain, 139
Stahl, Johannes, 14
staple foods, scarcity of, 47
state
    agency, 97
    analysis of the, 191–94
    control over forest, 103–04
    farms, 2
    forests, deforestation in, 72
    investments in forestry, 48
    legitimacy of, 57
    methods for studying, 18–21
    officials, 13
    organization, 12–13
    privatization of, 1–25, 15–18
    property regulations, rejection of, 68
State Forest Company, 47, 48
status, value of forest to, 80
storks, 178
strategies, reform, 194–96
strips of land, ancestral, 28
subsidies (EU), 189

T
taxation, 194
    avoiding, 161
    Dragomirești, 28
    grazing, 122

terraces, 43
theft, 36
    of trees, 73–77. *See also* deforestation
thinning forests, 60
tigers, 116
timber
    deforestation. *See* deforestation
    exploitation of forests, 30
    transportation, 59
Tisza River, 184
tourism, 158, 160
    in Dragova, 40
    increase of, 189
    national parks, 131
    pastures, 131–34
toxic spills, 186. *See also* pollution
tractors, use of, 151
traditional land use, 96
transformations, 25–53
    economic, 56
    ethnicity and postsocialism, 65–67
    lessons of, 199–201
    of pastures, 125
    socialist societies, 57
transportation
    horse carts. *See* horse carts
    illegal logging, 78
    timber, 59
Transylvania, 2
    land ownership in, 10
    Mureș River, 171
    population of, 3
    relationship with Dragova, 37
trees
    in Dragomireștit, 28
    in Dragova, 39
    fruit, 32
    plum, 42
    sale of, 79
    theft of, 73–77
trucks, 84
țuica (plum brandy), 31
    orchards and, 155–57
    water quality issues, 183
two-row barley *(Hordeum distichum),* 154

U

Uekoetter, Frank, 41
uncollectivized villages, 43–48
underground waters, pollution, 55
USAID, 54

V

Vâlceni, 28, 29, 147
Valley of Povarna, 32
vegetable gardens, 122, 197
Verdery, Katherine, 10, 15, 16
veterinary care, 46
Vietnam, 4, 139, 140
    deforestation, 90
    land fragmentation in, 164
villagers, reactions to government rules, 11
villages, collectivized/uncollectivized, 43–48

W

wagon wheels, manufacture of, 30
Walachia, land reform in, 29
walnut trees, 32
water fern *(Azolla)*, 178
water mills, 172
water resources, 171. *See also* rivers
    capture of, 181
water snake *(Natrix tesselata)*, 128
Weber, Max, 13, 14
Wedel, Janine R., 56
Wegren, Stephen, 164
Western Europe, 4, 189
West Germany, fruit exports to, 44
wild animals, conflict with, 18
wild boar *(Sus scrofa)*, 17, 98
    role in economic changes, 197
    in pastures, 129–31
willow trees *(Salix triandra)*, 67, 178
Willow Valley, 33
wood mafia, 89
wool, selling, 159
worker-peasants, 144–46
    practices of, 146–55
World Bank, 9, 54, 61
World War II, 42, 190
    communal forests, 108
    fertilization after, 153
    industrialization after, 144
World Wide Fund for Nature, 115
Worster, Donald, 7, 152

Y

Yugoslavia, 4

www.ingramcontent.com/pod-product-compliance
Lightning Source LLC
Chambersburg PA
CBHW072150100526
44589CB00015B/2168